Beside the Golden Door

Beth Staas

BESIDE THE GOLDEN DOOR by Beth Staas

Book and cover designed by Ellie Searl, Publishista®

Copyright© 2012 by Beth Staas

All rights reserved

No part of this publication may be reproduced, stored in a retrieval system or transmitted in any form or by any means, including electronic or mechanical. Photocopying, recording or otherwise reproducing any portion of this work without the prior written permission of the author is prohibited except for brief quotations used in a review.

ISBN-13: 978-0615731919
ISBN-10: 0615731910
LCCN: 2012922087

This story is based on real people and historical events. Some of the names have been changed to ensure anonymity. German words have been italicized only when used by characters in America.

QUALIFIED PRESS
Westmont, IL

In profound gratitude to all those, both living and dead, who bared their souls and re-lived the past so that I could write this book.

CHAPTER 1

Chicago, 1927

THE WHEELS SQUEALED AS THE train rounded the bend, metal against metal. August rubbed his cheek, numbed from leaning against the cold window. The fading light said they were almost there and as the train slowed, he could see the flames atop the Gary refineries like so many Christmas candles. Eighteen hours from New York, limbs stiffening with every mile. Afraid to sleep, his hands dug into his pockets guarding his thin wallet and the small fortune sewn into his underwear. It had been an event, flushing the toilet and shaving with hot water right from the tap. He'd watched stubby grass and trees dusted with early snow, viewed red barns and ribboned paths leading to farmhouses, slopes dotted with dormant grapevines, their tendrils curling along fences, waiting for spring. Then came factories with chimneys belching black smoke, the stench permeating the train's closed windows, small towns nestled in the hills not much different than any small town in Southern Germany. Pretty soon it all looked the same.

August shifted on his seat. It would be good to use the toilet once more, maybe even shave. Two of his brothers would be at the station to meet him and he should be presentable.

Inside the tiny bathroom he did his business, buttoning the seat of his underwear when he was done. He bent down, tightening the shoelaces loosened when his feet began to swell, folding the long underwear once more into his socks. Standing up, he pulled out the soap, brush and straight razor from his improvised toilet bag. Once again there was hot water coming right out of the faucets. This would be something to tell Marichen and the children.

Finished, he wiped off the residue and combed his thinning hair, his muscles flexing at the simple task. There was a time when he might have been called handsome with a firm jaw, straight nose and piercing blue eyes. Many women thought so. But Marichen's high backside and breasts like ripe oranges made marriage necessary. After that came Siegfried, buried near the other family members who had died in infancy. Then came Herby, Trudi and now the baby, all in about five years. Half-past thirty, his short frame was gnarled from hard labor, his stolid stance a challenge to anyone who crossed his path, his mind sadly underused. Yet behind his stern demeanor lay a passionate intensity, exploding into unexpected rage or giddy excitement. And he did like his Marichen after all.

There was new activity when he returned as passengers gathered their things for the approach to Chicago, the city on the lake. He felt the train slow, curving past houses, squealing on rusty tracks, then into a dark tunnel with a roar. Arriving in the terminal, it stopped after a series of mechanical hiccups, the final rush of steam like an engine's sigh.

Hoisting his suitcase and coat from the overhead, he joined the line of passengers making their way to the end of the car, his knees nearly buckling as he stepped onto the platform below. Another line, this time as the baggage car unloaded. There would be two crates with goods to sustain him until he found a job and a place for the family – dishes, pots and pans, bed sheets and the featherbed that Marichen insisted he'd need to keep warm. The suitcase contained his immediate needs. Aboard ship, his pants had been placed under the mat overnight, pressed by body heat. He'd worked onboard for passage, small enough compensation for his military service on the North Sea, leaving him glad for a seat on the train to Chicago.

Locating the boxes, he dragged them off to one side, checking the ropes to make sure they were tight. They seemed much heavier, maybe waterlogged aboard ship. People brushed past amid the clatter of carts and cash registers inside the ticket cages. Uniformed redcaps gestured toward the revolving doors, offering transport to the curb. He pulled at his overcoat and wrapped the scarf around his neck, tucking it over his ears. "No speak English," he muttered, looking away.

This was much different from the train station in Essen where public buildings were designed to make a statement. There the entrance was flanked by carved statuary, the doors of polished brass that shone like gold, the marble floors gleaming and the frescoed dome depicted heroic machinations of Germanic myths. August had been there only a few times, the first to his navy post in the Great War, the last to the ship that took him so far from home.

The crowd was thinning and he could see across the enormous terminal. Otto and Fritz said they'd meet him but he recognized no one. Surely they knew when his train was to arrive. He looked around for a phone booth and then remembered he didn't have any change, the last of his coins spent for a sandwich in New York. Maybe the ticket man could make nickels from one of the precious dollars. But then again, how could he be sure?

He shifted his weight feeling his stomach growl. A coal miner was used to being hungry. But here in America he would save his money and buy a grocery store where there was always something to eat. He sucked in his belly and threw out his chest, stretching his frame to stand tall. He was a man after all, not a rat scurrying below ground brushing coal dust off his lard slathered bread and cheese, gulping cold coffee, with no sausage to sustain him through the long afternoon.

Then he saw them coming through the revolving door, scanning the busy terminal. He gestured, trying not to appear too eager. Calling out would have been unseemly.

A pause, then a grin broke out on Otto's face as he elbowed Fritz, pointing in August's direction. "Halloo" and "*Ach Ja*" echoed along the walls as they broke into a trot. They pounded on his shoulders then stepped back for a more formal handshake. "So another goose has crossed the ocean. Welcome to windy city." Fritz looked him up and down. "But you don't pay attention. I wrote you to bring a warm coat."

"This gives good enough. Maybe next year I buy new." It had been a year since August had seen his older brother, now even more dapper with a thin moustache and a soft gray fedora tilted at a rakish angle.

Fritz's face turned serious. "I know. You need to leave money for the family. So how is Marichen? The children – Herby, Trudi? The baby? All is good?"

"Everybody crying when I go, even the baby. But I tell them we come back together soon."

"And how is our *Mutti*?"

August lifted his shoulders. "Is too far gone. TB is a terrible thing. So now we can only pray."

Otto cleared his throat and bent down, tugging at one of the boxes. Barely twenty, it had been hard for him to leave. "So enough already. We can talk more at home. 'Lisbet cooks supper and if we come late she be mad." He looked at Fritz. "We got lost – a little bit."

The two brothers hoisted the boxes on their shoulders as August walked behind with the suitcase. Burying his chin into his scarf, Fritz pointed over his shoulder. "The wind comes from the lake. We go the other way."

They trudged about a mile in single file, past shoppers darting in and out of brightly lit stores, past businessmen ducking into cafés to make a last deal before the end of the day. Along the curb an occasional worker busied himself with broom and shovel picking up droppings from the horse-drawn wagons or capturing bits of newspaper that whirled in eddies along the ground. At Halsted Street they joined a small crowd huddled on the safety island waiting for the streetcar.

The clanging heralded its arrival and they pushed through the surge, gaining access to the rear platform just before the conductor closed the outer doors. Fritz pulled out a quarter for their fare putting the change in his pocket. He mumbled something to the conductor who gestured toward the corner. They could leave the boxes on the platform until they got off. Meanwhile August stood watch as the streetcar lurched forward to sway side to side, stopping every few blocks for passengers to get on or off. Soon they were past the tall buildings and the street narrowed, flanked by small factories, shops, and an occasional church spire. They got off at Orchard Street.

Loaded once more, the men passed several parked cars then down two blocks with three and four story buildings, facades smudged with city soil, the paint around the windows an uncertain color. Otto pointed them toward a gangway and a stairway around the back. Arriving at the third floor, the door was flung open before he knocked.

"*Ach* Otto, you are late and we had worry. Is he here?" The woman's face was rosy from the heat of the stove, her dark hair a mass of ringlets, her lipstick a little smeared. The gentle bulge under her apron said she was pregnant.

"For sure, 'Lisbet. But first let me put this down," he said, making room for the others to come in. "We got a little lost but not too much."

She turned toward August, grasping his free hand with both of hers. "And you are now in America! Was it a good journey?" She turned to her husband hovering in the background. "Look at his face, Rudy, how thin. We need to feed him."

August shot a sly look at his brother. "I see you and your wife been busy. Once a man has his own bedroom, you better watch out."

Rudy laughed. "What else we do on a hot summer night? Maybe we have eighteen babies like our *Mutti*."

"No, no. One, maybe two. We find you some places to sing like in Germany. It keeps you busy at night," 'Lisbet called from the kitchen. "Now show August where to put his things. Is time to wash up. Supper is almost ready. Then we talk some more."

Otto joined them in the front room, gesturing toward a double door. "'Lisbet and Sophie have the bedroom. Rudy sleeps with Fritz and me on the Murphy bed for now. Is okay. We sleep sideways. You can have the couch. There is a drawer for your things. The boxes you keep in the corner by the windows."

August halted mid-step. "Sophie? When did she come? I thought that was over. How come nobody tell me?"

Otto busied himself with the boxes. "'Lisbet invited her."

"'Lisbet!" August snorted. "And who else?"

"Yes, 'Lisbet. They're best friends, you know. And this is

'Lisbet and Rudy's flat. We only stay here for a while."

"Oh yes, I know. And they gonna fix her up with you. She just looking for a man, you dumb ox." August sucked in his breath. "And she not even German."

"Yes she is. Is only her family lived in …"

Just then another door opened and Sophie emerged from the bathroom, her broad Slavic face mottled from crying. "Greetings, August. I hope you had a good trip. I'm through in the bathroom. You can go in."

"Greetings from Germany, Sophie," he replied stiffly. "How long you are here?"

"Not to worry. She leaves tomorrow," Otto replied.

August stood for a moment, then went into the bathroom to wash up for supper. Otto had always been willful. The family had rescued him from the police at enough Communist rallies in Germany to endanger their own lives, finally spiriting him across the ocean to safety. But he still slathered after Sophie like she was a bitch in heat. He looked around and finding no towel, wiped his hands on the seat of his pants and went back out.

They were crowded around the kitchen table on un-matched chairs and stools. "Come sit, August," 'Lisbet cried. "We all hungry. And you too."

August squeezed onto a chair between Otto and Fritz, eyeing the food on the table. Where was the pot roast, the brown gravy, the red cabbage or succulent goose his mother would cook for their boarders? Wasn't this supposed to be the land of plenty? "What gives with this American food?"

Rudy laughed. "*Ach*, now we teach you something. What day you land in New York? I tell you. It was Thanksgiving. Is big American holiday with Indian food from long time ago when Italian guy comes to America and they have a cooking to celebrate food they grow all summer. So I tell 'Lisbet we wait so we celebrate with you too. Because we all come to visit like Italian guy but then we stay."

August helped himself to the fowl that was as tasteless and dry as it appeared. Then there was a red jelly that you ate without bread, something called yams that was so sweet it hurt his teeth and a cold pie made from squash that was treated like dessert. But it filled his stomach and after sipping a glass of homemade wine he began to feel warm and mellow.

"Now give us the news about home. How goes *Mutti*? Is Papa well?" Rudy's smile was enhanced with gold caps on two upper teeth, a mark of fashion. It was enough to dazzle parishioners at the Lutheran church or the Community Theater and regional opera where he'd been a rising star. It made women swoon and won 'Lisbet who pursued him until they were wed. Rudy, handsome and vulnerable, surviving a childhood pocked with illness through *Mutti*'s grim determination. Now it was *Mutti* who was near death.

"We all pray God's will be done," August replied. "Papa prays with her every day."

Otto had taken Sophie's hand under the table. Neither was paying attention.

"And Marichen? The baby?" Rudy smiled at 'Lisbet. "Tell us about the baby."

"Werner was baptized before I left. Marichen said we wear out the baptismal dress. She say three children is enough." August took a deep breath. "He is a fine boy."

"And the others…?"

"No change. Women in the kitchen, men working in the mines. Wilhelm stays in Germany because he has good job. The rest…" He looked at Sophie. "They think America will be too hard."

Sophie picked at a small piece of turkey. "For one person, is hard but if you have family…"

"When you are young, anything is possible," 'Lisbet insisted. "Look at us. Here just a year and already we have a flat, Rudy has good job and today we praise God with Thanksgiving. Come summer, we have baby."

August tightened his jaw and looked away. Rudy was heavily in debt to 'Lisbet's uncle, owner of the butcher shop where he worked, the man who'd sponsored their arrival in America. "We have family," he conceded. "At least, some."

"And more will come," Sophie cried, her face suddenly radiant. Then she looked down and everyone laughed – all except August.

"Maybe someone you know?" Rudy teased.

"I didn't mean…" She looked at Otto who was turning red.

"Women talk too much," he growled.

"For sure," declared Fritz, pushing back his chair. "But we sit too long and I am too full. So we take our wine to the front room and women clean up. They can talk more in the kitchen."

"I will help," Otto offered, reaching for the empty plates. "'Lisbet needs to sit down from working so hard."

So the men retired to smoke and stroke their wine glasses, pretending to be rich burghers, while Otto and Sophie cleaned up in the kitchen, following 'Lisbet's instructions, chatting about this and that as though there were no tomorrow.

At eight o'clock, everyone took a turn in the bathroom and after a murmured Good night the flat went silent except for the squeak of the Murphy bed and an occasional hiss from the radiator. On the couch, August gave thanks to God for his safe journey, praying that the Almighty would look after his wife, children and especially his mother whose life hung by a thread. Surely his coming was not a terrible mistake.

CHAPTER 2

Germany, 1928

CHAIRS LINED UP ALONG THE walls wherever there was space with a pot-bellied stove and small sink on one end of the room, a table at the other. A calendar and worn picture of the Last Supper were the only decorations.

Pauline sat atop a pile of pillows on the chair that had a high back and arms, her cheeks pink, eyes bright. Tuberculosis, the scourge of the poor. At fifty-seven, she looked eighty, a portrait of perpetual mourning. Eighteen children. It hardly seemed possible. Only eight had survived. Every year, a birth or a death. And now the family had shrunk even further, seduced by that siren called America.

Tonight the remaining four were together with their respective families for evening devotions. Marichen and the children would soon be joining August and the others in America. Their voices lifted in song. "Let our hearts be ever joyful, each day filled with sun - n – shine..."

At the last verse, Friedrich opened the Bible, his fingers etched with dust from the mines, his voice like pulverized coal. "*In my house there are many mansions. If it were not so, I would have told you. I go to prepare a place for you.*" His watery eyes focused on his invalid wife who seemed to have gone to sleep.

The room smelled of strong soap and bleach mixed with factory smoke seeping through the windows. Martha hooked her feet around the legs of the chair, trying to get comfortable. She peeked through her lashes at the sturdy clothes that were worn for special on Sunday, then at her own blue and white middy. At sixteen she already had a flair for fashion, skilled enough to become a fine seamstress. But Martha had other plans. She would be a model or an actress, eyes half-closed as she sashayed across a runway, her full lips in a seductive pout. She'd wave a cigarette holder in one hand, draping a fox pelt over the other. She would splash on perfume, bathe in fresh water and brush her teeth twice a day.

Completing the reading, Friedrich closed the Bible with a snap, bringing Martha out of her reverie. Hurriedly, she moved toward the stove. Tonight there would be good strong coffee made with fresh new grounds, her mother no longer able to cuff her across the shoulders for such extravagance. Checking to see that the water was boiling, she measured carefully then stirred it with a wooden spoon as its fragrance wafted into the room.

Joined by her older sister, she and Alma lifted the heavy pot and through a sieve poured coffee into the cups. Her father had gone to the pantry bringing out three flasks of schnapps. From another repository came platters of sliced sausage, their juices oozing over the edge. There was bread, not the dark kind laced with molasses but white bread so light and airy it barely sustained the weight of butter that melted in your mouth.

She glanced at Alma and Helmut's two children on the bench next to their father, happily munching on bread and jam, at Herby and Trudi across from them, their eyes wide as they followed the food passing by, obedient to their mother's admonition to stay seated. Such good children. It was cruel to make them wait. She would sneak them a piece of sausage as soon as she had the chance.

Amid the commotion, Pauline opened her eyes and looked about vacantly. Martha turned toward her mother. "Something to eat, Mutti? We have nice bread and cheese."

Pauline shook her head and motioned that she wanted to stand, whispering something in her ear. A quick nod and together with Alma guided her into the next room.

Fifteen minutes later, they emerged with Alma holding a chamber pot discreetly covered with a ragged cloth followed by Martha smoothing her rumpled skirt.

Disappearing out the back to the community toilet, Alma returned to the bedroom sliding the chamber pot below where Pauline lay wheezing softly. Then back to the sink to wash her hands in the icy water.

Alma had been called the pretty one, with soft blond hair and small even features, a title that remained hers until Martha was born. Extravagant and self-indulgent, she overspent and wore things out, frivolity that fascinated then alienated one friend after another. Aged twenty-seven and married with two children, her face had taken on a pinched look as though mourning her fading youth.

"Come now, more coffee, more bread," cried Friedrich as he moved around the room pouring schnapps into the emptying glasses. "Make hurry."

"Yes Papa." Martha scurried into the pantry to bring out another tray of food then to the coffee pot to provide seconds.

She stopped in front of Marichen who was seated in a corner, the baby asleep on her shoulder. "A little more?"

"Oh, yes. Such good coffee," Marichen murmured, caressing the cup. "August says they have coffee like this every day in America."

"And you will too," Martha promised. "Pretty soon come springtime."

Marichen patted the chair next to her inviting Martha to sit down. "You should come too. Make something of yourself in America. You are still young."

Martha's face was wistful. "There is no money, no job. And Mutti needs me here. Papa too. Maybe later."

Marichen's voice took on a conspiratorial tone. "If Sophie can do it…"

"Sophie has a real job here and a man waiting for her in America. I not so lucky."

"A job!" Marichen sneered. "She's a clerk in a store. How much good does that in America when you don't talk English?"

The coffee pot was heavy and Martha's arms were beginning to ache. If Sophie wanted Otto, and Otto wanted Sophie, what business was it of theirs? She placed the coffee pot on the vacant chair reaching to stroke the baby's cheek. "I think he is asleep. Maybe you put him in the bedroom. Is nice and quiet in there."

Marichen nodded. Alma's two children were moving about the room and Herby and Trudi were still on the bench close to tears. She should be getting them something to eat. You would think someone would step forward to help. Why was she always left to do everything herself?

Grasping Martha's outstretched arm, she stood and together they went into the bedroom where Pauline lay huddled close to the wall. The room smelled of camphor, the bedclothes damp from fever and sweat. It had been weeks since Marichen and her mother-in-law talked beyond a modest hallo. Not that Marichen had felt a part of the family. She'd caught on soon enough, hearing the whispers – outsider, ignorant, farm girl… Still, Pauline was dying. It was un-Christian not to feel sad. A lifetime of suffering and caring, one child after another. Each Sunday gathering could be her last. She placed the sleeping baby at the foot of the bed bolstering him with pillows. Then after a final pat followed Martha out the door.

By now the food was half-gone and Martha hurried to consolidate what was left, bringing out whatever remained.

It was getting dark and one brother and a sister had left for home with their respective families. Someone had moved a few chairs in a circle with one to serve as a table. Herby and Trudi sat on the floor with their two older cousins, nibbling from plates in front of them while Helmut and Alma looked on. "We have a chair for you," Alma said, motioning next to her. "I know you told the children to wait. But they were hungry."

"I know, Marichen murmured. "But it's hard being without August." She eyed the table. "Is there something left? I'm hungry too."

She returned with a plate brimming with pig's feet, liver sausage and cheese plus a mound of potato salad. "August says a nursing mother eats for two," she declared defensively.

Alma shot a warning glance at Martha who stood nearby rolling her eyes. "A woman needs to stay healthy so the baby gets big and strong. Especially in the winter."

Helmut turned toward Marichen. "And how goes it with August? Have you a letter?"

"Only last week. Five pfennig, air mail," Marichen replied proudly. "I know that spends a lot but it was special. He has bakery job. I already told you that. Work begins in the middle of the night when no one is up so he can do the toilet good and quiet. Still, is cold and far to walk, maybe four kilometers. The floor is dusty and full of flour, bad for the lungs. But the ovens make warm and 'Lisbet is glad when he brings home the leftover bread and biscuits for cheap."

Herby had finished eating and stood at Marichen's side holding the empty plate while Alma's children, Hilda and Gunter, busied themselves carrying dishes to the sink. "Mutti, can we have more?" Herby whispered. "Is that allowed?"

"Of course," Martha declared. "Come. I help you."

"August told me to look for boxes but not too heavy so I can begin to pack," Marichen continued. "We need to find out how much I take on ship. Clothes, sheets and blankets, some dishes, the Bible and maybe one or two hymn books."

"Is August making good money? Is he looking for a flat?"

"Pay is not so good but there is overtime and he saves. Everybody works in America. Fritz, Rudy, Otto…"

Helmut studied the floor. "He is lucky."

Martha had returned and settled Herby and Trudi on the floor with the plate between them. "Helmut doesn't need America for a job," she said staunchly. "He just needs to keep looking."

"They always have layoffs and then they call them back," Alma soothed.

Helmut shook his head. "Is because of the war. Ten years gone by and things are no better. America sends money to help but it goes to those who get richer and richer. Hilda goes to bed praying for a coat – not candy, not dolls, not pretty things. Just a coat for my little girl. And we can't even buy the cloth to make it at home."

"But the French are gone and new money is making inflation go away," Friedrich interjected, joined the group.

"When you have no marks, what does it matter how much each is worth?"

Marichen put down her plate and Trudi crawled onto her lap, rocking back and forth. "We all have sinned and fallen short…"

"We should start picking up. Everyone's tired and it was a long day," Martha said, hoping to forestall a lecture.

Marichen nodded, one arm around the little girl the other rubbing her back. "Ja. Is past bedtime."

"I get the baby." Martha reached for Trudi. "You can come and kiss Oma goodbye. But you must be very quiet."

Motioning to Herby, they tiptoed into the darkened bedroom where Martha lifted each to plant a kiss on the sleeping Pauline. As the children returned to the front room, she moved to retrieve the baby, enveloping him in her arms. Such a good baby. Sound asleep and still quite cool in this overheated room. Marichen would have to wrap him good so he didn't get chilled when they went outside.

In the front room, Marichen was putting on the children's coats and hats. Still holding the baby, Martha settled on the chair to wait, cuddling his soft body in the crook of her arm. Pushing back the blanket, she stroked his cheek and kissed his curled fingers. He didn't stir. She bent closer brushing her lips against his dark eyelashes, his tiny nose. His pink lips had a slight off color, no doubt tinged with jelly from the children's kisses. Surely that was all. She traced his lips with her finger, seeking out sticky. There was nothing. She gave him a little shake. Nothing. She lifted his arm, and it fell limp. Nothing, nothing. Nothing! A scream surged from the soles of her feet and echoed along the four walls. "Marichen! Oh dear God!"

Marichen turned sharply. "What's the matter with you? Are you trying to wake the baby?"

"No! No, look. There's something wrong. He doesn't move. He's not waking up. Oh precious God, have mercy!"

It took only a glance. Frantically, Marichen snatched the baby and tried to open his eyes. She looked into his mouth. She lifted him to her shoulder, pummeling him on the back all the while screaming, "Take a breath, breathe, breathe…" Back on her lap she fastened her lips over his, trying to force her breath into his tiny lungs as his body heaved in response, all to no avail. Meanwhile the family stared in horror.

"Martha! Alma! Someone get a doctor! Anyone! Go!" Friedrich leaped over the chair, pushing the children aside.

Jerked to attention, Martha grabbed her coat and ran into the bitter cold screaming to the darkened sky. "Help, help! Someone help us! Anyone, please help!"

There were neither carriages nor autos in the street. Sunday was a day of rest. A few lights came on in the surrounding buildings and someone opened a window calling down. "Who's there? What's wrong?"

"We need a doctor. Are you a doctor? No? Can you get a doctor?"

"A doctor living here? You must be crazy!" And the window slammed shut.

Martha began to run, still shouting. There was a clinic about a kilometer away. As she turned a corner she was stopped by a policeman. "What's the matter with you? Don't you know it's Sunday?" He blocked her with his motorcycle ready to write out a ticket.

"It's the baby. He isn't breathing. Oh, help me!"

"What? Someone hurt? Why didn't you say so? Where?"

She couldn't think. Where did she live? Where did Marichen live? What was the address?

He grabbed her wrist turning her around. "You show me."

She headed back the short distance holding her coat closed as he coasted along beside her, finally pointing to the house.

"I'll get the doctor. You go inside and tell them." He turned, his motorcycle emitting a thin spray of gravel as she raced to the door.

Inside Marichen rocked back and forth hugging the motionless baby while Friedrich stood helplessly by. Alma had gone into the bedroom tending to Pauline who was babbling, unable to comprehend what the commotion was all about. The children clung to one another sobbing while Helmut tried to comfort them.

"A doctor is coming," Martha cried breathlessly. "He's on his way from the clinic."

It was another half hour but by then they knew it was over. He entered the front room and ordered the baby to be laid on the cleared table, poking him here and there with the stethoscope, looking into his mouth, his ears, tapping his belly while everyone stood back and watched in silence, the children sniffling softly. Finally he looked up. "I'm sorry. It's no use. He's already getting cold."

"Oh no! Oh, my baby, my baby…"

Alma reached out her arms but Marichen was beyond comfort and brushed her aside taking the stiffening baby in her arms. "Why did this happen?" she sobbed looking at the doctor. "He was such a good baby. Look at him. Was he sick? Did he fall? Why, why, why? You should know. You're a doctor. Just tell me why."

The doctor shook his head. "Sometimes it just happens. A baby dies for no reason and we can't find out why."

Marichen collapsed in the chair. "How am I supposed to tell August? What do I say? What if he blame me? What if he say I no good mother? What did I do wrong? Oh, my baby…"

"Every year a birth or a death," Friedrich murmured. "August will understand."

"You have the others," Alma said softly. "They are healthy and strong. And you are young. You can have more."

"I don't want more!" Marichen choked. "I just want my baby!"

"God works in mysterious ways," Friedrich admonished. "He made Job to suffer and put Jonah in the stomach of a whale.

Do not question the works of the Lord. He was a beautiful baby and God took him home. That is all."

It was no comfort.

Finally the doctor left. There were things to be done – the funeral, the preacher, the notification to family and friends. Alma went home with Marichen to help put the children to bed and prepare baby Werner for burial.

The next day Marichen bought a tiny white casket lined in satin. It meant they'd eat less for the rest of the month but that didn't matter. Werner would be buried in his baptismal gown surrounded with flowers. A picture would be sent to August.

The funeral was in a small chapel that smelled like roses. Sitting in the front row, Marichen sobbed quietly ignoring her punishing breasts bound tight to keep from making the milk no longer needed.

At first Alma came over every day to see how she was doing. Then someone came twice or three times a week depending on who had time. Pretty soon it was only after church on Sundays. The women had each lost one or two children of their own and Marichen seemed to be doing all right. And if she wept alone into her pillow at night her tears would help with the healing.

Three months later, she and August would share their grief in one another's arms. By then the pain would have numbed to a steady ache. There would be no point in examining it any further.

CHAPTER 3

Chicago, 1928

August walked from one end of the flat to the other. Everything was in place, the double bed, a dresser and two floor lamps. To the right a tiny bedroom held a daybed and a chest of drawers bought second-hand. Four rickety chairs and a table had been improvised from orange crates found at the back of a grocery store. There was also an inside bathroom with a porcelain tub, sink and a coin-operated water heater, ten cents per tank. On the other side a water closet against the ceiling and a chain to pull for a toilet flush. He'd moved there two weeks after 'Lisbet's baby Eleanor was born when sleep became impossible. The flat was cheap, yet even second-hand furniture cost money. Then there was the ocean fare for Marichen and the children as well as for Martha, for after her mother died there was no reason to stay behind.

The clock over the dresser pointed to four. The train was due at five. Wiping the sweat from the back of his neck he smoothed the featherbed and, locking the door, went out into the bright sun.

He'd allowed an hour for the walk to the station but Fritz would be there in case August was late.

Marichen and the children! It had been almost six months. Would he kiss them hello like Americans did? Would they cry? He'd prayed over Werner's picture every day but the night before he'd tucked it in his underwear drawer. Maybe they could talk about it later. Maybe they could talk about Mutti. Maybe later.

Leaving Huron street he turned south onto Ashland, a long stretch before going east toward the station. His heart beat faster and he lengthened his stride. Maybe he was excited after all. Yes, he would kiss them, even Martha. Then they would take the streetcar to their new home as Martha and Fritz continued to Rudy's. Maybe they'd gather once more on Sunday. Maybe, maybe. Everything was maybe.

Brushing by the crowds, he swung through the revolving door into the terminal. Six months in Chicago and already he'd learned his way around. At the baggage area he found Fritz who had established his spot and after shaking hands, they leaned against the wall to wait. Fritz had helped him move but he hadn't seen him since.

"You all settled?" Fritz asked, lighting a cigarette.

"Not much to settle. A chest and two beds. But when the shipment gets here there will be enough." He looked at his pocket watch, a confirmation gift from many years before. "Are they late maybe?"

"It's Friday. Everything comes late on Friday. Why? You got something in mind?"

"Don't talk dirty. I'm a married man. You know what I mean."

"Then you should smile," Fritz declared. "And give her flowers. Don't expect anything from Marichen if you can't smile and give her a kiss and maybe some candy."

"Don't you ever think of anything else?"

"You are the one looking at the watch. I'm just here." Fritz turned toward the depot gate. "And there they are!"

Marichen came first, pulling a large cardboard box, her other hand dragging Herby along as he stumbled to keep pace. Martha followed clutching Trudi's sleeve while balancing suitcase and a huge pocketbook, the surge of people propelling them forward.

"Marichen! Martha! Over here!" Relieving them of their goods the men guided them to a safe corner.

Taking a deep breath, Fritz reached down pinching Herby's cheek, then looked up at Martha. "You like the train? Or was it not so good?"

"Everything was too much." Martha straightened the collar of her dress and plumped the sides of her hair. "What I need is a real bed and a pillow. But first some fresh air and sunshine."

"Was it cold aboard ship?"

"How should I know?" She eyed Marichen. "We stayed all the time below deck."

"And good reason too," Marichen declared stoutly. "All those strangers, men in straw hats who wanted to give candy. We know about those kinds…"

"Some were goodly German, nice and polite. I can tell the difference," Martha sniffed. "I would have given the candy to the children anyway."

Fritz placed the box and suitcase along the wall. "You have ticket stubs for baggage?"

"I come across the ocean and all you want is tickets? I think maybe I should go back home."

"*Ach*, always the Martha. So come here and I give you a little kiss. I even give you a hug nice and tight." Fritz put his arms around his sister and kissed her soundly on both cheeks. "And Marichen too." Taking Marichen's face in his hands he brushed her forehead with his lips before turning once more to the children.

Now it was August's turn. Reaching down he tousled Herby's hair and asked if the little boy remembered him.

"*Ja wohl, Papa,*" was the shy reply.

Smiling, August lifted him and held him close until Herby squirmed to get loose.

Then August turned to Trudi who had buried herself in her mother's skirts, her eyes filled with terror. "Trudi will you come to Papa and give a little kiss?"

Trudi shook her head.

"Maybe if I hold her," offered Marichen. "Six months is a long time for such a little one." She picked up the child so their faces were level. "You got an American haircut. And maybe gained a little…"

"No exercise," he replied. "Just work, work, work." He reached out to touch Trudi's arm wrapped around her mother's neck, stroking Marichen's cheek instead as the child shrank back. "Haircut was yesterday. It will grow back."

"You look fine. Like American." She smiled. "Trudi made a surprise for you. But now she scared."

August hunched down so he was looking up at them. "Trudi made a present for Papa?" He chucked under her chin as she buried her face into her mother's shoulder. "People like when you come with presents. What do you think?"

"*Ich liebe dich, Papa.*" The words were muffled and barely distinct.

Marichen drew in a choking breath. "We practiced it on the ship all the way over. I think Americans talk like that. I told her how it means but she's so little…"

"Already talking sentences!" August smiled. "And she only just past two."

"*Ich libe dich auch, Papa.*" This from Herby standing next to his mother.

August gestured, groping for something to say. "I hope you were a good boy for your Mutti." Turning to Marichen, he breathed a kiss on her lips feeling his cheeks burn with emotion. "And God be praised for bringing you safely home," he whispered, the words tumbling forth.

Fritz nudged Martha and they turned away, the scene too achingly tender to watch, moving toward the crates and boxes arriving from the baggage car.

When they returned August was bouncing Trudi in his arms and Marichen's face was dried of tears. "Papa says we take streetcar home," Herby announced.

Six months before it had been freezing cold. Today it felt like the middle of summer, the breeze fresh and clean. Seated on the straw-woven seats the children gazed with awe at the colors and shapes as they bobbed to the streetcar's rhythm.

At their stop they gathered their things, waving to Martha and Fritz as the streetcar pulled away.

Pausing while cars whizzed by, August balanced the box on one shoulder, dragging the suitcase with the other hand. "What you have in here?" he demanded. "I told you heavy should be shipped."

"These are some dishes from your Mutti. Shipping breaks everything so I carry them with me. The rest is what you said." She reached for the handle to lighten the load. "I can help you."

"No, I do it. Just watch the children."

The apartment was a block away. Unhooking the front gate, August led the way down the steps into the cool interior. The dim light seemed eerie after the bright sunshine and Marichen reached for the lamp.

"Not yet. Is still light outside." Then August's voice softened.

"I show you around the flat." Taking her by the hand, he moved toward the children's bedroom, the bathroom and back to the front room and the adjoining kitchenette with gas stove, icebox, sink and double cabinet overhead. "The bedroom closet is nice and big," he offered.

Marichen ran her hands over the appliances. "Easy for cooking," she smiled. "Where do we eat?"

August gestured toward his homemade dining set. "But pretty soon we get real table and chairs. I saw some at Salvation Army store. Maybe after payday." He pointed to the icebox. "There's already milk, butter, eggs and sausage. I bring bread and biscuits every day from work. We eat good in America for sure."

Marichen stood motionless. "You call these chairs? You think us gypsies?" She paused seeing the stricken look on his face. "Well maybe you right. We buy when there is money."

Trudi had commandeered a spot on the corner of the bed and fallen asleep. Herby was on the other side of the room peering out the window at some children sitting on the steps. "Mutti, can I go outside?"

"You can go if you be where we can watch you. But first put on your hat." Marichen turned to her husband. "He had earache on the boat. After a while some yellow stuff came out. Then everything was good, wasn't it, Herby?"

Herby nodded, taking his hat from his mother. "I stay right in front."

With Trudi asleep and Herby outside, August and Marichen busied themselves unpacking. The rest would arrive in about a week.

As the sausage sizzled on the stove, August arranged the makeshift chairs alongside the wobbly table still pleased at his resourcefulness. Turning on the lamp he placed plates on the table with forks and spoons next to them. Herby had returned from outside and Trudi was awake tugging at her mother's skirt to be picked up.

Herby pulled off his hat. "I want to play but the children laugh at me. How come they talk so strange?"

"Americans talk different. You will go to school and learn," Marichen replied, filling their plates. "Papa and I learn too. It will be easy."

"In America, everything is possible. Now sit down. We gonna eat," August said.

Once more shy, Herby clambered next to his father while Marichen took Trudi on her lap murmuring, "Come Lord Jesus, be our guest…"

After supper Marichen washed the dishes and prepared August's lunch while he read aloud from the Bible. Walking around the block, they examined their new neighborhood with August pointing out directions, proving how much he had learned. By eight o'clock the children were ready for bed.

The wash-up was in cold water. Hot water was reserved for Saturday night baths and Monday's laundry. Shivering, the children snuggled in their respective spots on the daybed with Herby giggling about being toe to toe, upside down.

The front room was dark when Marichen emerged from tucking them in. August was in his underwear sitting on the edge of the bed. "I get up at three you know."

"But maybe you wait a little for me?" whispered Marichen.

The window shades were curled around the edges with soft shadows that danced along the ceiling. Slowly, Marichen took off her dress and petticoat draping them across the makeshift chair. Next came shoes followed by bloomers, long stockings and finally the corset, her naked body outlined against the opposite wall.

"Your hair? You take down your hair?"

Two long hairpins and her hair spilled over her shoulders. "Do they do it here like in Germany or is that different too?"

"We find out." He squirmed out of his underwear, letting it drop to the floor. Grabbing her fiercely, he threw her onto the bed. There was no preliminary, no foreplay. It didn't matter that the mattress sagged, that there were crumbs on the bed, that he was functioning on four hours sleep. Barely started, it was over. "I wake you before I go to work," he promised, breathing hard. He touched her cheek brushing her hair from her face. "You are my wife."

Sliding over the side of the bed, they knelt in silence, their thoughts going to heaven. August began reciting the Lord's Prayer and they finished with a soft Amen. He was asleep almost immediately.

Marichen lay listening to the streetcar's clang, the wailing siren in the distance and the sound of footsteps. The air was heavy and she wondered if it had begun to rain. Bone weary yet restless she couldn't rouse herself to look out the window. At midnight there was the sound of church bells tolling the hour. At three August woke her and she sleepily responded when he turned her over for a more lingering repast before leaving for work. She had begun to doze when she heard the children in the other room. Her day had begun.

Hot oatmeal cut through the morning chill. Along with biscuits and a glass of milk it was a substantial breakfast.

Picking up the dishes, she allowed the children to play with her button box on the table. Finding a sponge under the sink she washed the windows, polishing them dry with a tattered towel, then scrubbed the floor, wondering at the worn spots on the linoleum. The bathroom was another matter. How did one scour a water closet so far over her head? She'd have to ask August when he got home.

By mid-morning she'd moved toward the dresser, discovering Werner's picture beneath August's underwear. The funeral, the flowers, the photograph, everything had cost more than she thought possible. After a long time, she put it back. No need to keep looking. The image would be seared into her heart forever.

August had left a house key hanging on the nail over the sink in case she wanted to go out. Oh yes, indeed. She was ready. Calling to the children, she ushered them out the door.

They walked west with the sun warming their backs. Marichen counted the streets in one direction, the house numbers following each turn, keeping mindful of the sun. Then wonder of wonders they came upon a playground with swings, slides and two teeter-totters. Nearing lunchtime it was almost deserted except for a few young mothers with babies and two children building a bucket village in the sandbox.

Ignoring her cries of caution, Herby rushed forward and was already on the swing by the time she caught up. Catching her breath she sat on the one next to him holding Trudi on her lap, rocking gently back and forth. "A park so close! Is good we came."

He nodded, his eyes bright with excitement. "I know how to pump. Tante Martha showed me. See how high I go!"

The boy and girl in the sandbox had left their project and commandeered the other two swings staring at them with curiosity. "Give me a push?" asked the little girl looking at Marichen.

Marichen smiled apologetically. "No speak English."

"What's that?"

"I speak *Deutsch*. Germany, you say."

"It's okay. I'll do it." The little boy jumped off his swing and sent the little girl soaring as she screamed with delight. He moved behind Marichen. "Give you a push?" Without waiting for a reply he gave the swing an off-center push careening from side to side.

"*Liebe Gott!*" Marichen's hands jerked off the chains sending her crashing into the dirt landing almost atop Trudi.

The two children gasped in horror. Then the girl leaped off her swing as both dashed across the street and down the block, laughing hysterically. By the time Marichen dusted off her torn stockings they were out of sight.

Holding the howling Trudi in her arms, Marichen examined her bruises then crooned words of comfort while Herby stood in stunned silence.

Two of the mothers had come over to help but Marichen brushed them away angrily. "No speak English." Then, "Is okay."

After a while Trudi's tears diminished to a sniffle and she buried her face in her mother's shoulder. "Go home," she wailed.

"No, no. We go to sandbox," Marichen said. "Boy and girl left buckets so we take them with us because they gone."

Herby looked skeptical and walked over to see. His mother had said that there would be real toys in America not just buttons or empty boxes. And here they were. Pretty soon he was happily adding to their half-finished architecture brushing away his sister's efforts to re-do his work, watchful in case his mother took Trudi's side. When it was time to go they confiscated the two sand buckets adorned with pictures of fish and seashells with handles that moved up and down, their first American toys.

August returned from work at three. The children had had lunch and were taking a nap. Marichen was on the bed reading the Bible.

"It's getting hot outside," he announced. "The bakery was like an oven. But is nice here." He placed his key on the hook next to hers. "The children sleeping?"

She nodded. "We went to the park and they found buckets for playing in the sand. We took them home with us."

"And you didn't get lost! See? Is good in America." He eyed

the rumpled bed. "Maybe I take a nap too."

"A boy pushed us off the swing," Marichen continued. "He ran away. My stockings are torn and Trudi has scrapes on both elbows. I put on iodine and she cried."

"After laughing comes crying. But you can darn the stockings. The rest is still good, no?"

"Trudi cried and cried and say she wants to go home," Marichen said.

"So?"

"She means home to Germany."

August scowled. "You listen to baby? Baby not boss."

"I told her we already home but she just keep crying."

"Let her come crying to me. I give her something to cry about."

"They wanted to play with the children in the park but they not understand."

"They will learn," August replied grimly. "You will see."

"Is hard," Marichen said softly, her chin quivering. "I did not know that so much."

His voice softened. "We will visit 'Lisbet and the baby tomorrow. Here we have Family Devotion like always and you will get used to it." He perched on the edge of the bed. "And maybe we have another baby so you not cry so much anymore."

There was a rustle in the other room and Herby came tottering out his face flushed. "Mutti, my ear hurts again. It hurts and hurts."

He brushed by his father who reached down to feel his forehead. Startled, August got to his feet. "He has fever. Didn't you tell him to wear a hat when you went out? Where's the aspirin?"

"I used it up when he was so sick on the ship." She gestured pleadingly. "The sun was shining. He didn't want his hat."

August reached for the house key, then stopped. "I don't know where is a pharmacy!"

"Just go ask around. I will give Herby bath to cool him down."

Nodding, August checked his pockets for money and was halfway out the door as she called out, "…and buy some sweet oil for his ear."

It was an hour before August returned to find Herby half asleep on the bed, hot and shivering intermittently. The aspirin helped and he said the warmed sweet oil in his ear made it feel better.

Supper consisted of fried potatoes and leftover sausage eaten in snatches as they watched over the restless boy. Even Trudi sensed the drama and clung to her mother. At bedtime August slept with the little girl while Marichen watched over Herby, laying moist cloths on his forehead, his stomach, his arms, soothing him as he moved from one side to the other all the while murmuring an urgent prayer. Dear God, not again.

The fever broke at dawn and Herby fell into a restorative sleep awakening periodically to take sips of milk or water.

After breakfast August walked the two miles to his brother's flat explaining why they would be missing the Family Devotions. And if Marichen had wept in front of the children her tears were carefully wiped away by the time August returned.

CHAPTER 4

Germany, 1930

WHEN DOES A MARRIAGE TURN bad? Is it when the familiar is no longer a comfort and the daily becomes dull? Is it when there is nothing to say except in anger? When there is grinding poverty and no hope of joy or a welcoming smile? Alma smoothed her dress and stared off in the distance, half-listening to the pastor's voice. Helmut had moved out to live with his sister. Or maybe Alma had thrown him out. It was too painful to remember. She just knew that the marriage had never been good. She'd expected much more, maybe a nice flat with a couch, a modern stove and food in the pantry.

A hero who had earned the Black Cross, Helmut had gotten a job in the mines and suddenly Alma realized he was a dirty, smelly coal miner just like the rest. And like the rest, stopped at the saloon after work, coming home drunk. Payday was the worst, remaining until the money was gone. By then Hilda was born and Gunter on the way, so that was that.

Then Helmut was laid off.

Renting out a room in their flat was of little help. Oh, the boarders thought her pretty enough and Helmut didn't interfere, his eyes watery from too much wine, wordlessly watching as she mounted the stairs.

Rousing herself Alma shifted in the pew to look at Guste, her younger sister, and the newborn asleep in her arms, at Siebold at the end of the row now a proud Papa. Her eyes moved to Wilhelm, her eldest brother and his wife Ida seated with their four daughters, the picture of health.

She stroked Hilda's hair, smoothing the wisps over her ears. It was dirty and should have been washed. The Director at the Children's Home was supposed to take care of that before Hilda's weekend visitation. How long had it been this time?

The music swelled. The sign of the cross and the blessing said the service was over.

Alma reached for her pocketbook containing pictures drawn in school and colorful stones gathered along the way. The orphanage didn't have much to offer beyond safety. But after the separation, child-care had been more than she could afford and no one stepped forward to help. Guste and Siebold were living with Papa, the place already crowded, and Ida had her hands full with the four girls.

It had happened after Gunter and Hilda forgot their house key, huddling outside before returning to school with pinched cheeks, ice-cold hands and nothing for lunch. That evening Alma came home to an empty house. Frantic visits to neighbors, then the report on child neglect. Who had generated the charge? Why? She never knew.

Foster care came next. The first family was good to Hilda, treating her well. The next was on a farm along with a case of head lice. She was moved to the orphanage, her brother Gunter sent to a location even further away, both children placed with strangers.

"Do we have to go now?" Hilda whispered.

"Yes. Tomorrow is school," Alma replied. "And you have to go back. You know that."

"We will walk a little with you," Guste offered. "It keeps you company a little bit. But first would you like to hold baby Elvira?"

Hilda sat down to make a lap, her face brightening. "Someday I should be a Mutti and have a baby too."

"After you finish school and get a good job," Alma declared firmly. She rummaged in her purse. "Here, take my handkerchief. Wipe the baby's nose."

Guste laughed. "Mutti is right. Babies always need wiping."

The hall had emptied. There could be no further delay.

Outside the air was still warm, the sun winking through the bright autumn leaves. Loosening the blanket, Siebold shifted the infant to one arm taking Hilda's hand with the other. "So in school you need to study and get a job that pays good money. Ladies need to work too."

"Papa studied hard but he has no work because of the war." They were approaching an overpass and Hilda pointed. "I remember the French soldiers. I pushed through the barbed wire to beg for food. But the soldiers pointed their guns and I ran fast…"

"Guns and lice. That is all we get for our troubles," Alma muttered.

Hilda looked down, ashamed. Tante Guste was not supposed to know about that.

Siebold moved closer. "I tell you something funny. Is real, not a joke. But it will make you laugh. You know how Tante Marichen just had a new baby in America? It was in a real hospital not with midwife. And Onkel August waited downstairs until the doctor come and say baby is fine and so is Tante Marichen. And Onkel August say Thank you and he goes home and never sees Tante

Marichen or the baby. He thought baby was a boy but it was really a girl." Siebold clapped his hands. "Is funny?"

Hilda looked uncertain. "Is joke?"

"Onkel Siebold wants to make you to smile," Guste said gently, "so you be happy."

They had reached the intersection where Guste and Siebold would be turning off. Before them was the orphanage with gaslights glowing.

"We go the other way," Siebold said. "You be good and we see you next week. Pray that Mutti finds a job so you live together again with Gunter. With God, everything is possible."

The orphanage was sturdy and formidable, the first floor containing a foyer encircled with offices and meeting rooms, the second floor a dining hall surrounded by dormitories.

Hilda began to tremble. "Take me home with you Mutti," she whispered, clutching at her mother's hand. "I'll be good, I promise. I'll clean the house and cook. You can go to work…"

"We did that, remember? And the school reported us." Alma grasped at Hilda's shoulder. "And don't start to cry. Because they think I beat you when you come back crying." She reached for the doorbell.

Just then the door swung open with Frau Klepper, director of the institution, framed in the light. She looked at Hilda's woebegone face then back at Alma. "A little early I see." She paused. "Well then maybe you can stay and eat with us. A little soup with some bread… I know is hard when time to leave." She drew Hilda toward the stairs as the little girl's sobs echoed through the halls causing doors to open with children peering out. "Go back, go back," she cried, waving at the interlopers. "This has nothing to do with you!"

Turning back to Alma, her face was stern. "Mother's visits are supposed to be happy."

"Once a week is never enough." Alma's voice could barely be heard over the din. She tightened her jaw, determined to speak up. "So how come Hilda comes with dirty underwear? You are supposed to take care of that."

"She could have told me," the Director huffed. "She can talk plenty when she is supposed to be quiet."

"…and her hair is dirty too."

"Again, I tell you…" Hilda's wailing had declined to shuddering hiccoughs her face awash with tears. "Maybe you should stop coming until she gets used to us here."

Alma's head snapped around. "Never!" She thrust herself forward, trembling. "And don't you try to move her away from me again." Then as Hilda's sobs reached a new crescendo she turned and stormed out, running most of the way with Hilda's cries echoing in her ears.

Out of breath, she entered the room she could barely afford, sparsely furnished with a straw mattress atop a wooden platform, an armoire and a small chest. Next week's rent was due and there was not enough money to pay. She threw herself across the bed pressing her face against the rough pillow remaining fully clothed to deal with the cold. One door after another slammed shut no matter how hard she tried. She'd listened to an array of men making promises, offering a pittance then calling her filthy names when she asked for more.

Turning on her side she fell into a dreamless asleep waking as the sun lightened the morning mist. Her back was sore and would be more so by the end of the day.

Being a live-in maid wasn't hard. The hours were long but one could pace oneself. Work in a boarding house was harder, cleaning up to fifteen rooms and two toilets by lunchtime, serving men who were like pigs, their disgusting habits used as a sign of manhood. It would be bending, reaching, scrubbing and scouring while keeping an eye on the clock. After lunch came kitchen cleanup. Yet it was something she would gladly do, given half a chance. A job. A pay envelope. It had been so long she could hardly remember. In the meantime she'd lost everything.

Her chin was set as she rolled out of bed. Today she would not stay home looking at the walls. No, today she would grit her teeth and do what had to be done.

It was about a kilometer away and her movements slowed as she entered the courtyard. Then up two flights of stairs where she paused and taking a deep breath, knocked on the door. No answer. She knocked again, this time harder. Finally footsteps and the door opened.

"Hello, Helmut." She could barely get it out. "Can I come in?"

He looked startled running a hand over his unshaven chin, the other trying to smooth his rumpled hair. "Ja, sure. I didn't hear you at first because I was reading."

"That?" She gestured toward the Bible on the table.

He nodded. "I have now time."

She stood, uncertain. "Can I sit down?" She cleared her throat. "Can we talk?"

"Ja, sure." He pulled out the chair. "My sister is still at work. She works nights." He hesitated. "Can I give you coffee? I think there is some left."

She shook her head tucking her reddened hands under her sweater. "I need to get back pretty soon. I take in a little sewing…"

"At least you have something to do." The edge on his voice echoed their final quarrel, soft but cutting. "So tell me what you came for. I will not keep you."

She took a deep breath. "I was with Hilda yesterday all day. Gunter is so far away I can't even see him once a week. Hilda cries so much she makes herself sick."

"So? Why come to me? I told you not to do this. I said this would happen. I begged you to be a good wife, to stop with the men, to stay home and take care of the house, the children…"

"What else was I supposed to do?" she cried. "No food on the table, no meat, cabbage, not even potato peel soup. No soap to wash the face or clean the clothes. Go to the toilet and what is there to wipe your bottom? Not even newspaper." She dropped her face in her hands. "What I was supposed to do?"

"Look to have fun? That is what you did. Two children and a husband out of work but you go out and want to have fun. Like a cabaret queen dancing and singing while everything falls apart."

"I did nothing wrong. They took the children just because we leave them at home alone."

"Not we – you! And why they were alone? Where were you, little Mutti?"

"I was looking for work, Helmut. That was your job but I did it."

"For sure. But why didn't you do that before you threw me out? I wasn't garbage." He drew himself up. "And I not garbage now. So what do you want from me? Why you here?"

She shrunk down, small and vulnerable. "They say we can take the children back if we come together again. The Reichstag is promising jobs. We could go to the Rathaus and put in for some new Welfare. I'd find work and we could live, you know, like brother and sister…" She spoke rapidly afraid she'd lose her nerve. "Oh Helmut, you should see them the way I do, Gunter and Hilda so dirty and sad. They don't deserve this."

"I do see them," he said dryly. "I go every day to the orphan home and look through the windows. I walk all day to look at Gunter even when it's far away. They are my children too."

"We could make a contract. I stop going out. You stop drinking."

Her voice softened. "We do it for the children."

He was quiet for a long minute. "I think about it."

This was not what she expected. "You think about it?" she shrieked. "You live here like a beggar while your sister works nights? All day you read or go out and peek in windows. Is it too much to ask you to stand up and be a man?"

"I think about it," he said firmly. "Because I am a man and will not have my wife running around like some Jezebel, like some harlot. The children not should see such things. And they not need to hear us fighting all the time. I pray every day that God gives us a better way to live. So tonight I will pray for a true answer and not one from the devil – or from you. I don't drink no more and I read the Bible every day. I will pray God to tell me what is really in your heart."

"I cannot do this anymore, Helmut," she whispered. "I cannot look in the mirror for shame. Life is too hard and I cannot go it alone. If we go hungry let us do it together. If the world, if Germany dies, let us die together. God should be the judge not you."

"I did not break the Commandments. I did not break my marriage vows." He pointed at the open Bible. "A sin is a sin."

Her voice was hoarse. "Can't we try? At least try a little? For the children. I beg you."

"You beg now do you? So how does it feel? Do you cry in your pillow at night? Yes, I am a man but I cried. What else could I do? I no can shoot this man and that man and the next man. I not strong. The Kaiser took that away along with half my stomach in the war. I not can fight. But I am still a man. And I am proud. You shame me again and again. How do I know you not shame me once more?"

"I will not do anything that makes me give up my children. Never again. May I be damned to hell if I do. I swear it to you and to Jesus and to God."

He stared at her for a long time. "Then put your hand on the Bible and promise. So Help Me God."

Slowly, she took her hand from under the sweater and placed it trembling on the Bible.

"You will not ever again call me names or tell me I'm no good. And you will clean and cook and be a wife." He looked deep into her eyes. "…not like brother and sister but like a real wife."

Alma sucked in her breath, then nodded. "So Help Me God," she whispered. "For the children."

He sat back. "Good. So now I can tell you. I have a little job. Is not much, only two days a week filling holes in the street, painting and cleaning up. But like you said, soon there will be extra money for men who lost jobs in the mines. Or maybe they start to hire again now the Occupation is over. I go find out." He studied her face then got up and walked around the table touching her shoulder.

She tried not to cringe. "We will need to find a flat. My room is not big enough. Then we have to tell them so the children can come home."

His hand slipped under her sweater. "We still married you know. And my sister will not come home for a while. You can stay a little. Do us good, a new beginning." His voice was soft and caressing. "It's been a long time."

An oath sworn on the Bible. Jesus and God would be watching. She got up slowly. Yes, it had been a long time. She could barely remember why she'd married him. But it no longer mattered.

She felt herself being led into the bedroom. It was just for the children.

CHAPTER 5

Chicago, 1933

MARICHEN SAT STARING INTO SPACE. She'd been doing that a lot lately, drained of energy and ambition, indulging in comfort food until she swelled out of her clothes. They'd moved out of the basement flat on Huron Street after their clothes turned moldy and the children got one chest infection after another. Then the new baby developed double pneumonia, and was baptized at the kitchen sink with Fritz and Martha as godparents. That was three years ago. They moved once more and got bedbugs and cockroaches. Next it was a first floor flat on Division Street with two bedrooms and an eat-in kitchen, a place that seemed promising despite the rat carcasses in the alley. Still, they dared not let up on the bugs, spraying kerosene around the beds and bed-springs, leaving the flat to reek from one week to the next.

Meanwhile, the two older children attended church school and Marichen was able to do some day work if she were allowed to bring the baby, leaving her to play on the floor while she scoured, dusted and did laundry. Later she was steered to the night shift at The

Chicago Women's Club, substituting for the regulars when they got sick or went on vacation, reasonably scheduled so she could plan accordingly. But sometimes a telegram would summon her for that very night, a shift without sleep. Still, any job was a windfall in the heart of the Depression. They'd even managed to buy a few pieces of second-hand furniture. Then it turned into a lifeline for August was laid off a month before Christmas.

"The shoes are nice in a row," declared Elsie from under the sewing machine. "Now what should I do?"

Marichen looked at the three-year old. "You will take a nap pretty soon. Then Papa comes home and I go to work."

"Is Papa at work now?"

"Not exactly." Marichen pictured the storefront, the massive corn poppers, the copper kettles for mixing corn syrup with shredded coconut or pecans, the squares of wrapping paper, supplies and equipment that took the last of their savings. Pop-P Corn & Candy Company. The brothers had launched a business, embarking on the American Dream as captains of industry. "He's with Onkel Rudy making popcorn balls to sell on Sunday. Maybe he brings some home."

Elsie didn't much care for popcorn balls especially the coconut kind. But she didn't dare say so. Eat! And you ate. Sleep! And you slept. When someone raised a threatening hand you scrambled. "C'n I go out on the porch? It stopped snowing."

Marichen nodded pulled out of her reverie. "I watch you through the window." Taking down Elsie's coat she added a long scarf wrapped twice around the little girl's neck then inserted her own gloves inside a pair of woolen socks to keep her hands warm. That would have to do.

Scampering onto the porch Elsie began scraping the snow from the railings, piling it into a mound on the middle of the porch only to find that it clung to the improvised mittens refusing to turn into any kind of shape. After a half hour she was about to go back inside when Mrs. Still, the lady next door, came down the gangway with her young son Jake.

"I have a Christmas tree!" Jakie cried, waving an evergreen branch over his head. "The man said I could keep it."

"That's not a tree," Elsie snorted, looking to Mrs. Still for confirmation.

"Don't be mean and spoil it. To him it's a tree and that's good enough." She bent toward the steps urging the little boy into the flat, sending an angry scowl over her shoulder.

Seeing her mother gesturing through the window, Elsie went inside hoping she'd not done something wrong.

"Lunch is ready and you need to dry off." Marichen placed the makeshift gloves next to the stove. "What did Mrs. Still want?"

"She said Jakie had a Christmas tree. But I told her it wasn't a real tree. Only a branch. I was right, wasn't I?"

"Jews don't believe in Jesus so they think a Christmas tree is a sin. Jakie will learn about that later. He's still young." She put a sandwich in front of the little girl. "See how lucky you are?"

Elsie nodded. Jesus belonged to the God family. He was supposed to save her from the Devil whose presence throbbed through the dark in wild patterns as she tried to go to sleep. It was something she dared not tell her mother. *If I should die before I wake...* The bedtime prayer terrified her.

She lingered over her sandwich unready to take a nap but her mother lay down next to her and soon they were both asleep.

Herby and Trudi came home from school at three and August arrived shortly thereafter. Newly awake, Marichen stretched and yawned then moved to the bathroom to get ready for work.

Suddenly there was a banging on the door. Marichen turned

toward the children with a questioning look.

More banging, this time louder. "Mrs. Zahn?" It was a woman's voice. "We are here from the church."

A look of terror came over the children's faces. Had the teacher followed them home? Had they done something wrong?

August cautioned quiet with a finger across his lips.

"Mrs. Zahn?" the voice continued. "We're here about Christmas."

"I have to get to work," Marichen whispered. "I can't be late."

Another bang. "Anyone there?"

August gestured helplessly and went to the door.

Festooned in red and white Santa hats, two smiling young ladies stood surrounded with gaily wrapped boxes filled with cans of peas, beans, corn and something that smelled like a turkey fresh out of the oven. "Oh, we're so glad you're home. We were about to leave! Merry Christmas!"

"Merry Christmas," August muttered. "What can I do for you?"

"We're from the Lady's Aid Society at St. John's. We brought this for you."

August eyed the boxes suspiciously. "We don't need nothing. My wife has to go to work. Excuse me, please. We can buy for ourselves."

"We're not selling anything," the lady cried. "This is a gift from the church. Every year they take up a collection for people like you. We know how hard it can be."

August sucked in his breath. "Give it to someone who needs it. We are okay."

Marichen stood beside him, hugging her coat. "They doing this in the Christian way, August," she whispered. "We should thank them, thank God..."

The children were staring at the boxes, their eyes wide with wonder.

"Is free?"

"Yes, of course. Christmas dinner. And a little something for the children. We'll put it on the table." The ladies moved inside eyeing the mismatched furniture, the threadbare rug, aware of the peculiar smell. "Santa Claus left these with us. He said your children have been good. Is that true?"

Herby and Trudi nodded, nudging Elsie to do the same.

"They like Sunday school," Marichen declared. No harm in establishing credentials.

"I'm sure they do. My sister and I grew up in the church. We know how important it is, especially for children." They stood for a moment at the open door shifting from one foot to the other. "Well, we have a few more deliveries and it's getting late." Patting the children on the head, they turned and left.

August closed the door his expression a mixture of wonder and shame.

"I have to go," Marichen declared, breaking the silence. "They won't want me again if I not on time." She paused, clasping her hands together. "God works in mysterious ways. Oh August, we are blessed."

"Yes, yes. You have to go. I cover the turkey and put it on the porch to stay cool. You can put everything away when you come home." He surveyed the boxes. "Maybe we take the turkey to 'Lisbet for dinner. I go tell them tomorrow. It will be a surprise."

He looked at the Christmas tree decorated with lights and ornaments. Other indulgences included a bag of unshelled nuts and a three-pound box of chocolates. Presents for the children would be simple – a doll for Elsie, a folding blackboard desk for Trudi and a pair of high-cuts for Herby with a pen-knife tucked into its side pocket, all purchased before August had lost his job. They would be distributed before the Christmas Eve church service, a practice carried over from the Old Country. The gifts from St. John's would be opened at 'Lisbet's house. Santa Claus? A pagan concept. There was no such thing.

On Christmas Day they dressed in their best and headed for Orchard Street, walking past empty saloons and the darkened movie house, pausing in front of the Salvation Army storefront as a brass trio played Christmas carols, each moment a delight in this winter wonderland. Within a half hour they were there.

The children ran ahead eager to see their cousin Eleanor and Aunt Martha who had married the incredibly handsome Wally, a man who smoked cigarettes, drank beer and laughed at his own jokes. Aunt Sophie, expecting her first child, greeted them with smiles and an enveloping hug. Eleanor whisked them back out to visit some of her friends after the caution to be back in an hour.

The men settled in the front room, sipping homemade wine or beer while the women chatted amiably in the kitchen. The flat was less crowded now that Martha and Otto were on their own. 'Lisbet and Rudy had turned the bay window into a private space for Eleanor. The Murphy bed was largely unused, for Fritz had moved into the storefront on Montrose Avenue to protect the popcorn equipment. Rudy continued working for 'Lisbet's uncle, ensuring a steady income.

Meanwhile, August and Fritz would make the popcorn, going out on weekends, one hawking east-west the other north-south, hoarse and chilled or dripping with sweat depending on the season. "Buy popcorn balls, two for a nickel. Coconut, pecan, plain, give one to your sweetie-pie lady friend. Only five cents, Mister. Only a nickel." If they were lucky, there would be a child or two sitting in the back seat. "Little princess, tell Daddy you want some. Only a few pennies." Sometimes Wally would join them, his teasing grin disarming all but the most impatient drivers, while the others took turns in his car between surges of traffic.

"There is a store on the next block that will be vacant in a few months," Rudy began. "We could expand and sell things like in a candy store. The school's close so we might stock pencils and paper too. Then we have another store, then two and three stores all over Chicago. Pop-P Corn and Candy Company. All of us together like a big company." He lit a cigarette blowing smoke rings toward the ceiling. "Is nice, no?"

August was dubious. "Marichen scrubs floors all night then comes home to sleep one, two, three hours before the children are up. I make popcorn and sell two, three baskets on Sunday. The milk in our icebox goes sour because we can't buy ice. Once I get a job there will be money but no more extra time."

Otto turned to Wally. "You have a good job and Martha works in Marshall Field's stock room. But Sophie and me, I don't know. We need furniture and with baby on the way…"

"We're not hungry any more. There is no war. And if we work hard…" A deep draw from his cigarette sent Rudy into a paroxysm of coughing.

"You better put out that cigarette!" 'Lisbet called from the kitchen.

"Here, give it to me," Martha whispered, sideling into the room.

Wally laughed and patted her behind as she leaned against him taking a deep drag.

"Maybe we make Pop-P Corn and Candy Company for ladies, too. Brothers and Sister."

Martha settled on the arm of her husband's chair. "What you talking about?"

It was simple enough. There was a vacant store just a block away. They could continue popcorn production opening the smaller place as a candy store. "'Lisbet can take care of customers. She speaks English pretty good now." Rudy's eyes were bright with excitement. "Then we open another store, then another. Candy stores. School stores. Ice cream stores…"

"You already owe me money," August interrupted, "and I have nothing left. My girls wear two dresses, one on top of the other because they have no sweaters and their coats are almost worn out. I fix shoes with rubber soles from the dime store but children outgrow them and get crooked toes."

"It's not easy for any of us but that is why we came," Rudy insisted. He turned to Martha. "You and Wally like being in business, yes?" He began coughing again.

Marichen stood in the doorway, hands tucked under her apron. "You need to drink hot milk with honey and butter then stay in bed to sweat it out, Rudy. And you should stop sleeping with the windows open. It's not healthy."

Just then the children came in, their cheeks rosy from the cold.

'Lisbet turned from the stove. "Eats are almost ready. After that we open presents."

But first, supper. Then warmed with good feeling and a full stomach the men went back into the front room to smoke and drink while the wives cleaned up. Wally tried to teach the children to sing "The Little Brown Church in the Wildwood," beginning, *Oh come, come, come*, forgetting the rest of the words, prompting gales of laughter. Everyone knew *Silent Night* and sang as the twilight gave way to the lights on the Christmas tree. Finally it was time.

The presents had no nametags. The children would simply have to pick, youngest first.

Elsie walked up to the tree choosing the smallest box, hurrying back to her mother's side.

"You have to open it and show us," prompted Marichen.

Undoing the wrapping Elsie drew out a coloring book and a box of 16 crayons holding them up for all to see.

Next it was Eleanor's turn. Sitting on her mother's lap she unwrapped a fluffy brown and black Teddy Bear. "You can take it to bed with you," 'Lisbet offered.

"And stop asking for a dog," Rudy added.

There were two boxes left. Eying them carefully, Trudi said eenie-meenie, then unwrapped a pencil box filled with ruler, sharpener, scissors, rubber bands, colored chalk, bringing forth another chorus of oohs and ahs.

There was one left and everyone leaned forward. It was Herby's turn.

"The best shall be last," Fritz called out reassuringly.

Sitting in the middle of the floor Herby unwrapped the colorful package revealing a tattered shoebox.

"So what did you get, Herby?" Fritz prodded. "You got shoes? Show us."

Herby lifted the lid drawing out a handful of dusty coal. Dumbfounded, his face flushed then turned white.

Fritz eyed the bewildered boy. "What's that we see? Are you a bad boy who gets only lumps of coal for Christmas?"

"I wasn't bad," the boy protested, close to tears. "How come the others got nice things and I didn't? What did I do wrong?"

"Church people must know everything," Fritz insisted. "You better tell Mutti tonight when you say your prayers. There should be something you did."

"The others could have picked this one," Herby wailed. "How come I got it?"

"Okay, that's enough, Fritz," Martha declared, taking the box from Herby. "Such a bad joke. America has Santa Claus, not Nicklaus. Now give him his real present before I give you a hit on the head." She reached down and lifted Herby to his feet. "Go wash your hands. Onkel Fritz hid the real present. He only makes fun." She glared at her brother.

The little boy retreated into the bathroom and they could hear sobbing through the door.

"Leave him alone," admonished August as Marichen started to get up. "He will come out when he's ready."

"*Ach*, it was only in fun," Fritz muttered, pulling out a small box from behind the couch. "He should not be such a crybaby."

"He's only a boy," Marichen stormed.

"Life is hard enough for a man," Fritz replied. "A sissy boy will never make it. He has to learn to fight, to be strong…"

"*Ja sure*, Mr. Soldier Man. Like you in the war, so smart you get captured then escape three times so you get plenty beatings after you caught. Is that how you got strong? What good did the beatings do?" Marichen was trembling. "Better you not try to be Mr. Tough Guy."

"Enough!" August thundered. "It's over."

When Herby emerged he received his real present, a small harmonica with a songbook and instructions on how to play. But after a few tries Herby put it back in the box spending the rest of the evening sitting quietly next to his mother.

By nine o'clock the air hung heavy with cigarette smoke and the lingering scent of pine. Christmas was over. August and Marichen wrapped the children in their coats and hats and after soft goodbyes went out into the cold, taking the streetcar home.

Elsie fell asleep and August carried her the rest of the way, an unexpected tenderness as the others trotted behind.

"Tomorrow you can play with your nice new things," Marichen declared as they prepared for bed. "You are lucky. The only present I ever got was a ball and that was just once."

Closing the door, she sank on the couch next to August, watching as he took off his shoes.

"Don't start with me, Marichen," he growled looking up. "Fritz is a stupid fool but he's my brother and a good person most of the time."

Reaching into her pocket, she withdrew a brown booklet with smudged markings and the title engraved St. John's School. "I wanted to show you this but waited until after Christmas." Her eyes reddened. "Herby thought it was his fault."

"Something you not tell me? Because why?"

"The teacher said we owe them money. They will not let Herby go back to school or get report card if we no pay. The same with Trudi." Her lips trembled as she handed him the booklet.

He looked at it carefully and finally put it down. It said their tuition was three months behind. "We not have the money, Marichen," he said quietly. "There's rent and electric. And now we need to help grow the business. It is our future."

"The future is our children," Marichen cried. "They should be learning in the good Christian way." She reached for his hand. "Maybe if we talk to them," she pleaded. "They know we poor."

"They shame us and make us beg then give us a turkey to make themselves feel good." His voice was biting. "No. Let them keep their *verdammte* school. Public school will be good enough. The Christian way belongs to us right at home."

"But it's a nice school," she begged. "The teachers talk German and tell us the children are smart. Trudi comes home to teach Elsie songs and they sing themselves to sleep at night. The pastor likes them."

"We will find another church just as good or even better. One where nobody tries to be a showoff every Sunday." There was no arguing. Oatmeal instead of corn flakes, soup instead of roast beef. Extras were for other people. For them it was to be polite and hope no one perceived the difference.

So after the New Year, Martha and Wally helped register the children at the new school telling them about the wonders of recess with crackers and milk afterward. Their books would be free and they could even take them home. "Just remember to sit up straight and fold your hands on top of the desk. Then everything will be all right."

It would be another change mandated by the adults. A reminder of learning how to cope.

CHAPTER 6

Germany, 1933

THE CLASSROOM WAS DREARY AND dim, typical for late winter, early spring. It was Friday and Hilda was anxious for school to end. Not that much would happen afterward. Her parents had reconciled, and she was becoming reacquainted in this family of four. Now age twelve, she would go home to unlace her shoes and sit a while before starting the laundry. Maybe the clothes wouldn't need to be scrubbed so hard this time. Maybe her brother would help although that was less than likely, this being woman's work. Anyway, Gunter would be running relays for an hour, an after-school requirement for boys of ten.

Up front, Herr Schwartz was droning on about the Reichstag and the new Chancellor. Hilda moistened the tip of her pencil and dutifully wrote it down. Chancellor: Adolph Hitler. This would surely be part of Monday's test.

"And what happens now? A new government, of course. It will be Aryan pure, strong and independent, free of Jews, Communists and liberals who burned down the Reichstag," thundered Herr

Schwartz. "They will mete out punishment to the scum who cast such a plot." He made a circle with his hands like a bandleader. "And who are the ones responsible?"

"Communists!" the children cried in unison.

"Exactly! But Herr Hitler will destroy the Red Peril. It will be a national revolution." His voice softened dramatically. "There is work to do, preparing for a new Germany. Boys and girls active and strong, becoming heroes like the heroes of old." He leaned forward. "Each one to practice obedience and serve in the National Socialist spirit. Not just mothers. Not just fathers. No, it is much, much more. Children will be part of the fatherland, Aryan pure like Siegfried and Brunhilde."

The scratching of pencils had stopped as the children sat hypnotized, their eyes fastened on the teacher.

"There is room in this new German society," he continued, "to build strong bodies for the fatherland. Together you will join and make Germany what it was." His eyes scanned the room. "So I ask you now. How many of you boys have joined the Hitler Youth? How many are preparing for a brighter tomorrow?"

There was the scrape of chairs as some six or eight boys stood up.

Herr Schwartz waited a few moments, scanning the room. He cleared his throat. "How many will be joining by summertime?"

One by one the other boys stood up. It was unanimous.

Herr Schwartz clapped his hands together. "One hundred percent! You do me proud." He motioned the boys to be seated. "Now about the Bund Deutsche Mädel. How many to become strong wives and mothers for the Deutsche Reich?"

Hilda's heart began to pound. Her mother had been adamant that she not join. No amount of pleading could change her mind. "You want to be crazy like the others, marching, singing, dancing...?" Alma had growled. "Better you come home and be useful. We have no time or money for such foolishness." Hilda scanned the half-dozen girls who were standing next to their desks then lowered her eyes.

"How many will join the BDM by summertime?" crooned Herr Schwartz.

Hilda took a deep breath. She was the only one still seated. Would it be wrong to stand? Would they hold her to it? Obedience was a constant, but obedience to whom? Her mother? The Reich? The room was silent.

"I can see I have many good children in my classroom." Herr Schwartz scowled at Hilda then motioned them to be seated.

Hilda kept her eyes carefully averted for the rest of the afternoon. Herr Schwartz was one of her favorite teachers. Had he known about her mother's objection? Was he warning her or being cruel?

She walked home alone, lingering behind the others who skipped and laughed as they made plans for the weekend.

The air was heavy with steam when she arrived at their second floor flat, her mother having started the laundry pot on the stove, stirring the clothes with a wooden spoon, watching them tumble as the water began to boil. She looked up as Hilda entered. "Tomorrow we go to the Welfare Office. Sixty marks is not enough for growing children who need clothes, shoes, warm underwear. You have to tell them that." She shifted the spoon to the other hand. "Go change your clothes. Papa will be home pretty soon and I need to start supper."

Nodding, Hilda went into the bedroom to put on a simple wash dress, hanging the school clothes in the wardrobe that divided the room in two, the laundry lines already strung wall to wall. In a few weeks it would be warm enough to hang the clothes outside.

Back in the kitchen, she moved the washtub to the center of the floor. Pulling each piece out, she scrubbed the lingering stains before their final rinse. "Papa working today?"

Alma was at the sink rinsing off a half-dozen potatoes for potato pancakes tonight and potato peel soup for tomorrow's lunch, adding onion and a bit of lard for added flavor. Vichyssoise," she murmured hopefully. "Yes, Papa has a full day and I am sewing all day long. Never enough work yet always too much." She sighed. "And now Onkel Siebold is out of work, too."

"Herr Schwartz said everyone who joined the Jungmädel should stand up," Hilda said, rubbing a pair of wash pants against the scrub-board. "I was the only who didn't."

"Tante Guste is going to East Prussia to get money from Onkel Siebold's father, the Graf," Alma continued. She lowered her voice. "They are very rich."

It was a familiar tale. Siebold was the illegitimate issue of the housekeeper and the Graf's youngest son. The Graf had paid off Siebold's mother with a nice settlement, the money squandered by the man she subsequently married. Still, if he knew of their current straits he might take pity and help.

"The girls say they have fun at the Jungmädel meetings," Hilda persisted. "They sing and exercise outside. Sometimes they go on hikes and sleep under the stars." She had moved to the second pair of pants, rubbing carefully around the worn fabric. There were still three shirts and a dress to do, then all that underwear before she was finished. "Everyone looked at me funny because I'm not allowed to join." This last said more boldly.

"Looked at you funny? And will they pay for the skirt, the blouse, the jacket, the scarf, the leather slipknot? Because we cannot." Alma's scowl deepened. "This fancy mountain climber with his hand sticking up like a Doppelganger. Let Hitler first find jobs that put food on the table."

"Onkel Siebold saw Herr Hitler when he was in Dortmund. Cousin Elvira went with him. There were Brown Shirts and a big Nazi flag, so many they couldn't even get close. She said it was a fine parade."

"Just what I said," Alma sniffed. "Marching and singing. Onkel Siebold had time to go because he's out of work."

Hilda continued scrubbing. "Elvira will join the BDM when she's old enough. Tante Guste said she could."

"Never you mind. Just stop talking and get the laundry done. Papa will be home pretty soon." Alma looked at the clock. "What happened to Gunter? Did you see him after school?"

Just then Gunter entered. "I stopped at Heinz's house," he said, responding to her inquiring look. "We listened to music on their crystal set coming all the way from Berlin. It was so fine. Then his Mutti gave us each a glass of milk." He went into the bedroom to change his shirt. One more day and he could take a fresh one from Hilda's ironing board.

"Go empty the ash bucket before it gets dark," Alma commanded from the kitchen. "Papa will be mad if he comes home and sees it full."

Gunter smiled. Papa never got mad at anything anymore. Back in the kitchen, he reached for the ashes to take down the stairs, stopping at the first floor toilet on his way back. Relieving himself he watched the tinkle. Yes, he was German through and through. Onkel Wilhelm's promotion to supervisor in the mines had required a family history all the way back to 1700. There might have been a few names that sounded Polish but not a single Jew among them.

Back upstairs, he placed the empty ashcan next to the stove just as his father walked in with Onkel Siebold merrily in tow.

"Look who I found!" Helmut cried. "Siebold has no one at

home so I told him to come for supper." He shook himself out of his jacket and motioned Siebold to do the same. "We can always find another plate at our table for family, right? Hilda…"

"Coming, Papa." Hilda hurried out of the bedroom where she'd begun hanging the clothes. Company was always special. Maybe Mutti would allow them to have some applesauce with the potato pancakes.

Alma reached resignedly for another potato. "Greetings Siebold. So Guste is already gone?"

He nodded. "Left yesterday morning. Took every penny to go."

Helmut threw out his arms dramatically. "But money is coming in pretty soon because Siebold has a new job."

"They're building an airport in Westerwald. Germany is going to have an air force again." Siebold put his fingers to his lips. "Construction workers will come from all over. I know a little Polish and English so…"

"Westerwald? An airport in the forest?"

"No, no. It will be nearby. Trees will help to hide the planes and hangers…"

"Since when do you fly airplanes?" Alma sputtered.

"I'm to make reports and write letters, that's all. But it pays good money and we'll be living in the country."

Alma stared at the two men then turned back to the potatoes. Clearly this was beyond Helmut's ability. Still, Siebold didn't need to be such a showoff.

Siebold turned to Gunter. "And what is happening with you?"

"I went to Heinz's house to listen to the radio. We heard the music all the way from Berlin," Gunter said proudly.

"Wilhelm teaches his girls to sing the old time lendlers and folk songs. Maybe he teaches you too."

"Like trained monkeys," Alma sniffed.

"Don't laugh. It can open doors."

"Oh sure. Like Ida's brother joining the Nazis. Does anyone know where he is?"

"Probably in some training program. They keep it secret."

"Or maybe he's dead."

Hilda had returned and was listening quietly. She knew her father preferred the monarchy or a strong republic but her mother was fearful of any change. It was whispered that Onkel Otto had been a Communist, escaping to America when the purge was on. But surely he wasn't that important and the whole thing could have been a lie. Onkel August used to talk about gleaning horse manure or bits of coal along the railroad tracks to burn in the family stove. Yet here was Onkel Siebold, so filled with ambition, begging supper from those who had even less. No, these were only coal miners struggling for every meal, praying for crumbs.

"Hilda, don't just stand there. Put the plates on the table. Take out a jar of applesauce in the pantry, Gunter. Come now, everyone. Pancakes are done," Alma cried. "Everyone sit. Gute appetite!"

The platter of pancakes came to the table, lacy edges crisp and crunchy, the applesauce adding just the right amount of zest. Kinder, Kűche, Kirche... the standard every woman should strive for. Hilda took a deep breath remembering Herr Schwartz's exhortation to send Germany back to their glorious past, to the days of Wagner, Schiller and Brahms, to the great Teutonic myths. If only it were true. Yet somehow, she was afraid.

CHAPTER 7

Chicago, 1936

IT WASN'T SUPPOSED TO HAPPEN this way. America was their bright future, its streets paved with gold. But just when things seemed bright, disaster followed. Worried at Rudy's persistent cough, August overruled 'Lisbet and dragged him to County Hospital, sitting for hours in the waiting room then more hours waiting for the X-ray results. *Spitting Forbidden,* displayed on the streetcars and busses. The diagnosis was TB. First Mutti, now him.

It was a lingering illness, with family visits at hospital bed, joking, laughing, spreading words of cheer. Letters and cards from Germany bolstered his spirits. But after paroxysms of coughing and splatters of blood, he knew. *Morgan muss ich Sterben,* a premonition of death, hoarsely whispered to August who'd been the last to leave for the night.

"The angels are waiting for you," August said softly, "where there is no weeping or gnashing of teeth," after which he went home to pray and silently grieve.

The following morning Rudy lay in 'Lisbet's tearful embrace, his prediction come true. *1901-1935, beloved husband, devoted father, leaving behind his own father, four brothers, three sisters...*

It was a beautiful funeral, the Germania men's choir singing, "Let Me Go," the flowers abundant. Rudy had made many friends in America. It was afterward that was so awful.

Maybe it was too soon to recall old debts. Maybe they should have waited, giving 'Lisbet time to grieve. But everyone was living month-to-month, week-to-week, day-to-day. How much did Rudy owe? How much did 'Lisbet have to re-pay? Who knew? August claimed one number, the others something different. Along with medical bills and the funeral, her debts were enormous.

The little store had opened only a few months before, the counters and shelves bought with money from August, Fritz and Martha, all decided with a handshake. 'Lisbet was an admirable clerk who worked long hours, reaping a small profit by selling pencils, popcorn and penny candy. But 'Lisbet was not family. How could she have known that Fritz was inclined to exaggerate, that Marichen was quick to criticize, that Martha was sometimes too frank? Each had benefited from 'Lisbet's generosity. But then was then; now was now. So the divided family divided once again. Sophie and 'Lisbet were best friends and clung to one another. Otto, a devoted husband and father, just went along.

It didn't take much to exaggerate slights, corroding the mix even further. Without a written contract recourse was limited and lawyers were expensive. So they turned their backs in the Teutonic way, refusing to speak forevermore or at least until the debts were paid, leaving 'Lisbet and Eleanor to move into the space behind the store, sleeping on cots, scratching out a living.

For a while Fritz and August continued making popcorn balls, hawking them on the road every Sunday afternoon. But without Rudy's enthusiasm they lost interest. Even Wally found it hard.

Pretty soon they went out every two weeks, then whenever there was inventory, and finally they stopped, covering the equipment with tattered sheets to ward-off any corrosion. Surely a buyer would appear at some future date. Copper had value.

Fritz found a job washing cars and started to tinker with automobile repair. He met Kate at a German saloon that had a dance floor, a weekend band and twenty-five cent beer that could last all night. A strawberry blond with bright blue eyes, Kate was a live-in domestic working for a successful doctor. Short and roly-poly, she followed Fritz around like a puppy, and was someone to his liking for the moment.

Meanwhile Martha's job at Marshall Field's was going well. Beginning as a stock clerk she charmed everyone from salesman to executive buyer. Soon she was modeling in the tearoom on Saturday afternoons then transferred to the hair salon and sent to beauty school, all expenses paid.

Ever mindful for something more, she kept her eyes open. What were the porters doing? What were the requirements? How much were they paid?

Soon she had August in the employment office, keeping his hand steady as he filled out the application form. Then the interview, one on one. No, he was not a citizen but was going to school to learn. His English was getting better. His teacher expected him to pass. No, he hadn't heard of Social Security but would study it out. How much formal schooling? Well, there was *volkschule* in Germany, similar to completion of eighth grade. Work experience? He rattled it off: coal miner, foundry worker, baker.

The interviewer leaned back in his chair. "I see your sister works here. You're Martha's brother?"

August felt his stomach flip. Why did he ask? Were there rules against it? He nodded, too tense to speak.

"Well, I guess that's good enough," the interviewer smiled. "Couldn't ask for a better reference."

"Is okay?"

"You can start the first of the month." The interviewer thrust out his hand. "Welcome to Marshall Field's."

Six months later it was Marichen's turn. She was strong, a willing worker. The children were in school and at age twelve, Herby could supervise his sisters in the afternoon. Latch key children, they were sturdy and independent.

Assigned as a dishwasher in the Walnut Room, Marichen was quickly moved to the linen department where she patched and mended the server's uniforms. It was tedious but together she and August earned thirty-five dollars a week. Carefully managed, they could save half. Forget the disaster of Pop-P-Corn and Candy Company. They would open their own Mom and Pop store, just the two of them.

Now it was spring. The snow was gone, the children's long underwear replaced by a shorter version hooked onto long cotton stockings. At Easter they received baskets filled with chocolate eggs, marshmallow chicks and jellybeans, a concession to Americana and eaten in a frenzy of delight.

The next event would be August's birthday. Forty years old! Martha and Wally would be there along with Fritz and the ever-present Fraulein Kate. Marichen had baked a birthday cake, slathering it with plenty of frosting, placing four candles in the middle.

But before that, the children went to the library to check out some books, a new Saturday ritual. All they'd needed was a copy of the gas bill to verify their address. Yet August had resisted. "You mean it's free? You take books home for nothing? Doesn't nobody steal the books? Then why they need to see the gas bill? Won't somebody look at the address and come to rob us?"

Marichen thought that library books constituted the devil's temptation, far from the hymnals at church or the Bible. It had taken weeks of begging before the parents gave in, leaving it in God's hands at the end. There was just so much they could monitor and reading English was still too hard.

Martha and Wally had already arrived by the time the children returned. Perfumed and slender, Martha's dark hair framed her face in soft waves, her eyebrows pencil thin. Always current, she rouged her cheeks and creamed on lipstick with her little finger in the most enticing way. Walking, her skirt swirled above her knees and high heels arched her insteps as she placed them just so. She smoked cigarettes, dismissing Marichen's frown with a toss of her head. August was no help, declaring that the children could figure out that she'd become Americanized and outside their domain. As for Wally, he was seen as harmless or useful depending on the moment, a likable clown with crinkly eyes and a booming laugh.

Fritz and Fraulein Kate arrived shortly after and the air turned tobacco blue. Marichen had made peace with Fritz after the Christmas incident and he'd stopped teasing the children. He would even take them out for a ride in his panel truck from time to time. As for Fraulein Kate, she had become a permanent appendage at family occasions, never understanding Wally's jokes but laughing anyway.

Marichen adjusted her apron. The house was clean for company. Amish-sparse, the front room contained a couch and one upholstered chair along with a player piano, a gift from Wally after his mother died. A few extra chairs were scattered about for company. Radio? Frivolous and unworthy of the Christian life. Telephone? Cost too much. Newspapers? Okay when a *Tribune* or *American* was left on the streetcar but pay money? Nonsense.

The two bedrooms were equally sparse with parents in one, all three children in the other. Jewelry, makeup and nail polish were absent as were slacks and shorts. Movie magazines were dismissed as risqué, the work of the devil. Beds, dresser, and maybe a chair were good enough.

Back in the kitchen, Marichen checked the food simmering on the stove. Pot roast and carrots were birthday festive. It would be followed by the German ritual of each approaching the person of honor. "I congratulate you on your birthday," spoken in German, followed by a handshake and a kiss on the cheek. For the children, it ended with being given a shiny quarter, promptly spent for candy or dime store junk.

But for now conversation was mundane and comfortable. Martha, August and Marichen chatted about work. So-and-so was being promoted or sent to another department. Someone else was taking a leave of absence, because she was with child and not yet married. Shame on her. A new floorwalker was hired in the shoe department but everyone knew he wouldn't last. A woman fainted in the bathroom and an ambulance was called. No further word.

Fritz and Wally talked about cars and the new Ford that came with whitewall tires. Buick could seat six with a wide running board for easy access. Desoto and Packard were expensive, beyond anyone's dream. "Maybe you should buy a used car," Wally said, looking at August. "Take the family out for a Sunday drive, stop for ice cream or maybe a little sightseeing. You and Marichen are making good money. Loosen up a little."

"Sunday drive?" August snorted. "I had enough Sunday drive with selling popcorn on the corner."

"You could drive to church. Wouldn't that be nice?"

"Tell them," Marichen whispered to August. "You can tell them."

"What? Tell us what?" Martha asked.

"*Ach*, it's too soon." August shifted in his chair, scowling at Marichen. "We still have to sign the mortgage and pay the rest of the money down."

Everyone stopped talking and stared.

"Well, okay, then you got it out of me. We gonna buy a house." A smile tugged at the corners of August's mouth. "West side on Addison Street. The papers say Leyden Township. Like in the country but the bus goes there. We gave them a hundred dollars earnest money last week. There are four hundred more for the rest of the down payment. We have six months."

"You have to save four hundred dollars in six months? Are you crazy?" Martha gasped.

His face took on a teasing aspect. "Maybe I can borrow from you. You a rich lady, got nice clothes, dollars to burn…"

"That's how much you know," Martha sniffed. "Anyway, I have my own secret. I gonna visit Germany next summer for my birthday. So I don't got any money to give you."

Kate leaned forward. "You should take the Bremen cruise line, Martha. Is a nice way to go. My cousin, she went on the Bremen. A little more money but…"

Fritz had done some quick calculation. "Mortgage needs twenty percent down. What kinda house you gonna get for twenty-five hundred dollars?"

"Probably a fixer-upper," Wally offered. "Makes good sense. August is handy. He can do the work." He thrust out his hand. "So congratulations, August. Get the kids out of this lousy neighborhood into the country. Give 'em some fresh air."

"Country is for farmers," Fritz sniffed.

"How can you save that much money in six months?" Martha persisted.

"We are careful. August gives me five dollars a week and we eat good." Marichen took a deep breath. *Gott kann machen.*"

"Like God provided for Rudy or little Werner? You think this time it'll be different?"

"You didn't need to say that, Martha," Wally murmured, "to step on their dream."

"Why you need a house?" Kate prodded. "You work, the kids go to school, nobody is ever home anyway." She pointed to the front room. "Spend your money on piano lessons for kids and send them to Germania Club where they learn how to read and write good German. Then if you lose your job you don't lose the house too."

"I write down every penny in my Want Book," August said firmly. "How much money for Sunday school and church, for electric, for food, for everything. We pray and God will make it happen."

Marichen rose and began picking up the dishes. Maybe they should not have told their secret. "Trudi, go get the cake out from the bedroom where it is nice and cool."

The great moment had arrived and the real birthday was about to begin. "No Mama! Let me!" Scraping her chair back, Elsie darted into the bedroom.

Marichen voice rose in alarm. "Herby, you go help her."

"No, no! I can do it!" Elsie cried. And snatching the platter from atop the dresser, she lifted her prize, moving slowly toward the kitchen. And just as slowly the cake began to slide. Darting forward, Herby grabbed at it but only scraped ridges into the frosting leaving dark crescents of chocolate under his fingernails. It landed with a soft plop on the linoleum as Elsie stood frozen, clinging to the empty platter.

"Omigosh," Martha cried as the others gasped in dismay.

Elsie braced for the inevitable, a protracted holleration if not something worse.

But not in front of company. Instead, Marichen stepped

forward and taking the platter from the quivering Elsie, gathered up the crumpled cake, carrying it to the sink while Martha wiped up the remains. "Mama can fix it. It was accident."

There was enough to salvage after the candles were abandoned. Everyone said the cake was delicious and none the worse for having fallen onto the floor. But Elsie slunk into the bedroom, ashamed and terrified at the possible repercussions. She came out only when her father demanded a polite goodbye. Eyes downcast, she offered her hand and whispered *auf wieder sehen* then retreated once more.

After a while Martha followed, sitting next to Elsie on the edge of the bed. "You tried to be a big girl and one day you will be. It's only a little mistake. The cake tasted good, didn't it?"

Elsie's eyes continued to smart. "Did you know we were moving?"

"I learned tonight just like you. But think about it. You'll have a yard and a cat and maybe a dog…"

Elsie wasn't sure. A house away from Columbus school, away from the butcher shops with chickens clucking in wooden crates waiting to be killed kosher-style, away from the saloon that played loud music all night and permeated the street with the smell of beer, away from the storefronts where gypsies covered their windows with colorful cloths to hide the black magic inside. Daily Vacation Bible School was fun even though her parents forbid a repeat after seeing games and songs, marking them as frivolous. Library books showed mothers in ruffled aprons cooking dinner, little girls in Mary Jane shoes, back yards banked with shrubs and flowers and adorable puppies cavorting in the grass. All this was nothing near Aunt Martha's world of cigarettes, cocktails and perfume. "I want to be like you when I grow up," she whispered.

"Then you have to smile a lot," Martha replied, "so people will see what a nice girl you are."

"Martha, are you coming?" Wally's voice rang out over the murmur in the other room. "I'll go start the car if you're ready."

Martha got up. "Mama and Papa are doing this for you and for your brother and sister. It's not old-fashioned to give them respect."

A gentle reproach but not what Elsie wanted to hear. She turned away as Martha stroked her hair. "Uncle Wally is waiting."

"You will grow up and be a beautiful woman, Elsie. But remember, you need to be beautiful inside like I know you can be." Martha smiled and waved as she went back out.

The front door slammed and voices drifted from the kitchen as the clean up began. Herby had talked about being handicapped and led her to the library with her eyes closed so she could feel what it was like to be blind. She'd read about little girls with curly hair, going to bed in clean, pink pajamas. It would never be for her. She wasn't blind, but she wasn't a real American either. German was German and she was stuck with it forever, no matter what.

CHAPTER 8

Germany, 1936

ALMA SCANNED THE KITCHEN. EVERYTHING was in order with windows washed, floors scrubbed, tables buffed, dishes polished in a bath of hot suds, the shelves wiped clean, ready for Sunday and the day of rest. This day would be all the more special with a family gathering at Wilhelm's to celebrate Martha upon her 24th birthday.

Lima beans simmered on the stove with carrots and pork rind floating on top. Hilda had completed Volkschule and the required Landjahr where she spent six months away from home learning a trade. She was now home, working part-time at a café across from the school, preparing simple dishes, expanding her skills under supervision. Her wages plus Helmut's as an oiler were making life bearable. They'd moved into a three bedroom flat and Alma had even bought a radio, listening to how the Saar was being returned to the Reich, and the coming military conscription and rumblings of war. At first it caused a tug of alarm but then she put it aside. Gunter was too young, Helmut too old to be drafted into the military.

She sank into a chair across from where Hilda sat knitting. "We see Tante Martha tomorrow. Do you remember her?"

"I'm not sure. I was only eight when they left."

"She's staying with Wilhelm and the family even if Ida made an angry face."

Hilda shrugged. "There was nowhere else. Tante Guste and Elvira are staying with Opa while Onkel Siebold looks for a flat in Westerwald. And we don't have any room. That's for sure."

"Ida has bought many new things since joining the Party. She even says she wants more babies. Hitler is promising extra money for women who do."

Hilda's fingers flew over the knitting. Soldiers were everywhere, clicking their heels and saluting. Even little children now raised their hands to chirp Heil Hitler. Still, the streets were scrubbed clean. The shop windows glistened, pedestrians moved with a lighter step, and women wore traditional dresses again, showing a sense of German pride, German order, the German Fatherland. There might be comfort in that.

"So tomorrow we go zum Sahl and then to Onkel Wilhelm's. And once more we will hear about all the good things in America." Alma's voice was edged in bitterness.

"Tanta Martha is still German," Hilda said easily. "You can't take away someone's birthright." She swung around as Alma approached with the dishes, nudging her aside.

"At least there should be plenty to eat."

"Family is family. It cost a lot of money for Martha to come visit. I will be glad to see her."

Sunday church services ended early and they walked to Wilhelm's house, nudged along the way by soldiers who marched briskly by. "See how handsome…" Helmut declared grandly.

"Yes. Still, it makes me a little afraid," Hilda murmured.

They had arrived and her comment was left hanging in the air.

It was an imposing house, with a brown exterior surrounded by a veranda that curved around the sides. Friedrich was waiting in the largest of the chairs dressed in a black suit, his back ramrod straight, the shock of white hair and bushy eyebrows adding to a stately presence. Inside was Wilhelm, his eyes that had danced with an inner song now weary and sad. Ida's body had become coarse and dumpy, its natural curves hidden beneath heavy black garments worn to grieve her assorted miscarriages. The four daughters, Teutonic maidens ripe as a basket of plums, greeting them with a polite curtsy and a solemn "Heil Hitler." Ida offered her hand for a handshake with another "Heil Hitler," before motioning them to join the others.

Hilda had been there before and admired the couch, upholstered chairs and tables flanked by knick-knacks and oddments worthy of respect and a certain amount of envy. Through the archway, she could see a heavy oak table was laid with platters of food.

"Hitler makes it all possible," Ida declared proudly, following her glance.

"Only after you found a good husband," Alma added tartly.

Just then Guste emerged from the kitchen where she'd been helping with the food. "Martha comes down in a few minutes. Wait until you see! So fancy dressed. I watched when she put her clothes away." Her voice dropped to a whisper. "Lace bloomers, a pink chemise and two rayon slips. She even has a pair of slacks like Marlene Dietrich. And her hair is all wavy like in the picture shows." She turned toward the kitchen. "Elvira! Come say hello to your tante and cousins."

Elvira darted in, her lack of prettiness overshadowed by a sassy sense of good health and energy. "Hello, Tante Alma. I go to school next year and Mutti says I can join the Hitler Mädel when I'm old enough."

"The backbone of the Reich," Guste smiled. "I'm growing her right."

"Ja sure," Alma muttered. "Just don't forget where you came from."

Martha emerged a few minutes later and the room was transformed with smiles.

The next few hours were filled with family gossip and frequent trips to the table, filling their plates, drinking coffee. They reminisced about Rudy's homemade sausage, about the cat trained to knock on the window when it wanted in, about their Mutti buying a bargain roast, not knowing it was horsemeat, about the siblings sitting around the table doing homework with Fritz the least inclined. Guste reported on her trip to Prussia where she'd asked for help from Siebold's family only to return empty-handed.

Then Wilhelm's four daughters stood up to sing three songs in harmony, proving their father's mettle as conductor of an award-winning miner's chorus. It had generated attention from higher-ups, rewarding him with the job of supervisor, prompting him to shorten his name from Salefski to Zahn to distinguish himself from the Polish grunts under his command. August had followed. If Friedrich objected, he never said.

Finally the birthday cake emerged, a delicate five-layered torte, a treat that would have been a miracle a few years back. America might be the land of plenty, but hard work and political will was paying dividends in Germany.

Then conversation began to lag, the effects of abundance and wine. "I am so full," Martha groaned, "and I need a cigarette and some fresh air."

"I go with you," Alma said. "We can take a walk and I show

you around the neighborhood." She looked around. "Anyone else?"

Hearing no response, the sisters retrieved their sweaters and went outside. Pausing to light her cigarette, Martha handed one to Alma, then arm in arm, they strolled past three- and four-story buildings, rounding a corner to arrive at the end of the street, now blocked by a huge windowless building.

"It's a new factory," Alma explained. "It's supposed to be making cars for the autobahn. But everyone thinks it's for munitions. Hitler says we should take back what they stole from us in Versailles. If it's war, I hope it's over soon."

"Do you suppose Gunter will…"

"Oh no. He's too young. And Helmut's too old."

"So you're not afraid?"

Alma had turned away, her reply lost in a sudden breeze.

"You should have come to America, Alma. It's not too late, you know. You can still…"

"How? You think money grows on trees?" Then seeing Martha's hurt look, Alma softened her voice. "Things are getting better. Gunter soon finishes school and there will surely be jobs. Then I come visit."

They were back on the main road, the streetcars clattering by carrying workers home. Buildings outlined against the variegated sky provided a moment of loveliness to herald the coming week. Martha remembered how she carried kettles of hot water for her brothers to wash up at the end of the day. In America she would take a nightly shower with more hot water than she'd ever need. "Does Helmut like his job? Is it hard?"

"He doesn't complain and I don't ask."

Martha glanced sidelong. "Everything else still good?"

Alma shrugged. "How goes it with you and Wally?"

Martha laughed. "Okay, so it's none of my business."

"We do what we have to do."

"You did right, Alma. They are good children." She pictured Hilda as a baby, her pale translucent skin, her eyes bright and eager yet guarded like that of a stray animal. Born the size of a kitten, Hilda had managed to survive. Martha had married at eighteen. At almost sixteen Hilda might not have long to wait. "I bet Hilda has a boyfriend, no?"

"There were boys at the café in Osnabrück where Hilda spent her Landjahr. They were Männerchor that rented a room to rehearse. One, named Rainer, liked her and they sneaked out to go dancing but that was only once. Later, he gave her a big bouquet of roses because he was going into the army. He writes letters sometimes, but just friendly. I know, because I read her mail."

"There's nothing wrong with having a boyfriend, Alma. I had many boyfriends before I married Wally. My brothers not know everything."

"We should go back. It will be dark soon."

Martha lit another cigarette and handed one to Alma. "Remember how Papa used to walk, swinging his gold-handled cane? You would think he was a prince, his thumb in the corner of his vest, chin held high. I thought he was so handsome, so regal."

Alma looked straight ahead. "I don't remember. It was a long time ago."

"But don't you think about it sometime? When we were little we didn't know about being poor. We thought Papa and Mutti would always take care of us. And they did. It wasn't until later when we learned how hard it was. But at first..."

"You were the baby and it was easier for you. I had to take care of all those who came after me. There was no time for anything else."

"Oh Alma, such a life you had," Martha protested. "Has it made you bitter? Is there no joy left in your heart?"

"I get up in the morning, make breakfast and pack lunches. I get work if I can. At night, I fix supper, wash up, and go to bed so I can get up and do it again. If Papa was handsome thirty years ago, I don't remember."

Martha felt her eyes sting with unexpected tears. "I tell you what. Let's you and me go out to a cabaret where we sing, drink a little wine and laugh at funny jokes. We will celebrate my birthday the right way. I brought some extra money. If Helmut does not want to go, we go together just you and me." She grabbed her sister's arm. "What do you say?"

For a moment Alma's face brightened. Then she took a deep breath. "I have no nice clothes, nothing to wear."

"I borrow you some." Martha eyed her sister's slim body. "A blouse, loose around the bosom with puffed sleeves. You wear it with a skirt and a silk sash around the middle." She laughed as she pictured the transformation. "My earrings will make you look like a gypsy, all spangles and beads. Remember how Wilhelm called me his little gypsy? He would pick me up and dance around in circles singing his crazy songs until I was dizzy and Mutti made him stop."

"…then came the war." The cloud across Alma's face was undeniable, and with that they turned to walk back with nothing left to say.

So began Martha's vacation, going on long walks with her father, stopping at a sidewalk café for a glass of wine and a pastry, visiting with Guste, getting to know Elvira as much as the energetic child allowed. In the evening, she might visit Alma, describing American movies, dancing the fox trot or the black bottom while Alma watched wistfully and Helmut scowled.

Saying goodbye was hard and Alma's eyes reddened when she was handed an envelope containing thirty marks, close to a week's wages. "Don't tell anybody," Martha whispered. "This is for you."

Back aboard ship, she reflected on the trip to America with Marichen and the two children eight years back. Then she'd spoken German, thought in German, a prisoner of her surroundings, yet wary of demands, requirements, exhortations, always wanting to be free, to soar, to travel her own path, eager to see what lay ahead, eager, eager, always eager.

She thought of Alma, Hilda, Guste, Papa and especially Wilhelm. He had constructed a pipe organ in their very kitchen, the parts scattered over the floor for weeks, the organ ending up at the Sahl where it was still being played on Sunday mornings. What if Papa had been rich? Would Wilhelm have become a famous musician? What if Alma had never married? Would she have been a courtesan or did she have enough style to be a chanteuse or even a movie star? What if she herself had remained in Germany? Would she have joined the Party in order to reap benefits and handouts? What more would have been required to receive these desperately needed favors?

There was no point in speculating. Then was then, now was now. Aboard ship, she was a married woman on the way home to America.

CHAPTER 9

Chicago, 1937

THE NEIGHBORHOOD WAS LITTLE MORE than a series of bungalows and an abundance of vacant lots with gas lamps at the corners. A new school was surrounded by mud, waiting for grass to take hold. There was a community center with a tiny library upstairs where the social worker lived, the downstairs offering arts and crafts during the summer and after school.

Poverty was still the great leveler but they were poorer than most. Granted, they owned a two-bedroom house but it was the shabbiest on the block, the previous owners having stripped it of anything they could sell including the bedroom doors. The basement floor was of crumbling cement, badly in need of repair. The back yard was choked with grasses encroaching on the raspberry bushes, the flowerbeds covered with weeds. Inside, their furniture was shabby and unmatched. Clothes were too big or too small, too faded, too drab, too out of style, too foreign. Marichen would arrive home, her fingers sore from a day of sewing and patching, her mind numb. Any catching up was on

Saturday, with Sunday their only day of rest.

Yet, for Elsie, summer was a time of innocence, spending the hours on the front porch steps with a coloring book and broken crayons. Summer meant watching boys digging a secret hut in an empty lot, running under the neighbor's sprinkler or going to the library for the latest *Bobsey Twins*. Afternoons were filled with hopscotch, roly-poly or jump rope, evenings playing kick the can or make-a-round-circle. If there were worries, they rested on the shoulders of parents, aunts and uncles who labored in the city, alighting from the bus at twilight, too weary to smile.

It was Saturdays that made demands, cleaning the bathroom, sweeping the porch or sidewalk, then standing at the ready to do more. Between time, she might sit at the player piano watching the keys bounce up and down, trying to learn how to play by imitation. After all, her father had taught himself to play the violin, zither and cornet, all without lessons. But the keys moved too fast and she didn't know where to begin.

So, she went downstairs to watch her father as he squatted with an anvil between his knees repairing the family shoes.

"Mom said I'm supposed to polish the shoes when you're done." Elsie's face was quizzical. "Are you done?"

He fitted a shoe onto the anvil and glued a rubber wedge to a rundown heel, shaking his head as he removed some nails from between his lips.

"You done with mine?"

"What does it look like?"

"How many more to go?"

He squeezed a dollop of glue onto the next patch. "How come you asking so much? You still in the question age?"

"What's the question age?"

"When you want to know everything."

"Herby says he wants to know everything. Is he in the question age?"

August pulled out a crooked nail. "No. Question age is when you are three or four years old. Then is when you ask lots of questions."

"Did I ask lots of questions?"

The glue oozed out of the tube, the scent of Man At Work. "You still do."

"When will it stop?"

"When you grow up."

"How long do I have to wait?"

"Maybe when you're thirty."

She threw up her hands in exasperation. And turning, she went back upstairs.

Her mother had been in the yard hanging out the wash. Elsie should have helped and she felt a pang of guilt.

Then suddenly there was a swish and framed in the front door stood Aunt Martha. "My suitcase is on the front porch." She began to cry. "I didn't know where else to go."

Marichen stared, her face aghast. "What happened?"

"That sonovabitch doesn't know when to take no for an answer." Martha tilted her head revealing a black eye.

Marichen turned toward Elsie, who stood frozen at the top of the stairs. "Go get Daddy. Then go outside and see if the laundry is dry."

"But I want..."

"Do it!"

Banished, Elsie delivered the message then sat on the back steps straining to hear. First, her mother's stern admonition, *Whosoever God hath joined together...* and her father talking in German. In between was Martha's tearful rejoinder. "How was I supposed to know? All you ever told me was not to buy a pig in a poke. What was that supposed to mean? I was so dumb and nobody told me..."

An airplane buzzed overhead and dipped its wings. Herby came around the back with a half-dozen *American*s in his basket, extras from his paper route. Trudi, back from the store, was sent outside once she'd placed the groceries on the table. Two sentences explained what was going on and together they sat in worried silence. Was Aunt Martha going to move in with them? Oh, heavenly bliss! But where would she sleep? And what about Uncle Wally? Were they going to get a dee-vorce? Were they supposed to hate him now?

The voices subsided. August had gone back to the basement and his hammering resumed. It might be all right to go back inside. "Just act normal," Herby whispered.

In the kitchen, Marichen was busy at the sink and Martha sat at the table, her nose carefully powdered, her swollen lips covered with a dab of lipstick. "I have a suitcase on the porch. I gonna stay here for a while."

Herby looked at his mother. "Should I...?"

"Just put it in the front room."

"We have church tomorrow," Elsie whispered.

"You can go to church without me," Martha murmured. "It will give me time to think."

Elsie's eyes widened. Not go to church? Surely that was a sin.

"We can make up our minds later," Marichen declared evenly. "Now you can go bring in the wash."

Back outside, Elsie folded towels and sheets bringing the rest into the kitchen, sprinkling the shirts and dresses for ironing later on. Herby moved to copy the songs for Sunday Service on the family hectograph, both straining to hear what the grownups were saying in the other room. Then the silent walk to the library for there was little to say.

Back home with a fresh stack of books, they ate a quick supper and took their baths, hearing the murmur of adults far into the night.

Morning saw the usual scramble for church with Marichen telling Martha to peel the potatoes by eleven, then shred the red cabbage to cook at a low simmer. August distributed the money for collection, tied into the corner of their handkerchiefs for safekeeping. Then off in single file along the edge of Addison Street like ducklings in a row.

Irvingwood Church was a mile away and even farther than St. John's in atmosphere and size. Seeded as a "mission" church, it now served fifty families, enough for Lenten classes and an occasional potluck. Built like a New England Meeting House, its steeple, high windows and dark brown walls towered over the landscape. The basement level included an all-purpose room plus kitchen and three classrooms where children heard Bible stories and pocketed colorful leaflets to take home. August and Marichen attended the adult class, an intellectual reprieve from their menial jobs at Marshall Field's.

After that came church in the upper level. Seated next to her brother, Elsie would study the fly on her arm and the folds in her dress trying not to drift off to sleep. She knew how many thorns were on the statue hanging over the altar and was convinced that Pastor Bittner's somber black robe sucked up the sun making the sanctuary dim. Then a final hymn, benediction, and the procession down the nave to shake Pastor Bittner's hand at the door.

Marichen had found a spot in the shade, motioning the children to stay with her as August joined a group of men to discuss current events, deploring Roosevelt and the farmers who dumped milk and cream on the roadside to protest against cuts in subsidies, grumbling about taxes and social programs, re-making the world as they saw fit.

Finally hunger demanded they go home.

Within sight of the house, the children ran ahead, eager to change into more comfortable clothes for play. But this weekend continued to be full of surprises, with Martha and Wally sitting on the front porch, the car parked at the curb.

"What are you doing here?" August's voice drowned out the children's cries of delight.

Wally stood up, offering his most engaging smile. "Greetings, August. Long time no see." He stepped forward. "I'm here to get my wife. She's coming home with me."

August stopped at the foot of the stairs, his jaw jutting out. "Who said?"

"We had a talk…" Martha began nervously.

"That's right. Hey, fella, we're still friends, ain't we?" Wally reached for August's hand. "You know how these women can be."

Marichen motioned the children into the back yard, placing herself between the two men. "Maybe you need to go inside and talk. The neighbors…"

"No, that's okay. We're civilized. Man to man, right?"

August flexed his muscles. "What you mean, man to man? She's too good for you, you lousy Polack coward bum. Pushing women around like some drunken pig from skid row. Wife beater! We should have figured that out long time ago when she first brought you to 'Lisbet's house."

"Hey, be careful who you call a bum," Wally scowled. "Your Little Miss Flirty-Flirty could hardly speak English when I got her. And who found her the job at Field's? Not you. That's for damned sure. You wanted her to scrub floors for the rest of her life like all of your crummy family, a bunch of foreigners. I taught her all she knows."

"For sure. All the stuff that nice girls don't do. Too young to know better but you learned her good and fast."

"Oh yeah?" Wally stood towering over the red-faced August. "Well, she's my wife and what goes on between us is none of your goddamned business. She wants to come home with me so you just butt out, you lousy greenhorn."

August turned toward Martha. "You gonna go with him? This filthy pig who pushes women around, who gives you a fat lip and a black eye? You going with him?"

"I started it," she whispered. "It was half my fault. I threw something…"

August was undaunted. "You go back to this animal, this dog who climbs on his bitch three four times a day or whenever he feels like it, then knocks her around just for fun? You go home with him, this Crawly Wally?"

Marichen threw her hands over her ears and Wally's face turned ashen. "C'mon Martha. Before I knock his block off." Snatching the suitcase at the top of the stairs, he grabbed Martha's hand pulling her into the car as August lunged forward.

"*Verdammte*! In league with the devil!" August stood with his fists clenched. Turning, he stormed inside the house where there was the sound of crashing furniture and splintering glass.

He loses his head, Marichen had admonished the children. *Be careful you don't make him lose his head.* For once the dam broke, the raw emotion came spewing forth like vomit, a cathartic rage held back too long, leaving him limp and exhausted, his victims terrified, after which he would retreat into silence lasting days or even months. It had happened with Otto and Sophie, with 'Lisbet at Rudy's funeral, with his boss at the bakery when his shift was cut short. No explanation, no discussion, no signal as the clouds gathered, nor hint of when the sun might re-appear. All this revealed after they were married with no clue before except for his delight in her body, his demanding, passionate hunger.

The children remained huddled in the back yard. Trudi finally broke the silence. "I guess Aunt Martha was just visiting after all."

Elsie could barely breathe for shame. The whole world was watching, for the scene had taken place in the middle of the street.

They waited for silence, then went in to help Marichen clean up. There were three broken plates and some capsized furniture, but no serious damage. Meanwhile, August had retreated to the basement and no one dared follow.

Sunday dinner consisted of sandwiches with Marichen taking a plate down to August, placing it on his workbench before turning to leave.

He came upstairs as darkness fell, his expression warning everyone away. Meanwhile, the house hung in silence, waiting for a signal that said the paralyzing rage had passed.

But one thing was for sure. After today, there would be no more Wally and Martha, at least for a good long while.

CHAPTER 10

Germany, 1937

THE CAFÉ CLATTERED WITH ACTIVITY, ending the mid-day rush. Dishwashers rinsed cups and scraped plates, plunging them into steaming water while cooks scrubbed down greasy walls. In front, servers and barmaids counted receipts, tallying the balance before going home.

Hilda was in the kitchen preparing salads, arranging the trays of cheese and sausage. She was there to learn, making cheesecake, steak tartar and soups, another step beyond her basic training at the country house.

She arched her back and resumed wiping the refrigerator walls. One more hour before her shift was over. She moved quickly, afraid the overheated room would affect the contents. In the walk-in cooler, sauerbraten was marinating next to salads on trays, with cakes and pies sorted according to size. Once a local roadhouse, the café now drew from nearby defense plants or soldiers on leave, everyone flush with money from the impending war.

She turned toward the shelves checking to see that salt and

peppershakers were filled. Prep-cooks would be coming in to par-boil noodles, potatoes and vegetables, preparing sauces for dinner. Growth had cramped the facilities but with all resources marked for defense, there was no chance for expansion. For the owner, it was pure profit.

The dining room was empty except for three soldiers finishing their meal when two more came in. The waitress was not pleased even though soldiers tipped well. After writing down their orders, she came through the swinging doors.

"That tall one says he's looking for you, Hilda. What do I tell him?"

"Me?" Hilda looked up. "Which one?"

"The one facing the door. He says he knows you."

Hilda peeked around the swinging door and suddenly grew faint. It was Rainer, the young man she'd met during her Landjahr. She touched her hair, damp and grimy at the end of the day. "Tell him I've gone home," she whispered. "I'll stay here until he leaves."

The cooks and bus boys turned and grinned. They'd seen what happened with soldiers and pretty girls.

Retreating into the cooler, Hilda re-arranged the chicken and sausage, adjusted blocks of cheese, moving cans of juice to make them more accessible. She'd been sweating and now her damp clothes felt like ice. After a half-hour she went back out hoping that the men had left. The restaurant was empty, closed for two hours between lunch and dinner.

Grabbing her purse, she sprinted through the back door. Getting home late would require an explanation.

Outside, the restaurant dog sat waiting for his customary treat. She had forgotten. Maybe tomorrow. Taking a deep breath, she hurried down the road as the dog followed. "Go home, Steiger," she commanded. "The door is locked and I have nothing for you."

The dog slowed down, pausing each time she turned around, whimpering. Soon she was in sight of home and the dog had disappeared. From the upstairs landing, she heard voices from inside. Surely her father was not home so soon. Heart pounding, she peered into the kitchen and saw her mother and Rainer chatting amiably.

Terrified, she moved toward the bedroom window that faced the tiny porch. It was slightly open in the early summer air. Maybe she could slip in and hide. She pressed at the window sash until there was enough space to toss in her purse. Bent nearly double, she followed, landing with a thud on the glistening floor. Gathering her skirts around her, she huddled on the edge of the bed, wanting to see him, but not like this.

"She'll be home any minute. She's already late." Out on the landing, Alma leaned over the railing. "Oh, there's the dog. So she must be around here somewhere."

It was hopeless. Taking a deep breath, Hilda emerged from the bedroom. "How come you were late?" Alma demanded. "Rainer has been waiting."

Hilda mumbled something about bringing the soiled linen home to launder for a few pennies extra, then reached out to shake hands. "It is good to see you again."

He stood up and bowed slightly. "I was coming home on leave so I thought I would stop and visit. Your mother was good enough to let me wait."

"We've been having a nice talk," Alma smiled. "He told me all about how his Sing Verein traveled over Westphalia giving concerts just like your Onkel Rudy. You don't remember, of course. You were still so young."

Hilda's eyes had not left his as he stood so handsome in his uniform. Towering over her, they had laughed at the disparity during their one and only date when she was fifteen, an evening of dancing. Then the music had slowed and she'd put her head on his shoulder, an image visited each night before falling asleep. Why was it so different at seventeen? And why was her heart pounding so?

"You should stay for supper," Alma declared. "Hilda is a good cook. My husband will be home soon. Then we sit down and eat."

"That would be nice. I can help." He offered a shy smile. "I am the youngest of eight. I know how to cook. "

"Ah, you learned from the others. But first you can have coffee with Hilda." She bustled around to find another cup for her daughter.

It was hard to make small talk. Rainer, his muscles slender and smooth like an Olympic swimmer, easy and relaxed inside his crisply pressed uniform, his brown hair cut military style, his jaw strong and manly. A soldier of the Reich. But his eyes were soft and gentle, his voice sweetly melodic like a Schubert caress. And such an expressive mouth, like a movie star. "I'm sorry I don't look better. I should have cleaned up. I just came from work," Hilda stammered.

"I know. I remembered the address and came to see you."

"I must bring Frau Keller the dress I made for her," Alma said. "I be back in an hour. Gunter will be home soon."

They sat across from one another, both silent, as Alma's footsteps faded. "I wrote as often as I could," Hilda began. "But my parents…"

"I have two sisters. My father was the same way."

"I should wash up a little," she continued nervously. "The restaurant is always so hot and I didn't have time. Maybe you wait a little, then we talk."

"You look fine." He cleared his throat and leaned forward. "I like you very much, you know. Maybe it will be all right if we keep writing now and then. Your mother says it would be all right for now."

"I would write every day," she breathed, "because I like you too. And the war will not last long. Hitler promised."

"Still, bunkers are being built on the western front and Hitler is making friends with Mussolini. There are treaties with Japan and now Spain." His face was serious. "I might not come back."

"Oh, you will. You will!" she cried. "Then we have good jobs and buy things like in America. Just you wait and see!"

The clatter on the landing announced Gunter's arrival and the two sprang apart.

Out of breath, he entered the room in a whirl, his belt-bound books tossed casually over his shoulder. In his last year of school, Gunter would soon join the adult world, one of the thousands grinding out a living as best they could. Still, factories were humming and the new regime was scooping up the unemployed, shaping them into soldiers with close-order drill, marching like Prussians who'd been trained to do this forever. Even the farmers were thriving, mechanized in response to a growing demand. There was real work in the Ruhr, not just in the mines. A young man might become a postal clerk or work in a defense plant earning good money.

Framed in the open door, Gunter stopped, then smiled broadly. "Halloo. You must be Rainer. She told me all about you." His eyes moved to Hilda then held out his hand as Rainer stood up to salute. "Is okay. We don't bother with that in this house."

Rainer hesitated, then shook hands, once more at ease. "So how goes it with the school boy? Still doing homework? I'm told your new math is about how much to pay on each Aryan child instead of giving everything to the cripples." His smile twinkled as he eyed

Gunter's damp hair. "Looks like you were running around the track."

"Yes. Many teachers are gone so we have much more time outside." He put down his books. "You staying for supper?"

Rainer nodded. "Is good?"

"Sure. Hilda says you're very nice. I think you should get married."

"Gunter!" Hilda's face turned bright red and she moved to push him out of the room. "Is not funny. Rainer is a guest."

"*I will be a soldier true, fighting for the fatherland...*" The melody echoed as Gunter went into the bedroom to change.

"Gunter tries to be funny," Hilda declared, still blushing. "He goes to picture shows and wants to be like the funny men. He says he's not handsome enough to be the one who gets all the women."

Rainer smiled. "A blonde blue-eyed Aryan with a flat belly and broad shoulders will do just fine in the army. The generals like to see them in parades, carrying flags…"

"Mutti says not to worry."

Rainer sat quietly and thought for a moment. "Well, maybe we should start supper. We can talk to your Mutti and Papa for a while and drink some wine I brought. Then after, we go for a walk just you and me." His voice was a question.

She could feel his warmth like at the dance two years before, gliding on the sawdust floor, feeling his hand on the small of her back while they moved as one. He was different from the silly boys that were her brother's friends. Rainer was a man. She struggled to swallow the tightness in her throat. "We could make potato salad with a little bacon on the side. Creamed carrots would be good too, don't you think?"

"Ja, I think." Taking off his jacket, he rolled up his sleeves. "I can scrape the carrots first and then you show me what else to do."

He smiled at her confusion. "Most chefs are men, you know."

They worked in tandem, another version of the dance. By the time her parents arrived the table was set for five with the food ready to be served.

"We have company for supper, Papa. Rainer has to finish his service in the Wehrmacht and stopped to see us before he leaves."

"Herr Schulte," Helmut murmured, offering his hand. "May God guide you and all the soldiers fighting for the Reich."

"And pray it be over soon," Rainer replied.

Hilda stood watching and Gunter peered from the bedroom door. This time, no matter what. A decent job, a roof over their heads. That was not too much to ask. Already they had more food than they could have imagined even a year ago.

"But I see that we are ready." Alma clapped her hands, directing where each should be seated. Bowing their heads, they murmured a prayer then filled their plates, marveling at the tasty food while Hilda pretended that this was just an ordinary meal, that they would not be fighting in a war, that their world and their families remained secure.

It was getting dark when they finished. Hilda stood up, starting to clear the table but Alma brushed her aside. "No, no, you have a guest. There's still time before the last train leaves. I'll finish up. Go for a walk and enjoy the night air. Then you say goodbye."

Hilda's eyes fastened on her father.

"Yes, yes. Go ahead. I go to bed pretty soon anyway. It must be the wine. It was good, more than I could pay."

Rainer bowed slightly. "Good wine for good people. But I think a little walk would clear my head. If I may…"

Hilda retrieved her sweater from the box under her bed, leading the way down the stairs. The street was deserted on this weekday evening, the air smelling sweet from a recent rain. "This is my favorite time," she said. "The stars are coming out one by one. Even the moon…"

"*Kennst du das Land*," he hummed softly, "*where the lemon blossom grows, in foliage dark the orange golden glows…*" He reached for her hand folding it in his.

"You have such a nice voice," she said shyly. "I remember standing outside the door at the café listening to your group rehearsing. I love the Schubert Lieder. It's such beautiful poetry. They were my favorites in school."

"Ours is the land of Goethe, Heine, Beethoven…" He shortened his steps to match hers. "It makes me want to dance." He looked into her upturned face. "Like we did before."

"Oh yes," she breathed. "Every night when I go to bed…" Her face warmed at the mention of something so suggestive. "I mean…"

"Was I in your dreams?"

She nodded, wishing she could find the words.

"Like a first love?"

They had arrived at the end of the street. Across was a small park, now dark and deserted. "I don't know what that means," she stammered.

"Shall we go and sit down? There are benches…" Without waiting for a reply he led her toward a bank of tall shrubs exuding a nighttime fragrance. "*A gentle breeze blows from the azure sky,*" the humming went on. Then releasing her hand, he seated her with a flourish and perched at the other end of the bench his eyes on her.

"*Still stands the myrtle, and the laurel, high…*" she continued, her voice a golden lilt.

He smiled. "Is that how your teacher taught you to recite?"

"That's how I remember it," she replied, flushing again. "I thought I had it right."

"You were perfect. I couldn't have done it better." He moved closer. "You are perfect now. I knew that from the beginning when I first saw you." He lifted her face so she was looking up at him. "Did you feel something too? At the beginning?"

She couldn't speak. It was nothing like the movies with sassy flirtation, the give and take of clever repartee. Instead, her limbs felt like they would send her to the ground, a puddle of skin and bones. "Oh, Rainer…"

He was so gentle, barely brushing his lips against hers, his uniform coarse and rough in his embrace. "Oh, my sweet," she whispered, "my dear."

Then it was a real kiss, urgent and warm. "I think you were glad to see me. Is right?"

She touched his cheek, moving to stroke his chin, touch his throat. "You make me so afraid. I didn't know what I would do if the war…"

"Then you need to be my sweetheart good and true. You must write to me and wait for me. Then I promise, I will come back." His voice was firm. "You will never lose me."

Far off, a distant whistle signaled a factory shift change. The mines were working around the clock with overtime to keep them running. Hunger had become a sad memory, and scavenging for coal along the railroad tracks a bitter joke, for it was easily bought in abundance. "It's time," she murmured. "You have to go."

"I'll walk back with you to say goodnight to the family."

The flat was dark when they arrived. Moving about in the silent room, Rainer gathered his belongings, bending to brush his lips over hers for a final goodbye. Then he was down the steps, his cheerful whistle fading away to nothing.

Too excited to sleep, Hilda curled up on the cot fully dressed, hugging her pillow in an ecstasy of love. The deep breathing of her parents in the other room added rhythm to her thoughts. Finally, she began to drift off to sleep without noticing her brother peering from the other room, grinning his approval.

CHAPTER 11

Chicago, 1938

LABOR DAY MARKED THE END of summer vacation, the children eager to be back in school. Marichen looked at the sink filled with dirty dishes, at the stove crusted with burned-on food, at cabinets crammed with open packages, their contents too stale to eat. They'd enlarged the kitchen, created another bedroom for Herby and poured fresh concrete in the basement to support a stoker to feed the furnace automatically. Yet little had changed. They still sprayed for bedbugs, staining the white wallpaper that no longer looked like fine linen.

August was trying to sell vacuum cleaners door to door for extra money, an opportunity presented by Pastor Bittner who said it would be easy – just a matter of buying a demonstrator and memorizing the sales pitch. But doors kept slamming in his face or producing a curt, "No Thanks," once he'd cleaned half of the lady's house.

She looked at the uneven stack of newspapers, leftovers from Herby's paper route. It brought in enough to pay for his lunch money, carfare and clothes, the rest frittered away on junk. In Germany, the money would have been turned over to parents, no questions asked.

When Rudy died, August had promised that they'd open their own Mom and Pop store. But lately he'd refused to discuss it. Still, she kept her eyes open, going to Wallerman's grocery two blocks away, watching how he joshed the ladies into buying more and more. August predicted that they'd soon be bankrupt from selling on credit, but the store continued to thrive. Today, Mr. Wallerman had even added a small bag of cookies to her order. "For the children," he winked.

Two blocks west stood an isolated storefront surrounded by weeds and crickets in the summer, in winter blanketed with snow and ice. Sometimes an entrepreneur would open – a bicycle shop, dry goods or hardware. It didn't matter. Within a few months it would close. August and Marichen would peer through the windows on their way to church, shaking their heads in puzzlement. Too isolated? Not enough capital to invest? Wrong product? Why was one store successful? Why was Wallerman's different?

Four blocks to the north, a line of dairy stores sold milk for twenty-nine cents a gallon if you brought in your own jug, two cents more for homogenized and business was booming. Marichen's new Frigidaire could hold enough for one of the children to make the trip twice a week. Maybe that was the kind of store they should consider. Everyone drank milk, and with the right price…

She turned on the hot water, putting the dishes in to soak. Trudi was baby-sitting three doors down but she spent most of the time listening to the radio, learning about worldliness and frivolous things. None of this was what she'd planned.

Suddenly the front door slammed, and Elsie stormed into the kitchen. "There's nothing to do, Mom. Dolores is visiting her aunt and Joanie and Janet went swimming without inviting me. Everyone else is at camp in Wisconsin."

"Go take down the laundry. Then sweep the porch and the front sidewalk. After that…"

Elsie wiped the sweat off her forehead and stamped her foot. "Herby and Trudi get to do all kinds of things but all you want from me is work. I don't even have my friends around. Summer camp didn't cost much and anyway, we're not *that* poor." It was an argument she'd lost months before. "So now I'm going back to school without getting to do anything all summer long. It's not fair!"

"If it costs a nickel and you don't have a nickel, it costs too much. And like I told you, that camp is with the German *Bund*. They try to act like soldiers, marching and singing, wearing brown shirts and black boots and yelling *Heil Hitler*. They're bad people."

"You are always talking about how great Germany is, how they do everything better. How come…"

"These are different. They will get you in trouble. I read all about it in the *Abendpost*."

"The *Abendpost!*" Elsie snorted. "They don't know what's happening in America."

"And how much do you know about what's happening here, little girl? Girls Scouts, Boy Scouts, drawing and painting pictures when you should be studying or helping out around the house." Marichen pursed her lips. "Daddy said no, and he was right. Now go outside and do what I said."

Too frustrated for tears, Elsie flung herself back outside.

"Ten years here, and for what?" Marichen muttered. "Supposed to be for the children. But the one born here has the biggest mouth of all. No respect, just another spoiled…"

She plunged her hands into the hot water – scrub, rinse, drain, wiping off the stove, the table, the counter tops. It wasn't true and she knew it. Their jobs were secure, the children were in school, their savings beginning to build. Marichen had stopped crying after their second year in Chicago, and August was being nicer to her. It might be good to go back to Germany for a visit, but she wouldn't want to live there, not any more.

Back at the window, she watched Elsie placing the laundry in the basket. Two houses over, Trudi was on the swing with little Sharon, rocking gently. Marichen had planted a few potatoes and carrots their first summer in the house but there was never enough time to cultivate them. Just too much else to do.

Suddenly, a commotion outside. Wiping her hands, she went to the front door and there stood Martha and Wally, arms loaded with packages. It was unexpected, but not a shock. Over the summer, Martha had sought out August at work – accidentally on purpose. At first it was an icy confrontation. But Martha had a way of getting around her brother, starting with simple chitchat. Hadn't this been a hot summer? What news from Germany? How about the kids? The next step was to promise August that things were getting better at home, that Wally was down to one or two beers at night. He was a good man – really. She told about Wally spending hours trying to fix his car, not realizing he'd simply run out of gas. It made August laugh and after that they were back to normal.

As for Marichen, her only concern was to keep August on an even keel. If he exploded, it was because he was a man. So when Martha appeared in the Linen Room with iced coffee after the midday rush or brought her a beautifully made sandwich, she accepted them as peace offerings. Family was family after all.

Now she greeted Martha with a smile. "Oh, what now? You make Christmas in the summertime? Is nobody's birthday. So maybe your head goes crazy from the heat?"

"For the kids," Martha murmured, placing the packages on the dining room table. "School starts tomorrow. Kids should have new stuff – pencils and notebooks. It makes school special." She turned to Elsie who had come in from the yard. "What you gonna wear back to school?"

Elsie gestured toward the back yard. "Maybe that yellow dress hanging there. I can iron it tonight so it'll be ready."

Marichen met Martha's glance. "Don't feel sorry for her. When I was her age I did the family laundry, and we didn't have no washing machine neither. With all my brothers and sisters to take care…"

"I know, I know. But these are different times, Marichen. Kids should grow up to be somebody, not just Mama's helper. They should like school and have friends. That means looking nice."

Wally had gone back to the car and returned carrying a large flat package. "A little something for you." He placed it in front of Marichen with a grin.

Inside was a huge replica of an eagle adorned with red, white and blue feathers, the talons clutching an olive branch, the entire figure attached to a piece of black velvet framed in gold. "It's to hang over the couch. It gives the room some decoration, some color. You don't have anything here to spruce things up."

Marichen stared dumbfounded. Mirrors belonged on the wall. Calendars too. But a bird made with real feathers?

"It'll look really good over the couch. Where is August? Not home? Wally, go downstairs and find a hammer. We'll surprise him." Martha began to laugh. "Wally won it at the Riverview arcade shooting ducks with a pop-gun. It took two hours. He wanted you to have it."

"You think it looks good?" Marichen asked dubiously. "Is that what people like?"

The fumes from the Addison Street bus drifted through the

open windows and soon there were footsteps as August appeared, leaving the vacuum cleaner demo on the porch. "So what kind of horse crap is this?" he smiled, easing into the front room.

"Hey, August, *wie gehts*? Long time no see." Wally stood up and motioned toward the picture. "Look what I won for you! Took me two whole hours at the sharpshooters' booth."

"Two hours? I coulda shot that one down in five minutes." August put down his sales case and glanced at the eagle resting against the couch. "No wonder you wanna give it away."

"It will look good over the couch," Martha insisted.

August stared for a minute then shrugged. "So we keep it. Why don't you stay for supper? Just let me put my things away."

Trudi and Herby had come home, and soon the table was set, the laundry put away, the boxes moved against the wall. After supper, the adults took their coffee to the front room as the children cleaned up.

"So how many vacuums did you sell today?" Martha began.

"Not a good day."

"You sold nothing?"

"Just shut up."

"Well, at least you tried."

Marichen shifted in her chair. "Tell us what's new from Germany. You get letters from Alma?"

"The headlines are about *Anschluss* and Sudetenland, but she doesn't say much. I think she's afraid." Martha reached for a cigarette. "Good thing we came to America when we did."

"I suppose. You want some cookies? I got them at Wallerman's yesterday. He gave them free so they're probably stale." Marichen went into the kitchen and returned with the open bag.

"Wallerman's? Isn't that the place you don't like? I thought you said…"

"I wanted to see why he's still doing good business on credit."

Martha shook her head. "Marichen, Marichen, you got this itch in your behind but you better not scratch it. What do you know about business? Nothing! None of us do. Fritz hangs on to those copper vats like he's going to get good money some day and 'Lisbet, lives behind her store, paying bills from penny candy." She smiled to soften her words. "Kate is right. Better you take care of the kids so they take care of you later on."

"Like in the old country?" August's voice held an edge. "I thought you wanted to be modern."

"How much longer do we wait?" Marichen added.

Martha looked away. There was no point in continuing. "Let's open the stuff for the kids. Tomorrow is a work day."

The children were called to the front room and opened the boxes, a new dress for the girls and a sweater for Herby along with new school supplies. "Blue for Trudi, Red for Elsie. You will look nice tomorrow dressed up in all new."

"So you say thank you?" Marichen prodded.

Shyly, the girls planted a kiss on Martha's cheek while Herby shook hands with Wally. At fourteen, boys did not kiss relatives, even if it was Aunt Martha.

"I like how it smells." Elsie buried her face into the tissued box. "And it's just the right size. I can tell."

"Puffed sleeves are in style. We figure out how to iron them later," Marichen nodded.

"Style is important. But nobody likes to be next to someone who is dirty, or missing a button and held together with pins."

Elsie looked away, once more ashamed. It was Aunt Martha's way of saying she could do better.

It was barely dark when Martha and Wally left. A hurried

bath sent the children to bed, eager for morning, the first day of school. Elsie had a new pencil box, something she could show to her friends instead of merely admiring theirs. Aunt Martha and Uncle Wally were firmly back in the family circle and that was the most important of all.

CHAPTER 12

Germany, 1938

Alma hung her sweater next to the door as Friedrich emerged with collar neatly in place, hair freshly combed. They had moved into larger quarters, a place with a real inside toilet. It took more to heat, yet a man past eighty had to keep warm.

"Hilda went to meet Rainer. I think they will walk down to the Oktoberfest after supper. He can stay overnight in the bedroom with Gunter." She sat down heavily. "Did you take a nap? Is good for you, you know."

He shook his head. "Too much noise. Already starting, you can smell sausage and sauerkraut. I walked to the newsstand to look at headlines. Who can sleep after that? Poland is after Czechoslovakia and Hitler makes nice-nice with France. It makes me crazy so I can't think."

She stood up, moving toward the stove. "There are new jobs and things are getting better. Gunter might even find work in an office or be selling men's clothes in a department store. No more coal miners in this family."

"Don't make your boy a sissy, Alma. Better the mines than going in the army."

She brushed it aside. "I saw Ida on my way home. Four daughters and a hard working husband but all she wants to do is run after Der Fuhrer. She even wants more babies. She says it's for the Reich."

"Maybe she wants to try for a son. But that's woman talk."

"I'm telling you, she's crazy," Alma insisted.

"Dreams have special power. Look at your Mutti."

"Papa, I'm a married woman. I know what brings babies. And it's not because of dreams."

His voice was stern. "Don't talk dirty. What goes on in the bedroom is nobody's business. Hitler's Herrenvolk won't live to see it anyway. So today I only pray for the joy of peace and heavenly rest."

The door opened admitting a light breeze as Gunter, Hilda and Rainer arrived together. "You wouldn't know what to do with joy and peace, Opa," Gunter laughed. "When was the last time you did anything for fun?"

Friedrich straightened up. "And how come you talk like that to your Opa, you fresh boy?"

Gunter patted Friedrich on the shoulder, then disappeared into the bedroom. Opa was all bark, no bite. But right now his only thought was to coax some money from his father to celebrate Oktoberfest down below.

Hilda smiled uncertainly. She and Rainer had been talking about marriage even though they knew the rumblings of war were getting louder with separation once he returned to his unit. She tried to make small talk. "Tante Guste likes living in Westerwald. All that fresh air and sunshine makes it a good place to live."

"They go on walks and pick berries and wild flowers like rich people," Friedrich grumbled.

"You should go visit, Opa," Hilda said. "I can give you a little money I saved…"

Alma had carried a round of cheese to the table, making room by moving the soup tureen and basket of bread and announced it was time to eat followed by a scraping of chairs as heads bowed to a murmured *Komm, Herr Jesu...* as the noise wafting through the open window.

The young people ate as quickly as they dared. Now Hilda shifted in her chair ready to leap up as the final bowl was emptied, preparing to clear the table then change her clothes for an evening celebration down below.

But before she could move, her father put his hand over hers. "You stay right there," he commanded, his voice resounding with authority. "We have some business to take care of first. Alma, get some glasses. Gunter, bring the wine from the pantry and make some space on the table."

Had something happened? Did someone die? She looked at Rainer but he was studying his plate while Gunter scowled at the delay. Her mother's face was impassive.

Holding his glass in front of him, Helmut began. "Last week, Rainer came and asked for permission to marry. Hilda is very young but I listened and gave it prayerful thought. We talked it over and decided to welcome him into the family."

"Oh Papa…" It was all she could say.

Friedrich fumbled for his handkerchief, noisily blowing his nose, breaking the silence.

"You have made us very happy." Rainer said softly, taking Helmut's hands in his. "I will take good care of her for the rest of my life. I promise."

"So now we will really celebrate," Hilda breathed. "Mutti, you and Papa come down to Oktoberfest with us. We will drink a little beer and dance together. Is good exercise. Opa, you come too."

Friedrich looked startled, then shook his head. "This was enough excitement for today."

Helmut eyed the open bottle of wine. "I stay and keep you company."

Making quick work of the cleanup, the foursome left, joining the crowds peering into booths, listening to merchants hawking trinkets. People were dressed in lederhosen and Bavarian dirndls bright against the setting sun. Soldiers wandered by, hair neatly brushed, uniforms crisp and starched, the smell of bratwurst and beer blending with cigarettes and cigars. A huge tent stood at one end of the blocked-off street, its perimeter lined with tables and benches, the center a dance floor. High-breasted women with three and four beer steins in each hand made their way around, serving those already seated.

They found a table and Rainer was sent to fetch their drinks.

"Papa will be all right, won't he?" Hilda began. "I mean, he wasn't really too tired..."

"They like talking about old times those two," Alma smiled, "fighting the wars over and over. It's an excuse to finish the wine. Then they'll go to bed."

"And when they go to heaven they won't know what to do with themselves because there will be nothing to complain about." Gunter turned to his mother. "But we know how to play and be gay. So you must give the first dance to me."

Alma couldn't remember the last time she'd gone dancing, certainly not with Helmut. She hesitated for a moment, then stood and took Gunter's hand.

First a waltz then a polka, with Alma's skirts brushing against the next couple as they swung around at a dizzying pace. Her son, so gallant as he smiled down at her. Any girl would be lucky to have him. But for now he was safe in her arms. Soon she was breathing hard, her heart pounding. "I think Rainer is back with the beer."

Gunter laughed. "You're out of practice, Mutti." Then his voice softened. "Life is good and Hilda is happy."

"Yes, but I do need to sit down," she insisted. "And they are holding a seat for us."

The crowd had swelled and their bench was now crowded with an additional four soldiers. Shifting to make room, Hilda smiled uncertainly at the young man who sat staring at her.

He smiled back. "Would you like to dance, Fraulein?"

Hilda stiffened. "I don't know…"

"My sister is with someone," Gunter declared in a loud voice, motioning toward Rainer. "They're engaged."

The young soldier grinned. "That's okay. I won't bite. You can watch from here." He leaned closer. "Just this once…"

Rainer squeezed Hilda's hand. "Go ahead. You can go." Standing, he towered over him. "He seems harmless," he added, and everyone laughed.

The boy was blonde with flashing white teeth. He was slightly drunk, but he danced well, a gentle waltz that invited small talk. "For the Fatherland," he began. "We are on leave, you know. I just finished training." He bent a little closer. "Are you from here?"

"Of course. Why wouldn't I be?"

The tips of his ears turned a little pink. "Sometimes I think everyone is from far away. I'm from Mittenwald. You know where that is?"

She shook her head. "I've never gone farther than Osnabrück for my *Landjahr.*"

"Then I don't have to explain."

They had gone full circle and she saw her family eyeing them as they danced by. She waved and smiled. "What is your name?"

"I am called Manfred – like in the book." He brought their hands closer, pressed against the serge of his uniform blouse. "And you are Hilda?"

"Well, yes…" Her cheek brushed against his insignia. He was asking so many questions.

"Just come from your time in Landjahr?"

"Last year." Her heart began to beat a little faster. Did he know about her not belonging to the BDM? How should she answer?

"And your young man is going in the army?"

"He just finished…" she turned to look for her mother. "He just came back from his two years in the army. We are engaged. My father and grandfather are at home. They were too tired to come." The words came in a rush. "My uncle is a supervisor in the mines. I have lived in Germany all my life. We are all German. Truly German." The music had stopped and they were in the middle of the dance floor. "I'm very warm. I think I'd like to sit down now please."

"Are you sure? Maybe just one more."

"No, no. Rainer is waiting. We haven't danced yet." Her voice was urgent. "We are engaged."

His smile faded and he dropped her hand, then led the way back to the table. The soldiers had moved to the other side of the tent, their spot now occupied by two elderly couples. Except for a small space next to Rainer, there was nowhere else to sit. A little bewildered, Manfred bowed and with a click of his heels, wandered off to join his friends.

Still frightened, Hilda sank down on the bench as Rainer put his arm protectively around her. "You were the prettiest girl on the floor," he murmured.

"What did he want?" Alma demanded, tugging at the trembling Hilda.

"Nothing. It's just that…"

"Maybe he should be reported. They think they can do anything, say anything, just because they have a uniform. What is his name? Maybe I go over and…"

"No, no, Mutti. It was nothing. I just get nervous. It's the wine and beer. Dancing is so hot and I was a little dizzy." She turned to Rainer. "You go ahead and dance with Mutti. Gunter and I can hold the table."

The lady next to Alma leaned forward. "We keep your seats for you. Young people should go and enjoy."

So they moved out to the floor, trading partners then trading again with friends and neighbors as the festival grew loud and boisterous. The soldiers had found some young women to their liking and drifted off two by two, leaving space for the locals. Gunter joined his friends but returned as the band began packing their instruments. It was close to midnight and Hilda was no longer tense. She looked at Rainer. "It was a good day, wasn't it?"

He smiled. "I'm happy. Are you?"

She nodded. "Every day it gets better."

"But much is to plan, to take care of," Alma interjected. "So tomorrow we go to church first, then we talk some more."

It had turned cool as they walked back, the streetlights flickering above the trees sending patterns of light on the pavement below. Hilda looked at the stars as a light breeze sent shivers along her spine. The soldiers were gone. She reached for Rainer's hand. Life was sweet and tomorrow would be better.

CHAPTER 13

Chicago, 1939

MARICHEN PACED BACK AND FORTH, WAITING for the bus. It might have been the onset of autumn that made her so restless. Or maybe it was remembering how violence begets violence. Letters from Guste and Alma described new food shortages and the ever-present soldiers. There were jobs, to be sure, but mostly connected to the military. Meanwhile, American headlines screamed about Germany moving into Czechoslovakia, nibbling at the Polish borders, then the horror of *Kristallnacht* with windows broken and synagogues ablaze, even in the Ruhr.

She peered in the window of Fusco's, a newly opened grocery store. She tightened her lips. Some day they too would open their own store and do it right. By watching pennies, they had saved a thousand dollars. The mortgage was manageable and improvements added to its value. The Frigidaire was filled with melons, cherries, grapes and sweet corn all summer long. Cans of soup lined the pantry shelf. The children were self-reliant, with Trudi in high school and Herby soon to graduate. Elsie had a house key, coming home for lunch to open a can of soup or make a sandwich from the cold cuts in the fridge. They went to church regularly and were respectful to adults.

August had given up on selling vacuum cleaners so the demonstrator now belonged to her. She had a wringer washer and a mangle to iron the sheets, yet the laundry kept piling up. She couldn't remember the last time the windows had been washed and Elsie's kitten kept doing its business inside so the house smelled like a zoo. Meals were haphazard and the only certainty was an early bedtime as August wrapped himself around her demanding his due. Then up the next morning to begin again. Surely there had to be something else like making plans for their own business – real plans.

But by December, August had had enough and forbid any further talk. Then the holidays were upon them putting everything else on hold.

On Christmas Eve, Elsie was given a dydee doll that drank water and wet its diaper. She'd wanted a Shirley Temple doll but no matter. She'd pretty much outgrown dolls anyway. Trudi got a wristwatch that broke a week later and Herby received a camera then spent a week in bed with frostbitten toes that lost him his job with no money now for film.

Then it was Sunday again and coming home from church they passed the familiar vacant storefront, its interior now brightly lit with two men measuring counters, ceiling and walls, stirring up tiny eddies of dust. They paused to peer inside and the men motioned them in. It was a chance for them to warm their fingers and toes before going on.

For once August bowed to their pleadings, using the moment to look around as they huddled near the door. "You getting ready for opening again? Somebody interested? What's it gonna be this time?"

The larger man flashed a smile and gestured toward the window. "Just fixing it up a little. New businesses are popping up all over Chicago where it's already crowded. But out here there's open space with empty lots just begging for houses. Depression's almost over. You're gonna see building answering the new demand – drugstore, dry goods, ice cream..." He moved closer. "Perfect for a Mom and Pop store. A real opportunity for someone who has the bug. Maybe like you...?"

The other man, a full head taller, squinted down at them. "We're only here to help out. You know about those absentee landlords, rich guys without a clue about what's going on. They rent to people who just sit on their ass – 'scuse me ma'am – and expect customers to come runnin'. Well, I tell ya, it takes planning and good hard work. That's what they oughta be looking for. Hard workers, salt of the earth."

August drew himself up. "Maybe so. But we saw more than one hard worker come and go belly up. I'm telling you, we been watching."

"And you should. This takes a lot of careful thinking and you look like a smart man. Checking out the plus and minus. Decide what it is you really want."

"Wanting is not getting," August muttered, edging toward the door.

"That's for sure. Unless you find the right price. Low rent keeps the overhead low, and when it includes heat and electricity like in here, it's practically zero. I keep telling the owner it's a steal, but the guy has a big heart and wants to help some little guys get a start. He just doesn't understand that it has to be the right person, someone with ambition and imagination who can stick to it." His eyes were locked on August. "Plain simple folks who might be thinking..."

"Oh no! At least, not yet."

"I understand. It's a big step. Ya gotta look around and find the right spot." He smiled at Marichen. "So what did you have in mind?"

"Oh, I don't know. Bread and milk and maybe some canned goods. Just a start. But like my husband said..."

"Wadya know!" The first realtor's smile was dazzling. "A grocery store! This place would be perfect! We could prob'ly talk the owner into leaving all the fixtures. Then all you'd need is a cooler and Bingo, you're in business. When business gets good, you knock out that wall and add a few shelves, a couple more counters and expand." His bulk was blocking the front door as he clapped August on the shoulder. "The owner would take a six-month lease. Even a better price if you sign for a year. That would be the smart thing to do. Save more money. By then you'd be established."

"We just came to look," Marichen said nervously. "We always talk things over, have to sleep on it."

"And so you should," he boomed. "I can tell you been down this road before. Good German stock. *Sprechen sie Deutch?* I knew it, I knew it!" His voice lowered. "You and him together make all the difference, Missus. Two heads are better than one I always say. Behind the counter with a friendly smile from the pretty lady. That's all it takes. Hard work and a big smile. Some people make like they understand business but they don't want to put in the hours. But I can tell you both are hard workers."

"It's America, doggone it!" the tall man added. "Where else can you pull yourself up by your bootstraps? How long have you folks been here? I'd guess about twelve years. What? Only nine? Well see, I wasn't able to tell. You sure talk good for only nine years. And your kids are real Americans already, for sure. I'm tellin' ya, give it a year and you'll see what can happen. With everyone helping out, this place can be a gold mine."

"Someone else is looking?" Marichen asked timidly.

His smile was non-committal. "Things are softening up. But no promises. Close the deal with a handshake and you can take it to the bank. You have an honest face. We know we can trust you."

They returned home, dizzy with excitement and terror. It was Sunday and God was watching. Now what?

Lunch was hurried and the children went out to visit friends while Marichen and August sat in the front room facing one another. "We can do it," Marichen said firmly. "I'll quit my job and work behind the counter. 'Lisbet ran her candy store all alone." She lifted her chin. "I can too. We'll live on your salary until things pick up. It'll be enough."

That she wanted something, anything, was almost unheard of. Marichen would buy sandwich spread and potato chips for the children, then consume the last heel of bread herself. They drank out of empty jelly jars and bought chipped dishes from Marshall Field's restaurant for a penny apiece, accumulating a full service for eight, now considered the good stuff. If August wanted a new suit, that was fine even when there was one already hanging in the closet. It wasn't a matter of depriving herself. Long before the concept of *want*, there was *the possible,* something reserved for others. Hers was the worn pocketbook, the coat frayed at the elbows, the rayon stockings, good enough if the runs stopped at the knees. When someone asked what she wanted for Christmas, she couldn't answer because she really didn't know.

But she wanted the store. It was to be their Mom and Pop, their reason for coming to America. It was for them, for the children, a lingering promise. August could see Marichen's jaw tighten. Others had failed but somehow they would succeed.

Sometimes that is how decisions are made.

They had a little more than a month to complete the transaction, clean the floors, windows and shelves, stock a small inventory and prepare for the grand opening.

The minute the FOR RENT sign came down, they were swamped with salesmen and solicitors. A friend from church sold August a second-hand cooler that broke down after a week. It was replaced by one that cost twice as much, with an extra charge to haul the old one away. Next came the cash register that didn't work. A shoebox would have to suffice. Then a grocery distributor, dairy bottler, assortment of bread salesmen and those that sold the little cakes and pies that mothers packed into school lunches. Profits would be measured in pennies, compensated through quantity.

Their savings shrunk to half as they stocked the shelves. The rest was designated as operating expense. They had a year, having negotiated the lease accordingly.

Then it was time. Herby mixed *Bon Ami* powder into a paste, painting the opening date along with the prices on the front windows.

Grand Opening Special

Bread 10¢, Two for 15¢
Eggs 15¢ Doz. With $1 Purchase

The first Monday in March turned out to be blustery and cold. The wind was sharp, not unusual for Chicago, and temperatures were at the freezing mark. Marichen arrived at the store prepared for an eight o'clock opening. Everything was sparkling clean. The shelves held canned goods and paper products. Loaves of bread were arrayed on a center rack with little cakes and pies on the top to tempt the impulse buyer. The cooler held quarts of milk, both regular and homogenized along with blocks of butter, the quarters a penny more.

Smoothing down her dress, she turned on the lights put on an apron and after going to the bathroom one more time, unlocked the door.

Cars drove by, their lights cutting through the morning mist. Some slowed down, the driver peering through the window then going on. Traffic was aimed toward the city, the wrong side for a stop on the way home. They hadn't considered that, never having owned a car. Then it began to snow. By noon there were four or five inches piled in front of the door. There was no snow shovel so she went out with a broom brushing away what she could.

Early afternoon brought a spate of housewives, some with small children who slipped and slid leaving puddles of dirty snow on the newly scrubbed floor. They bought bread and milk, the amount dutifully written on a folded paper bag, to be transferred to the ledger sheets bought for a dime. Those who asked for credit were met with a scowl so they walked out leaving Marichen to return their items to the shelves.

August came in at six-thirty having stopped at home to eat, bringing his garden spade to clean off the walk. At eight o'clock they closed, locking the door. The paper bag listed sixteen customers for a total of nine dollars and thirty-seven cents.

"Who would have expected such bad weather?" Marichen muttered angrily. "I wouldn't go out either if I didn't have to."

"People have to get used to us being here. It takes time. Tomorrow will be better."

"You're right. In the spring, people will be going out, taking a walk, looking further…"

"Like we used to do."

She reached for her coat. August hadn't thought to bring her galoshes. It didn't matter. It was a short walk home. It was also the start of a twelve-hour day, taking them to the brink of exhaustion.

They had always worked hard with enough energy left in reserve. The two-mile walk to church could be relieved by a nap later in the day. If Marshall Field's was demanding, an hour on the bus allowed relaxation with an abandoned newspaper or a catnap on the way home. Evenings were spent on the couch whether or not there were chores to be done and Sundays remained a day of rest.

When the store first opened Marichen gloried in leaving the city behind, of abandoning the leaking bags of groceries as the bus bumped along or schlepping cans of juice for a mile just because the distant store was a penny cheaper. Now she could tuck a thing or two into a bag and bring it home, everything wholesale.

But the unrelenting work was paralyzing. In spring there was mud, and weeds surrounded the store adding to the dust and dirt. By summer, the tiny surge of customers declined to a trickle. School was over and Marichen hardly saw the children who followed their own inclinations. August would come home from work and throw together a meal of sorts then hurry to the store to work another few hours before returning with the receipts of the day recorded in the ledger, income always smaller than expenses. "When you go into business you marry it." The first time Marichen heard this she laughed. Now it added a bitter edge to her voice.

"A wife, three children, a mortgage and a store." August's voice was hollow, his eyes bewildered and frightened. "It takes every penny and there are no more savings. Maybe we should have started different."

"*Gott kann machen*," she declared firmly. "We just need to be strong and brave in our faith."

They had given themselves a year. She dared not say more.

CHAPTER 14

Germany, 1939

"Two letters from Rainer." Alma squeezed the thick envelopes. "He spends all his time writing to you. He better not get fired. With a wife to take care of and pretty soon a baby…"

"No one is going to fire him," Hilda declared, tucking the letters into her apron pocket. "He is a good worker."

"He should work closer to home. Why did he go there?"

"A job is a job and munitions factories need camouflage. That's what he does. That's what he knows. If we ever get bombed…"

Alma shook her head. "No, no. It will be over soon. Hitler promised. You'll see."

Hilda's stomach felt queasy. "I think I lie down for a while."

"When was the last time you wrote to Rainer?"

"I write when I have something to say, Mutti. Right now it's hard because I'm not feeling so good. Anyway, he comes home next week."

"He loves you more than you love him."

"One side always loves more than the other. Onkel Wilhelm loved Tante Ida more but now she doesn't want him at all. Divorce is a terrible thing. It was good that Tante Guste took him in."

Alma pursed her lips. "Took him in? When Siebold was finished in Westerwald, Wilhelm got him a job in the mines. Yes, Wilhelm lives with them, paying room and board for a small corner in the attic. We should be so lucky."

"Swallowing coal dust and getting TB is not lucky. If I never see another pair of dirty overalls it'll be too soon."

"That's why the army would be better," Alma declared pointedly. "The soldiers can sleep in clean barracks and spend all day in the fresh air. The food is good and there's plenty of it."

It was an ongoing argument as Gunter approached the end of school. Still underage, he had begged his mother for permission to join the Wehrmacht. Helmut had remained mute, deferring to Alma while Hilda cried out in tearful protest. "He's only seventeen, Mutti – still a boy! What does he know about fighting and dying?"

"Dying happens anywhere, especially in the mines. Gunter is strong and smart. He could get promoted, even make it a career. I can see him now, standing tall and handsome in his uniform..."

"Gunter will look just as good at eighteen – maybe better. By then the danger should have passed."

"...along with the opportunity."

Hilda couldn't think of a rejoinder.

"I told Guste I would help put things away," Alma said finally, taking off her apron. "She always needs someone to do things for her. I won't stay too long."

"Don't hurry. I can take care of supper." She picked up a small pot to put next to the bed.

Alma looked away. Hilda, less than two kilograms at birth and still fragile like a flower that folds whenever touched. Rainer should have known better. She followed her into the bedroom, covering her with a light blanket. "Eat some crackers when you get up. It helps. I be home soon."

Guste's flat had three rooms, more than most, yet she complained that it was in a poor neighborhood, the rent too high, the rooms too small. Her complaints were rewarded with the first month rent free. She was good at that kind of thing, always negotiating for something extra.

When Alma arrived, Guste was already in a sweat, her sleeves rolled up, her hair pinned back. "You're just in time. The wardrobe should be put to the middle of the room and it's too heavy for me to do alone."

Alma glanced around. There was the stove, the icebox, the sink, the open pantry door, the kitchen table pressed against the wall. "I don't see..."

"Upstairs. Come look."

The stairway was more like a ladder leading to an attic with a steeply slanted roof. "See? Two bedrooms upstairs. We can make it nice."

The larger one fit a single bed on either side, the wardrobe as a divider giving Elvira and Wilhelm their own space with long, thin boxes slid under the beds for storage. The second bedroom accommodated a double bed, the small dresser doubling as a night stand. As before, sturdy boxes slid underneath for sweaters, underwear and socks.

By noon they were ready for a break, with coffee and bread slathered with lard and a sprinkle of salt. "I'm glad you will be living nearby," Alma began.

"We had to make the best of it," Guste shrugged. "Jobs are still scarce – the good ones anyway."

"Gunter says teachers are scarce, a real shortage. It's because Jews are not allowed to work anymore and there's no one to take their place. Talk about planning…"

"Jew children become professors, lawyers, doctors…" She laughed bitterly. You'd never find any in the mines."

"I signed for Gunter to go into the army. Helmut and Hilda don't know it yet but I told Gunter and he is glad."

Guste nodded. "For someone young and ambitious, it is a real chance to make something of himself."

"But I do feel sorry for what's happening," Alma continued. "So many Jews tried to leave, some even went on a ship all the way across the ocean but nobody would take them so they had to come back… Almost like in the Bible with no place at the inn. That's why I think Ida is crazy. If Germany needs more room, why does Hitler want to make more babies?"

"And now Hilda, poor thing."

Alma nodded. "We always expect men to take care of that. She should have said something."

Guste took a final swallow, picking up the cups to rinse in the sink. "Well, enough talk. It's getting late and there's still work to do."

"Siebold will find a better job. You wait and see," Alma soothed.

"He will, if I have anything to say about it."

Alma stared for a moment then burst out laughing. "That's my little Guste! Where there's a will there's a way."

"We do what we have to do."

"I should be so lucky."

"It's not luck. You work to make it happen."

The bedrooms done, they turned to the kitchen and by mid-afternoon finished scrubbing the cabinets and sweeping the floor. Alma stood back and surveyed the room. She liked putting things aright. No clutter, simply Ordnung. It defined her. "I should go. Hilda wasn't feeling good and Papa is having his toilet troubles again. He says sometimes he can't piss even when he wants to."

"He should see a doctor. His Knappschaft always takes care of the bills. That's the only good thing about working in the mines."

"Try telling him that. He says hospitals are there to kill you."

A rustle at the door and Elvira bounced in, fresh from her first day at school. "Heil Hitler, Tanta Alma!" She pulled off her scarf and brushed away a few stray hairs as she turned to her mother. "We went outside and I showed them I could run faster than anyone and I knew all the words at singing time. Everyone was friendly and one boy showed me where to put my coat and what I would need for the new school."

"That's good. Now go upstairs and change your clothes. There's work to do."

Alma stood up, stuffing her apron into her purse. "Tell Siebold or Wilhelm to stop by tonight. Papa needs to have a man-talk about you know what. He gets mad if I mention it and Helmut is useless when it comes to such things."

Guste's thoughts had already drifted off. If Papa needed a doctor, let them look into it. She had enough on her hands.

It was late afternoon when Alma arrived home. Hilda was sitting at the table with a cup of coffee in front of her. The room was fragrant with sauerkraut seasoned with a bit of sugar and caraway simmering on the stove. "How do you feel? Did you take a nap?"

"I'm fine. It's only in the morning…"

"Is Opa taking a nap?"

"Yes. He was in the toilet for a long time. Then he took a walk to look for newspapers about East Prussia. I said we weren't interested and that made him mad, so he went to bed."

"He misses Oma," Alma said thoughtfully. "I remember seeing pictures from when they were young. It's too bad things got hard."

"With all those babies…"

"Just don't let it happen to you." It was as much as Alma dared to say.

"I'm eating lots of vegetables."

"You might think about being a midwife," Alma offered. "It's happy work and gives extra money. You do it in your spare time."

Hilda shook her head. "I've been trained as a cook. It's the best I can do."

"That's not true!" Alma cried. "You were good in school. Just because you're married…"

"I can tell when you've been with Tante Guste. You come home with all these big ideas like we're better than anyone else just because we're German. *We* have Teutonic blood! *We* are the Master Race! *We* can conquer the world like ancient Rome!" Hilda's face tightened. "Pray that it's over soon."

Just then Friedrich entered the room, his cheeks creased with sleep. "I listened to the radio, Alma. Poland has gone under. It's all over."

"Oh Papa, you shouldn't have taken the radio out. We're not supposed to…"

"You could hear all the bombs dropping. Boom, boom! Women were crying and babies too." He sat down heavily, smoothing his disheveled hair. "England and France sending ultimatum… Alliance and friendship? My ass! It's all about killing. And now the Russians, worse than the Polacks." His hands began to tremble.

"Rainer is coming home on Sunday." Hilda's face turned chalky white. "But his work is along the border."

"Put the radio back, Papa. And don't take it out without telling me. We could be shot if someone finds out."

Hilda pulled nervously at her sleeve. "We should have gone to America when we had the chance. Now look. Oh dear God…"

Alma stared at her daughter. "You think you'd have found Reiner in America?"

For a moment Hilda looked startled, not knowing whether to

laugh or cry. *If all the world and love were young, and truth in every shepherd's tongue...*

"Let her alone," Friedrich murmured. "God takes care of his own."

Alma took a deep breath and looked away.

"I will bake cookies tomorrow so Rainer sees how glad we are when he comes home," Hilda cried. "And I will make extra for Gunter because, God willing, he will not be drafted." She looked up at her mother. "Now aren't you glad you didn't sign him up?"

CHAPTER 15

Chicago, 1940

THE STORE SHOULD HAVE BEEN filled with pickles and pigs feet, with smoked herring and brown bread, friendly talk and a ringing cash register, Italian, Polish and German immigrants making it their home away from home. But instead, the interior created a chill, the shelves sparsely stocked, the windows empty, the walls without any sign of welcome.

Granted, she could help herself to anything, but the little pies tasted like cardboard, the Spam and tuna hard to digest. Even Wonder Bread, a previous luxury, was uninteresting. She might dust the shelves, sweep the floor, check the cooler, then do it over again trying to keep busy, the trip to the bathroom hurried in case a customer came in. They no longer had plums and berries in summer's abundance, for August rushed home from work to spend a few hours at the store while she herself was there from morning to night. Of course they might have tried selling fresh produce but didn't dare risk spoilage.

They were back to inserting cardboard insteps to extend the life of shoes, tying broken laces together to last a few more weeks. Elsie received a hand me down coat and swallowed her shame, for everyone at church would recognize it as Claire's. With no money for school supplies the children borrowed pencils and paper from accommodating friends, promising a payback that never took place.

At the store Marichen reduced weekly orders, returning items that did not sell, exchanging them for fresh. If salesmen refused or scowled, they ultimately complied, foisting returns onto the next stop.

Especially helpful was Mr. Hazard, the dairyman. Always in a suit and tie, he supervised his small region that trained drivers who were new, showing the more experienced how their accounts could grow. August's account was probably the smallest on his route, yet he would linger, giving hints about displays and tips on stock turnover, commiserating over the slow economy. He would tell anecdotes about his family, about other businesses and their success, all intended to bolster their spirits. It was a sunny spot in the day and Marichen liked him enough to lower her guard. He even charmed August, coming in on occasional Saturdays, acting like a cohort in the land of the entrepreneur. So it was no surprise on this wintry day that he stopped to collect on the monthly bill and pass the time of day.

"Hey there folks, how's it going?" He peered toward the steamed-up windows of the walk-in. "Looks like you've got enough milk for a few days. So I'll just tell your driver to give it a pass on Monday."

Perched on a ladder amid rolls of toilet paper, August glanced over his shoulder before coming to the floor. "We used to walk a mile to save a few pennies. Here people buy a quart of milk, then ask for credit."

"Penny wise, pound foolish." Mr. Hazard paused expectantly.

"I guess you came with your bill," August muttered. Moving to the shoebox, he smoothed a few dollars along the edge of the counter then cleared his throat. "Maybe this is the last time we see you."

"What? Why? Something happen?"

August shrugged. "Enough is enough."

Behind the counter, Marichen muffled a sob. Their lease was to expire in six weeks. What now?

"Hey, you guys aren't giving up, are you? Oh no! Good people like you need to stay in business," Mr. Hazard cried. "You're the salt of the earth."

"Sure, sure. But when there's no meat and potatoes, what's the use of salt?"

Mr. Hazard's face turned serious. "Listen, my friends. Let's be honest. You've got a lot of good ideas but business is all about location. You've been here a year and I can tell you've learned a lot. But now it's time to switch. I've seen it happen when a business goes bust then goes on to succeed. All you have to do is move. Set yourself up in another spot. How much would it cost? Maybe a hundred bucks. You're losing that every month by staying here."

August shook his head. "There's no hundred bucks left. When I pay you and a few others, it'll be all gone. Every penny. My kids need warm clothes and…"

Mr. Hazard leaned against the counter as two customers came in, motioning to the back of the store. "I know how you can fix it," he said softly. "I have friends."

Marichen squeezed her eyes shut before turning to the customers. She liked him. She trusted him. He was different from those realtors that sold them a bill of goods, signing them up to a year's lease when they could have had six months. Mr. Hazard had never steered them wrong. August should listen to him. Maybe, maybe…

Reluctantly, August turned and led the way.

Hunched over the makeshift table in the back, the younger man began. "I have a stop that's about a mile from here. The owner wants to retire. It's a going business with repeat customers. The store's a decent size with a partner who runs the butcher shop on one side. He is planning to stay and that splits the rent. Better yet, his customers will end up buying from you. The owner is selling it cheap because he wants out."

August shook his head sadly. "Cheap isn't enough. I'm telling you. There's nothing left and I have nowhere to turn."

"It's on a busy street with a drugstore, a liquor store and houses close by for foot traffic. No empty lots." He looked at August meaningfully.

"I can't afford another mistake." It was as much as August would admit.

"It's a lifeline, my friend. I'm showing you a way out. There's no harm in looking. Just go and take a look-see. I'll give 'em a call and tell them you're coming. They're really nice folks. Maybe they'd sell on contract. They know things are tight for everyone and I don't think they need the money right away."

It was a typical Mom and Pop store with hammered tin ceiling, tile floor and a side-cranked cash register that went *ding* as the drawer opened. August spent a few evenings across the street watching a steady stream of customers come and go, reassuring that it was indeed a thriving business. The owners were elderly with the Missus in poor health and everything that Mr. Hazard claimed it to be. All that was needed were a few new ideas to make it evolve from steady into something big.

The asking price including stock, fixtures and goodwill was negotiable as Mr. Hazard hinted. Martha quietly provided the down payment by taking out a personal loan telling no one, not even Wally, what she had done.

And so Modern Dairy was born.

They moved in on a Saturday night, using Sunday to prepare for Monday's opening. Penny candy was dismissed as unprofitable, so the children gorged themselves on Mary Janes, colored dots and Tootsie Pops throughout the night. One of the counters was moved into the back for storage, the open space to embark on a risky experiment called self-service. Gallon milk filled the cooler with prices listed across the front.

Window displays were arranged for a clear sight line into the store. Once more Herby dabbed a sign on the windows, GRAND OPENING, after which everyone went home exhausted.

Mr. Huntreiser arrived on Monday well ahead of August and Marichen, unwrapping pork chops and roasts, wiping down windows in his display case, arranging fresh meat on the shelf below lunchmeat and cheese. A white-haired man with wire-framed glasses perched on his Santa Claus nose, he would be a reliable associate as long as they didn't disturb his half of the store.

The next weeks were filled with terror and hope. Following Mr. Hazard's advice, August went with a supplier, pricing his wares according to their circulars distributed by Herby every Saturday afternoon. Reachable shelves were designated for canned goods and paper products. Eggs were a big seller, the rapid turnover keeping them fresh. Gallon milk, an innovation in this neighborhood, was a huge success, and Mr. Hazard's small account began to grow. Meanwhile, August's salary at Marshall Field's remained the lifeline.

Along the way, August discovered that the church treasurer was stealing from the Sunday collections. He urged Pastor Bittner to have the man excommunicated and the Synod agreed, but it was a Pyrrhic victory. The solemn verdict rumbled from the pulpit to an almost empty sanctuary. August was accused of destroying a once healthy congregation with his demands for confession and restitution. At first he was bewildered, then enraged. Truth, August's Holy Grail, had fallen by the wayside. And so he resigned from the church. God could be worshipped just as fervently at home. It was also more convenient. Elsie would go to Zoar Lutheran, a few blocks from the store for confirmation instruction while Herby and Trudi continued at Irvingwood's young people's group that had remained intact.

Now it was summer and as business increased, Herby was brought in to work behind the counter after school and on Saturday, a schedule that was to remain until graduation. "You have to be nice to customers," his mother admonished. "Remember, *The customer is always right*."

Then, at age fourteen, it was Trudi's turn.

The children were paid nothing. Paid nothing? Well, they were given carfare and enough money to buy lunch and a carton of milk that sold for a penny. If the children inflated the reported prices, their parents looked the other way. Petty larceny was not worthy of confrontation.

Then the delivery boy quit and Elsie took his place. Now instead of going home for lunch, she'd hurry to the store delivering an order or two, gulping down a sandwich on the way back, dropping a tardy excuse scribbled on butcher paper on the teacher's desk before slinking to her seat. After school there were more deliveries then biking back home to an empty house. She was paid the same as the delivery boy who'd preceded her, five cents per order, half coming from Mr. Huntreiser when it included meat. At the end of the week she could take the streetcar to Goldblatt's, buying a dress or sweater for a dollar. It was a far cry from Marshall Field's, but she was building a wardrobe, and doing it herself.

Meanwhile, Americans grumbled about Lend Lease and the

new military conscription pushed through Congress. August still felt a vague reverence for the disgraced Kaiser while Marichen struggled with modernism that was turning her children into strangers. Meanwhile, they struggled with divided loyalties, saluting the American flag, standing at attention for the Star Spangled Banner, then listening to Hitler's voice and feeling the *Horst-Wessel Lied* sending chills down their spine.

The children were feeling their own ambivalence, each yearning to belong but always on the fringe. Their futures were now tied to the business with little time for homework or extra-curricular activities in which Elsie begged to join the Girl Scouts or take Saturday dance lessons at the park, Trudi buying herself a dime store baton to teach herself but with no success. None of this was conscious, of course. Instead, they were grateful if there was clean underwear and a good night's sleep.

CHAPTER 16

Germany, 1940

THIS WAS GOING TO BE a big baby, no question about it. Hilda had continued working, coming home to dab lotion on her swollen hands as Rainer massaged her aching feet. They had gotten a telephone to call the midwife at any moment as things got better. Finally Alma insisted that she stay home.

Hilda didn't mind. She would go back to sleep after the others left for work, nestling deep into the pillows, inhaling the scent of her husband, feeling warm and secure. Later she would linger over coffee with her grandfather listening to his rambling about East Prussia, about how the government used to do things right, or retelling a Bible story reminiscent of when she was little. Today he was talking about relatives that might still be in Poland.

"Part of Oma's family," he murmured. "One was the mayor of Neidenburg."

"I think you miss her."

"We will meet again. Someday soon in heaven." He reached for his cane. "I will take a walk to the corner to look at the news.

But first I go to the toilet. I shouldn't drink so much coffee. Excuse me please. It will take a while."

Hilda eased herself out of the chair, looking down at her swollen belly. Pretty soon there would be diapers and baby clothes. It would be like having a real live doll.

Finished with the dishes, she made the beds and straightened up, looked for something to occupy herself until lunchtime. There were socks to darn, a handy excuse to sit for a while.

At noon Friedrich re-appeared, flushed with exertion. "Too many steps," he puffed. "Third floor is getting too much for me."

"It keeps you young," Hilda smiled, "so you live another twenty years."

"I don't feel so good. Maybe I lie down for a while."

"Are you all right? I can heat up some soup or make you a sandwich."

He shook his head, moving toward the bedroom. "First a nap. Then we see."

She waited as he crawled into bed, turning toward the wall, his even breathing signaling that he was drifting off. In his eighties he was about to be presented with his first great-grandchild. Strict and gruff he had been there to help with schoolwork despite her being in and out of foster care. He was there to scatter ruffians taunting her on the way home, bellowing in his own distinctive way. When she was too frightened to climb down from a tree he was there to catch her when she let go. Opa, the man who drank too much and made too many babies, yet was gentle when others were harsh, understanding her yearnings.

She glanced toward the other room. Maybe she would take a little nap herself.

She awoke with her mother leaning over her.

"You left the mending on the table. It's almost time for supper and you haven't even gone to the store."

Hilda rubbed her eyes and looked at the clock. "It's okay. I can still go."

"Never mind. I'll do it. Just let me sit down for a minute. Where's Opa?"

"Taking a nap. He said he was tired."

"No he's not," Alma declared. "The bed is empty."

"Then he's sitting in the toilet or gone to look at the headlines again."

But he wasn't on the toilet and when Alma stopped at the newsstand they said they'd not seen him since morning.

By the time the men came home, Alma was in a panic. "Go over to Guste's. Maybe Papa went there and stayed too long."

Helmut nodded. "If not, we will go to the police station on the way back."

Just then the telephone rang.

Alma reached for the receiver, her hands trembling.

"Frau Schweike? Are you related to Friedrich…?" It was the hospital nurse. He'd been brought in by two soldiers who'd seen him staggering along the street. At first they thought he was drunk, then realized he was beside himself with pain. "Would you like to talk to him?"

Alma nodded into the phone, her hands still shaking. "Liebe Gott, Papa, what happened?"

The voice crackled through the receiver. "I'm good, Alma. They fixed me for now. But I need to be operated. Let me talk to Helmut."

It took a few minutes, punctuated with "Ja, und so, and ganz gut." Satisfied, Helmut signaled to the others that all was well. "We come see you after supper. Don't worry. They take good care of you." Hanging up, he bent toward Rainer, whispering, "They put a hose in the you-know-where until they fix it for sure. Something called prostate…"

Rainer laughed in relief. "At least he will sleep good tonight."

The following day, they gathered at Guste's to figure out what to do when he was released from the hospital, for there was no way Friedrich could negotiate the stairs after surgery. "We might find space in the kitchen. There's a little alcove where we could put a bed…" Guste's voice trailed off.

"We can bring his things over," Alma nodded. "He doesn't need much."

Hilda felt the baby burrow under her ribs. "But it's only for now. Be sure to tell him that."

So it was settled. A day of tests then four to six days of recovery before he came to stay with Guste.

Friedrich was not a good patient and nothing suited him. Medics came in at all hours and there was always noise coming over the loud speaker. Nurses violated his privates, and that wasn't right. Visiting hours were short and in between, there was no one to talk to except a man in the next bed who wasn't friendly at all.

The women clustered in the waiting room on the day of surgery. When it was over, the doctor came out to report that everything had gone well. Friedrich might be impotent but at age eighty-two it didn't matter, did it?

The following day Hilda brought in a container of lentil soup and plumped his pillow conveying the latest news about Elvira and her new school, re-telling stories about her own childhood, deflecting questions about the war. She sat in silence while he dozed then tiptoed out when the loudspeaker announced that visiting hours were over.

By evening he could sit up and talk when Helmut came to visit. If Helmut was bored, he tried not to show it.

And so it went, with the women visiting during the afternoon hours, the men at night. When the nurses came to shush them, it was another complaint that Friedrich added to his list. It was his prerogative and he intended to use it.

On day five Friedrich was still doing fine. He could go home tomorrow.

At Guste's flat everything was in place and waiting. The bed from Alma's was a nice fit next to the steps. Frau Brosn next door said her boy could drive Guste to the hospital and bring them both home. If Guste gave the boy a few marks he would be grateful.

Sleepy-eyed nurses were going over reports with doctors making rounds when Guste arrived, the shuffle of housekeeping added to the muffled activity. Guste told the Brosn boy to wait downstairs, asking the receptionist to alert him when the call came that they were ready. Then she proceeded upstairs.

Friedrich's ward held ten beds each separated by a canvas curtain. This morning all the curtains were closed as nurses busied themselves with bedpans and sponge baths. Hurrying past the first few cubicles Guste smiled to herself, picturing her father on the edge of his bed waiting impatiently.

But instead, the bed was empty, its ends turned up like a giant locust ready to pounce. A woman in scrub clothes was vigorously washing the springs and rails, the smell of disinfectant rising from the steaming bucket.

Guste counted the cubicles. Everything seemed so different when the curtains were closed. "Was he moved? Did something happen?"

Just then a nurse appeared and the scrubwoman scurried off. "Frau Koerner? I'm so sorry. We tried calling your neighbor but the telephone couldn't get through." The nurse cleared her throat. "Your father died last night. It was unexpected. He was having trouble so we called the doctor but it was too late. He went fast."

Guste stared at the nurse. "My father is supposed to come home today. I cooked him a special supper. My husband even bought some wine. The family expects to be together tonight when he comes home. All of us will be together…"

"We have him downstairs in the morgue," the nurse said softly. "You can see him if you like. You'll want to make funeral arrangements of course."

Guste sank onto the chair next to the bed. "Funeral? But he was so good last night. My husband said they were laughing and joking."

"We tried our best. He was old. He had a full life."

"The doctors said he was supposed to go home." Guste's voice was becoming shrill. "Nobody just dies in a hospital. This is where you go to get well. You must have done something…"

"I am so sorry, Frau Koerner. I know this is a shock. Just take a deep breath and pull yourself together. I'll take you downstairs where you can make arrangements." She glanced outside the curtain. "Is there someone we can call?"

"I have someone waiting for me downstairs." Guste's voice was shaky. "Mrs. Brosn's son. But he has to go to work pretty soon. He has second shift. Someone should tell him. He has to go to work, to work…"

"I'll call downstairs," the nurse offered. "They'll take care of it."

Guste put her hands over her pounding heart as the nurse left to make the calls. Papa dead? But how? What was she supposed to tell the family? That Mrs. Brosn's telephone wasn't working? And what about Papa? Would he be delivered like a load of coal? Would there be someone to take him in? She reached for her purse not sure whether she'd brought enough money for carfare.

"Frau Koerner?" The voice drifted in from behind the curtain. "Frau Koerner? There is something you should know."

Guste drew back the curtain to see Herr Hoffer, the not so friendly bedmate, now sitting up, his face flushed and anxious.

"I saw some funny business going on," he whispered putting his finger to his lips. "Last night they came and gave your papa a shot. I watched between the curtains until they told me to close it up. Then someone took me downstairs but I just sat there for a long time, waiting. They didn't do nothing for me. They said because it was too late. When they brought me back, your papa was gone."

"A shot? What kind of shot?" Guste stood up, reaching for the bed to steady herself.

"I don't know. But it was a funny business to happen in the middle of the night."

The nurse had returned, her crisp uniform rustling imperiously, her footsteps muffled. "I called downstairs for the boy to go. He said you should take the streetcar home. If you need money…" She paused at the foot of the empty bed, noticing the gaping curtain. "This has nothing to do with you, Herr Hoffer. You need to mind your own business."

"I was telling her about last night. About you coming in and giving him a shot."

"You don't know what you're talking about," the nurse snapped yanking the curtain shut.

"He was telling me what he saw," Guste declared. "There was no reason for him to lie. How come you give my Papa a shot? What was in it?"

"Never mind. We did the best we could. He was old. It was just too much for him."

"Too old? Liebe Gott! You poisoned him!" Guste shrieked. "I heard about such things but I never believed it." She grabbed her purse and clasped it in her arms rocking back and forth. "You killed him when no one was around to see it. He didn't just die. You murdered him!"

"Be quiet! Be quiet. People are sick. Your screaming is going to make them worse." The nurse's voice was sharp and firm. "You can't behave like this in a hospital."

"No, no," Guste cried. "I heard about what you were doing. Our pastor said we should write to the Rathaus complaining about how the Nazis get rid of the old people, the crazies, the Jews, the foreigners. The pastor said it was against God. I didn't believe it at first but he was the pastor," she continued, her hands beating her chest then flailing against her thighs, "and pastors don't lie. He said there were priests and professors who wrote and we should too. Now I see it's true. You killed my Papa. You poisoned him!"

"Frau Koerner, you must not act like this. Your father is dead and you need to go downstairs to make arrangements. They're waiting for you down there. Come, I'll show you where to go." The nurse reached to take her arm.

"Don't you touch me, you murderer!" Guste cried. Swinging open the curtain, she pointed an accusing finger at Herr Hoffer who sat trembling on his bed. "You know what they did. You have to tell. You were there."

"I only saw a little," he muttered, "and just what I told you. The rest you made up out of your head." He looked up at the nurse. "I'm sorry. I just thought she should know."

He was rewarded with a withering look. "I'll take care of you later." She turned to Guste. "And now you must leave. You must. Or I'll have to call someone." Her eyes narrowed. "And you know what that means." She steered the protesting Guste toward the elevator.

There were uniforms in the hall, soldiers, police, doctors in white, all surreal and menacing. Everything was moving in slow motion, as though the very air was as thick as porridge, her feet barely touching the floor. It was like her papa hovered over her barely out of sight, bewildered, pleading.

She didn't remember going to the office. She didn't remember taking the streetcar home, telling Wilhelm that their father had died, telling Siebold and Elvira that he was not coming after all. And when she went to bed that night she didn't remember saying her prayers.

The next morning Friedrich's body was delivered in a wooden box. The women washed him from top to toe. They brushed his thick gray hair into place. They shaved his cheeks clean and dressed him in his dark suit and best white shirt. He was certainly a handsome man. His strong frame had become frail over the years but his face held an expression of peace.

At the end, he'd just wanted to go home.

CHAPTER 17

Chicago, 1941

MODERN DAIRY WAS LESS THAN three thousand square feet, yet business continued expanding. By now, August was not just a grocer but a butcher, complete with blood-stained apron. It had happened when Mr. Huntreiser mentioned retirement, a dizzying concept. What was he going to do with all that extra time? He was barely sixty.

His response was vague. Well, he would read, walk the dog, play a little golf…

At first August brushed it off. But pretty soon there were inquiries. Now August had another worry. What if Huntreiser sold out to someone less amiable?

Maybe August should buy him out. But that would require being there all day, for Marichen would not be able to handle it by herself. Coal miner, baker, now butcher? He'd kept his eyes on Mr. Huntreiser, watching him cut the chops and tie the roasts. Maybe he could do it himself. The village didn't require a license if it was the owner himself serving as the butcher.

Mr. Huntreiser was a good man. He liked August and said he'd sell his half on contract, no money down. So August took the plunge, swallowing another monthly payment and double the rent.

They'd had an in-store telephone from the very beginning. Now one was installed at home, its pay box stacked with nickels that the children weren't supposed to use – but did. Orders were placed at dawn. "How much is chuck roast? No, no, too much. I have some left. I wait until tomorrow. How about some nice lean spareribs? How much? I thought you said the price was going down..." Then on to lunchmeat and cheese. "Waddya mean there's a trucker's strike? How am I supposed to do business? Don't talk to me about unions! A bunch of gangsters, that's all they are."

By then, the entire household was awake, Herby to his job at Western Union, having graduated a year early, the girls getting ready for school.

But Sunday was still a day of rest. In that, August was firm. They'd bought a radio when President Roosevelt was challenged by Willkie, then discovering the world of commercials. Now they could eat a leisurely breakfast, settle on the couch to read the Sunday papers and listen to the preachers in radio land, going from one Bible-thumper to the next, from glorious choir to a soprano trilling *Amazing Grace* or an off-key tenor singing *Nearer My God to Thee*. After supper, they'd gather for The Goodwill Hour and Mr. John J. Anthony's advice to people in distress (no names please), extolling Carter's Little Liver Pills and the secrets of Arid deodorant. Then to bed, ready for the coming week.

But this weekend was different. August, suffering from a headache, had gone home early, grateful that the meat department was required to close at six, leaving Marichen and Herby to finish the day, Trudi being out with Aunt Martha, a rare and special treat.

Then halfway into the final rush, Trudi called, asking for

permission to stay overnight. Harried, Marichen had said yes.

Spend the night? August hadn't been consulted. This would be a first.

Now it was Sunday and instead of *Blessed Assurance* filling the room, the kitchen was silent with Marichen sitting across from August, her hands folded in submission, her eyes on the blue vein throbbing over his left temple. Meanwhile, Elsie and Herby had escaped to church with Herby lingering while Elsie returned at noon, fleeing into the bedroom to read a book.

Martha and Trudi's return at one o'clock broke the silence, with Trudi resplendent in a new dress, her hair coiffed and curled. Marichen and August were on the couch, waiting.

"What do you think of your little girl? Isn't she pretty?" Martha stood in the doorway waving her cigarette like a magic wand.

"Who said you could…?" August's voice was like thunder as he rose to his feet.

"I called the store and asked," Trudi stammered. "Mom said it was okay. She told me not to call home because you would be asleep."

"Oh yeah? Oh yeah? Well, you don't just ask Mom," August roared. "You ask me." He bent toward Trudi as she grabbed for the chair just inside the door.

"August really, what's the harm?" Martha cried. "See how nice she looks? I'd be proud to have a daughter like her."

His eyes were ice. "She's not your daughter. Yours would get all painted in the face and with red fingernails. And cigarettes and movie shows. Trudi's mine and I take care of her myself. We buy her the right kind of clothes and dress her like a good woman. She does what she's told."

"But Mom said…" Trudi protested.

"Never you mind. I take care of Mom later. For now you take off that dress and give it back. And next time…"

"Oh for God's sake, August. She's been wearing the damned thing all day," Martha cried. "I can't take it back. Anyway, it looks good on her. She's an American girl, not one of those little greenhorns just come over on the boat. In this country more than ten years, haven't you learned anything?"

"What? You swear in my house? And on Sunday? Don't you come here and talk like that! I'm still master under my own roof. I'm king in my castle. What I say goes. So you just take yourself and your cigarettes and your stinky perfume out of here. I take care of this myself."

Martha's smile faded and her lips began to tremble. "My God August, what's happened to you? Where's my big brother? You used to want nice things, try new ideas. That's why you came here – why we all came. Not like when we were back home." Suddenly her eyes blazed and she pointed toward Marichen, her finger shaking. "It's all her fault! Her and her ideas, making these poor kids all crazy about sin and shame, giving them nightmares about the devil." She gestured. "Skirt – too short. Nails – too long. Hair – too curly. Lips – too red. No dancing, no picture shows, no nothing. What are these poor kids supposed to do? How do you expect them to love you when you're so mean? We came here as family, and then…" She paused, lifting her head defiantly. "Don't you talk to me about cheap! I know why you got married."

August swung around, his hands balled into fists. "How dare you talk about my wife like that! She is my wife and you better respect her." He took two steps toward her.

"I didn't mean…"

"Yes you did. I could see it from the beginning, before we even came from the old country. Wanting this, wanting that. Nothing ever good enough, always wanting more. So just get out of my house! Get out!"

Emitting a tiny yelp, Martha grabbed her purse, and without looking back, ran out the door.

Trudi stood facing her father, frozen in terror.

"What you looking at?" he demanded. "Go take that dress off. Then wash your face and comb your hair. Just remember the Commandments the way you're supposed to. That's all you need to know."

Flinging herself into the bedroom Trudi joined Elsie at the window, craning to see Martha as she ran for the bus, neither of them brave enough to follow and say they were sorry, or say they were ashamed.

"You should have known better," Elsie whispered. "Dad never lets us do anything."

"You're just jealous 'cause she invited me."

She was right. But it would have been bearable had it not ended this way.

August's rage was followed by more days, then weeks, of punishing silence. At home, the children would look away when August entered, then quietly leave. At work, they tended to business as though he wasn't there.

Then spring turned to summer and the sun helped clear the air. As before, no questions or explanations; only relief when August slowly became approachable. Meanwhile, he continued sending Martha her monthly payments by check, shrinking the loan a few dollars at a time. And wonder of wonders, the business continued to grow.

In addition to night classes at the junior college, Herby had switched jobs to work at Montgomery Ward, using his discount to buy a Philco radio-record player with high frequency and short-wave band, the house now filled with the sound of Wagner and Mozart, Frankie and Bing. He continued with the youth group at church and Joe became a best friend despite being raised Catholic. Trudi would be graduating soon, entering the adult world. In between, everyone worked at the store.

Then it was December and another Sunday, a day that was unseasonably warm with bright sun and a clear sky, Elsie's last chance to roller-skate before the sidewalks were covered with snow.

Pulling on a heavy sweater, she set out to find Joanie or anyone else who might join her, but no one was home. No matter. Clattering down the front steps, she tightened the skate clamps, striding with a metallic *tsing tsing* around Fusco's corner then back.

Inside, the radio droned with the preachers' voice and soft music like a warm blanket. The Sunday paper was bright with Christmas ads and smelled of newsprint. Marichen sat dozing, her head slipping against August's shoulder, rousing herself to change stations or go for a snack of grapes and leftover Thanksgiving turkey. Returning, she parted the curtains to watch Elsie skate, the streets too cool for neighbors to be outside.

Suddenly there was Herby running down the street, taking the front steps two at a time, slamming into the front room out of breath.

Immersed in the Sunday rotogravure, Trudi looked up while Elsie pulled off her skates to follow him inside. "What's wrong? What happened?"

"Joe and I were listening to the football game when they made the announcement!" He reached around his mother and flipped the radio dial.

"Hey, what do you think you're doing?"

"Listen up, Dad! It's important!"

The voices drifted in and out, crackling with static. "I can't understand a thing," Marichen declared impatiently. "Turn it back."

"Mom, the navy is under attack!"

August pulled himself up, suddenly alert.

Fifty bombers armed with armor piercing bombs, air control and strafing... Over and over, *air Raid, Pearl Harbor. This is not a drill... Cruisers, destroyers, aircraft, all destroyed or sunk, those left standing, beyond repair.*

They stared at the radio. Hawaii? What were Americans doing over there? *Battleships, cruisers, airplanes...* August had been on a battleship, manning guns that wreaked devastation during the Great War. A battleship was an arsenal in itself.

None of this made sense. Words like *Export Control Act, Indo China* and *Manchuria*, foreign sounding names of *Mitsuo Fuchida...*

August turned to Herby, his eyes a question.

"Oh, I won't go. I'll be deferred because I'm in college," Herby declared reassuringly. "By the time they want me, it'll be over."

Elsie had pulled off the sweater and gone into the kitchen, coming back with a sandwich. "Anyone hungry? There's plenty of turkey left. I have half my Christmas shopping done," she continued. "And it's still almost three weeks away."

"War should help the business," Herby continued. "Defense plants pay good money and people will be buying steak instead of hamburger. Maybe you should invest in an apartment building. Strike while the iron is hot."

His joke had fallen flat. "If you weren't so big..."

It went on all afternoon, reports muffled by sirens wailing in the distance. Members of Congress, aides to the president, news commentators and university scholars interjected their analyses. Japan had attacked an island belonging to America, a place where ships routinely docked for safety or repair. This, even as the Japanese ambassador arrived in Washington D.C. to negotiate a trade agreement.

The following day, teachers struggled with questions they

barely understood. At noon, every radio in America was tuned to hear President Roosevelt's somber words, *Yesterday, December 7, 1941 – a day which will live in infamy..."*

Within the hour, Congress declared war. Germany's own declaration came a few days later, based on its alliance with Japan.

Recruiting stations were now jammed as the isolation movement collapsed. Herby could be called to fight his own cousins on foreign soil. Worse, they hadn't heard from the family in Germany for weeks. What now?

CHAPTER 18

Germany, 1941

THE CLATTER WAS CONSTANT AS the baby explored an array of pots and pans. Hilda picked him up, deflecting a final bang. "Here you go, Peter. A little milk, and then time for a nap."

Almost four kilograms at birth, the baby continued to thrive, thanks to government subsidies and rations. He'd walked at a year and was beginning to form sentences. "When your Papa comes home he will see how you have grown. Maybe you learn some new words and tell him you are a big boy."

His rhythmic sucking slowed as his eyes drifted closed, dark lashes brushing against his cheeks. The night had been filled with rumbling, signs that the bombs were close. They'd been drilled on the shelter's location, but with a baby...

There was news of the Bismarck, a warship the size of a village being sunk in only a few days. Maneuvers to attack the oilfields forced Hitler to face a dwindling supply of fuel with no reliable backlog. Meanwhile, a sense of emptiness permeated each day with Rainer and Gunter in the army.

She sighed and got up, placing Peter at the foot of her bed. Her father worked long hours even on Saturday and her mother was out to deliver some sewing. Guste and the rest of her family would be coming for supper. She began to prepare a batter of noodles, making sure there was enough. Coal miners had enormous appetites. She might add some bratwurst, a festive touch to go with Guste's streusel cake. Onkel Siebold and Wilhelm would like that.

When Peter awoke she changed and fed the baby once more, then lifted him onto her lap, holding him close for a long time even as he squirmed to be put back down.

The men arrived at suppertime with Guste and Elvira out of breath. "Everybody needs to look at the dress Elvira made. She just finished it." Guste declared, twirling Elvira around as the others nodded their approval.

"Elvira should open a dress shop like they do in America," Hilda offered. "Begin at home with a sign in front, then rent some store space."

"There would be plenty to choose from," Guste declared, "with so many shop keepers being deported. But I want Elvira to stay in school, get a good job and marry the boss."

"I saw a man with a yellow star on his jacket," Elvira said thoughtfully. "I never saw that before. Have you, Papa?"

Siebold shook his head. "I stay away from those shops. And you should too."

"No, not in the store, Papa. This was on the street."

"Pay no attention. It has nothing to do with you."

"Enough talk," Hilda declared. "It's time to eat. We can leave Peter on the floor to play."

Settled in, they sipped the wine, the food conveying a sense of plenty. Hilda related how Peter had climbed up on a chair and then couldn't figure out how to get down. Elvira described embroidery she was working on that would surely capture a prize at the next Jungmädel meeting, one more advantage garnered through the new regime.

Helmut turned to Siebold, his face becoming serious. "Guste should not be sending a letter to the Rathaus about how Papa died. It could get us in a lot of trouble."

"I do not tell Guste what to do," Siebold laughed. "That's even less safe."

"I said I *wanted* to write," Guste grumbled. "Anyway, nobody would read it. They're too busy with banners and songs and marching up and down."

"But for once there's plenty to eat." Siebold reached for another helping. "So it's not all bad."

"War is always bad," Wilhelm muttered.

"Rainer is being trained as a paratrooper," Hilda said worriedly. "I hope he doesn't get sent to Russia."

"Oh my!" Elvira cried, clapping her hands. "They wear such handsome uniforms. I should knit him some woolen socks. May I, Mutti? It's our duty to take care of soldiers who fight to keep us safe."

The rumbling had intensified and Hilda shuddered as she began clearing the dishes. "The bombers are getting close."

"These are our own cannons in Belgium and the Netherlands, Siebold said reassuringly. "It's nothing to worry about. The bunkers are safe."

"Not at 800 meters away. We could all be dead by the time we get there," Alma sniffed. "Or rolling on the ground from mustard gas or something worse. I asked Fritz. He was gassed in France during the war."

Guste nudged Wilhelm who was beginning to nod. "Finish your cake before you go to sleep. Then we go." She began gathering her things.

It was cold outside and they did not linger at the door. From down below, Siebold waved, then called to the others. "There's a post in your box."

"It must be from Rainer," Hilda cried, grabbing her coat. "His last letter said he was coming on leave." She ran slipping and sliding down the icy steps.

Retrieving the piece, she raced back upstairs to begin ripping open the envelope. Only then did she see the government seal. The letter was addressed to her father. *We regret to inform you...*

"What does it say?" Alma demanded.

"It's about Gunter. He's been wounded."

"Wounded? Where? How?" Alma grabbed the letter, scanning it before she handed it to Helmut. "I have to go see him," she cried, moving toward the bedroom. "I just have to. There's a little money saved in the jar. I can take that..."

"He's in a hospital, Mutti. Stop and think. You would just be in the way."

"No, no. I have to find out for myself. It says he in Tilsit. That's only a few hours..."

"It's at the Russian border. You couldn't even get close. Anyway, I need you here for Peter while I'm at work."

"He can stay with Guste. She likes him. Elvira can help." Alma looked toward the sink. "I have to get ready. You can..."

"Tante Guste will say no because her heart is giving palpitations or the weather is too cold..."

"Then I take him with me. He goes free on the train."

"Take him with?" Hilda cried, horrified. "No! I will not let you."

Alma's back was ramrod straight. "Then I go alone." She lifted her chin. "I am a mother too."

Hilda imagined Gunter in his mother's embrace, of him

being cheered at the sight of Peter. "Peter is my responsibility. I have to answer to Rainer."

"And Gunter is your brother – your only brother. Rainer is not here. So you have to decide." Turning, Alma marched to the bedroom and closed the door.

Her father followed after emitting a helpless shrug. Kinder, Köche, Kirche... Elvira might dream of marrying her boss, but this was reality.

Finishing in the kitchen, she got Peter ready for bed. Splashing water on her arms and face she lay down, not sure if she could sleep. Was this her mother's torment after signing papers for Gunter to join the Wehrmacht? Did she weep when she was alone? Was she weeping now? She pushed her face deep into the pillow. If only Rainer were here.

She awoke with a headache, remembering the wine, then the letter. Voices from the bedroom rose and fell, an argument about train fare and schedule. It was pointless. Alma always won.

She swallowed some water then knocked on the bedroom door. "Papa and I don't leave for work until tomorrow. Surely you can wait until then."

Peter was on the bed, watching Alma pack. "Oma go bye-bye."

"I'm just getting ready." Alma's hands were mid-air as she folded a sweater.

"We need my wages, Mutti. I don't dare take time off. You know that."

Alma's expression softened. "We won't stay long. I just need to see for myself." She resumed packing. "The trains are not so crowded on Sundays."

"I would go if I could," her father said. "And you would too."

Hilda cleared her throat and picked up the little boy. "Oma

will be bye-bye on the train, far, far away."

The little boy squirmed out of her arms and ran to his grandmother.

Hilda shook her head resignedly. "I guess that's your answer."

CHAPTER 19

Chicago, 1942

IT WAS LIKE A PIPE organ with all the stops pulled out, a blast from the Tyrolean Alps, echoed by Herby's bass-baritone as his latest platter resounded throughout the house.

"Turn it down," Elsie yelled, rolling out of bed.

"Touch that machine and you're dead," he roared back.

"Just because you bought it doesn't give you the right …"

He emerged from the bathroom, a towel around his hips. "You need to respect the music. Wagner wanted music to be loud. He's making a statement."

"Boom, boom, da-da boom…" Elsie scowled. "What's the good if you can't dance to it?"

"That's not what it's about. The classics are an intellectual experience." He switched the record then disappeared into his room. "When do you start work?"

"Gotta be there for morning deliveries. Mom's now letting me take care of customers too. I'm in training. What about you?"

"Nine-thirty." He closed the door to finish dressing.

"*Jeepers, Creepers, where'd you get those peepers...*" Elsie voice rang out over the music. "Trudi's got a boyfriend," she called out. "God help her if Dad ever finds out. Bad enough she cut her hair and got a perm, especially after that big thing with Aunt Martha. Pretty soon she'll forget to wipe off the lipstick when she gets home. That'll be real trouble."

"She's breaking ground for you. I should be so lucky."

"I don't know why we're so scared. We're three against two." Elsie hadn't worn braids since sixth grade.

"Just don't push it."

"You could be clicking your heels and saluting if they'd stayed in Germany. Hitler loves Wagner."

"Never happen. It's not my style." He emerged, grabbing his jacket. "Turn off the phonograph and lock the door when you leave. You left it unlocked last week and Dad was mad."

She was on the couch, her feet tucked under. "Aren't you scared about the war? The Japs are pretty bad but Dad says you could be killing your cousins in Germany."

"Men don't get scared." He slammed the door and with a swing to the right, sprinted for the bus.

Elsie replaced the record, humming along as she got dressed. Tucking a library book in her pocket, she left the house, hopping on her bike for work. The wind was brisk, waving branches against the sky. Crocuses peeked out along a fence or two and a stretch of prairie saw a tethered goat nudging the damp earth. It was spring break. She'd be at the store all week, giving her mother a small rest.

Around to the back of the store, she banged her fist on the metal door.

After a moment, it swung open. "I keep telling you not to bang," her mother frowned. "You're going to break it."

"Sorry. I wasn't sure you heard. Any orders come in?"

"Only two. Daddy is busy with Mr. Hazard. Keep your jacket on and go stock the cooler."

When she emerged, Mr. Hazard was in the front talking with her father about a new ice cream freezer that had just been delivered. "You should have come to me first. I could have gotten you a better price."

"You sell ice cream?"

"Better than that. I sell the mix to make your own. Put a machine in the window where people can watch and pretty soon they start coming in, just out of curiosity. By the end of summer there's more business than you can handle."

August's silence invited him to go on.

"The machine is free when you buy the mix from us. After five years, it belongs to you, free and clear." Mr. Hazard's arms swept wide, gesturing toward the window. "I'm telling you, they'll be beating down the door."

"And profit? How do I know...?"

"Groceries are a thin margin, my friend. A penny on a can of applesauce. You can make three times that much on one ice cream cone. And there's no spoilage because it's frozen." He looked meaningfully at the meat counter.

Two customers had come in and Marichen signaled Elsie to put on her uniform to help.

"I can crunch the numbers and get back to you," Hazard continued. "If you're not convinced, just say no. I haven't steered you wrong yet, have I?"

August was doubtful. "The war..."

"Exactly! Soldiers and sailors coming home on leave, taking the girls for a walks..." He nudged August. "Food rationing is around the corner. Pretty soon you'll be counting coupons too. But milk and ice cream will be exempt."

"I have to sign a contract?"

Mr. Hazard nodded. "But at the end of five years, you can switch to some other purveyor and still keep the machine. No hard feelings."

"Five years is a long time. We could all be dead by then."

"Then we'll attach the contract to the business so the wife and kids are protected."

Within minutes they were measuring the space. "You'll need to keep a small meat case for cold cuts. That's fast. The fresh meat can go." Mr. Hazard moved toward the bread display. "Bread and dairy. That's the draw."

The store began to fill and suddenly there stood Martha. They hadn't seen her since the argument over Trudi the year before. Following close behind was Wally in military uniform, his hat cocked in a most un-military way.

"Oh my!" Elsie gasped. "When did…"

"Hey there, Kiddo. Long time no see. Surprise, surprise."

"He's going overseas," Martha said softly. "We thought you'd want to know."

August turned to Mr. Hazard. "My baby sister and her husband. They're the ones with all the money."

Martha's eyes were luminous. "The store looks good, August. I knew you could do it."

"We were talking about ready-made ice cream," Mr. Hazard began, "made right there in the window where customers can watch. After seeing that, they'll come in to try some. Takes it in a whole new direction."

They had gone into the back with Martha perched on a crate, tapping a cigarette before lighting it. "And when did all this happen?"

Hazard looked at his watch and Martha burst out laughing. "I see! He's got to think about it. Well maybe next year."

"Don't be a smart aleck. It just happened."

Her face turned serious. "You have to strike while the iron is hot, August. If it makes sense today, it won't look any different tomorrow."

"Now that's a girl after my own heart!" Mr. Hazard grinned. "I can tell you have a feel for business."

They talked for almost an hour. Then as they moved toward the door, Martha nudged her brother. "Do it," she whispered. "I will help."

Hazard's team arrived a few days later, handing out samples for customers to judge. By six o'clock the contract was signed.

Once more, inventory was reduced, making room for the new equipment. The walk-in cooler remained along the back wall with a long counter, room enough for two clerks. Lunchmeat would be at the right with shelves along the left wall for basics, the bread display remaining in the middle. At the entrance, two freezers with an aisle between, one to scoop out cones, the other for pints and quarts with a shelf facing the door from which the customers were served.

Within a week people were coming in by the dozen, drawn by the image of August at the window, measuring out flavors like a white-coated scientist, weighing overrun on his tiny scale. Grocery delivery was discontinued, an enticement no longer needed. Elsie was assigned to the front, serving ice cream or frozen malt.

Meanwhile, other events bowed to the convenience of business. At Easter Elsie was confirmed at church a mile away from the store. They'd bought a dress at Marshall Field's made of ruffled white chiffon. Aunt Martha attended the ceremony, praising her recitation, making the day festive. A month later Elsie graduated from elementary school, walking back to the store with her mother to finish the day.

The war was now entering its second year and throughout the country the mood was fiercely patriotic. It was *Praise the lord and pass the ammunition.* Buy war bonds to help the war effort. Uncle

Sam wants YOU. Gasoline was rationed and automobiles were running on re-treads, keeping people at home or taking public transportation. An overall price freeze doubled the work of the administration and created the hated OPA but ensured that inflation was kept at bay. Elsie's friends were learning the boogie-woogie but Elsie spent fewer evenings in Joanie's basement play room, her schedule now overwhelming.

In late fall, Herby was inducted. Three missing teeth made him ineligible for the Air Corps, his first choice. Instead he was assigned to Basic Training at Fort Benning, Georgia, learning to shoot, bivouac and march, earning medals for machine gun and rifle marksmanship. An IQ test got him deployed to the University of Cincinnati in the Army Specialized Training Program. His request for the language program sent him to engineering. It didn't matter. Within a year the ASTP would be cancelled resulting in his transfer to Camp Campbell, Kentucky, some of the best and brightest to become another class of grunts waiting to be shipped overseas.

Elsie wrote to him every week. She tried to include news about the neighborhood, but there was little to tell, their six-year age difference now a yawning chasm. *Today I started menstruating* – she had to look up the spelling. Start over. *I think I'm cutting wisdom teeth. It must mean I'm smart. Ha. Ha. Howie Querm is in the army. Trudi says you used to know his girlfriend. I try to read the papers every day like you told me to do. This is living history. When high school starts I'm going to work really hard. I hung a blue star in our window to show that you were serving our country and Mom took it down. She said it was unseemly. But I'm proud of you anyway. Sure hope you get a furlough and come home soon, even if you play your records too loud. I miss you. Please, please, please stay safe.*

Meanwhile, the family saw events from overseas like a strange configuration in a museum. They were in America. They were safe. Defense spending had lifted the economy out of the Depression. This was still the land of opportunity and the future looked bright although with events galloping at a blinding rate, it seemed oddly unreal.

CHAPTER 20

Germany, 1942

THE FEATHERBED WAS HEAVY ON Rainer's legs. He was home on furlough, ostensibly to assess damage and relocate the family that was bombed out, moving them to a two-room attic flat that had been spared. The move happened while Alma was in Prussia assessing Gunter's injuries, his wounds serious but not enough to send him home. Meanwhile, Rainer's leave had been extended to allow his toes to heal from frostbite in the unrelenting Russian cold. It was small enough comfort in the ever-expanding war.

Sounds were coming from the other room and he struggled to get up, fighting a prevailing weariness. Frostbite was hardly glamorous, but enough to turn someone into a cripple. The doctors had said he was lucky they'd stayed frozen. Premature thawing could have caused permanent damage. Almost ready to return to his unit, there was a strong chance he would be sent back to the Russian front.

Here at home, the nights were filled with sirens and thunderous crashing as they raced to the bunker, Rainer's arms wrapped protectively around his legs or hugging the whimpering Peter. Then as things quieted, hobbling home to crawl into bed for a few hours of sleep, inhaling the lingering smells of fire or sulfur, listening to workmen clearing roads or covering damaged windows and walls with scraps of wood. Then another night, and another and another. Sometimes it was a false alarm and there was only throbbing silence punctuated by a child's cry or the murmured conversation between insomniacs. One was worse than the other.

He kept thinking of the broken concrete and deep craters on Russian streets, the percussive bombs vibrating like kettledrums. His unit might move inches or not at all, distances invisible under ice and snow with no sense of horizon or time. No *blitzkrieg* there, just rain and mud, then the ground freezing over, trapping trucks and tanks, making them useless. Useless, too, were the weapons that jammed in the rain and cold, the ever-present cold, the pervasive and endless cold that remained in his bones even now. After that, the twisted bodies tangled deep in the furrows or under blocks of mud and ice. When it thawed, the bodies would heave forth without a place for burial. And in the midst of it all, unspeakable cruelty on both sides as fear, then rage, took over. Russian barbarians? What about the SS shooting and killing women and children? How was that in accordance with a Just War? Ultimately, even that was discounted as hunger and cold wiped out any noble concerns. Survival. That's all that mattered in this far-away land of emptiness and cold.

"Papa? Where is my papa? Is papa gone?" The voice was barely a whisper like in a dream. Peter was almost three and not at all shy, a sturdy little man who'd saluted the picture of his father every night at bedtime, willing to be hugged and soothed into drowsy sleep when things quieted down in the bunker.

Rainer took hold of the mattress edge to pull himself up. "Peter, I am here," he called. "Don't be afraid. You can come in and say hallo to your papa."

The door creaked and a little face peered around the edge. "Mutti went to work. Oma said I should not wake you."

"Your Mutti went where?"

Alma peered in over Peter's head. "At the café. They were short-handed and it means a few extra marks." She studied the rumpled bed. "How do you feel? Did you get any sleep? Can I get you something?"

"A million marks and a house in the country." Rainer tried to smile.

"Besides that."

"I'm fine. It just takes a little to get moving." He swung his legs over the side, his feet red and swollen but looking much better than the variegated purple they'd been before. "See? I can even wiggle my toes." He winced. "A little..."

Reaching down, he swept the little boy in his arms, tossing him onto the mounded featherbed as the child squealed with glee. "We could go to see Guste. I need to walk and get the circulation going."

"Do you need help?"

He shook his head. "Just don't bump me." On his feet, he established his balance and limped to the chair, pulling on a pair of heavy socks to protect his sensitive toes. "Did you look outside? Is it bad?"

"Some shrapnel. They say the planes aimed for the railroad yards, but the way it looks, it must have been more than that. No use pretending."

"Not like in Tilsit?"

"East Prussia was quiet. The hospital was clean and Gunter said the food was good. He is getting stronger and expects to return to his unit." Alma shook her head. "Soldiers are like dogs sent to chase after robbers. Nobody cares if they get shot and killed. He was glad we came and Peter was a good boy. But after three days to come home to this..." She turned and went back into the other room leaving him to finish dressing.

Untangled from the featherbed, Peter climbed onto Rainer's lap. "Bouncy-bouncy, Papa!"

Rainer winced, shifting his weight. "Papa has to get dressed. Then we go for a walk outside. Is good?"

Peter slid to the floor. "Mutti says I should always go pee-pee first."

Rainer nodded. "Mutti is right. So you go and let Papa finish dressing."

When finished, he went into the kitchen where Alma was moving about, looking for storage in the less than adequate space. "Back in a few hours," Rainer called, motioning Peter to take his hand.

"Be careful. Don't step on any glass and stay away from loose wires," Alma warned.

Outside, Rainer stood for a moment surveying the front of the house, the street, the building next door. It had been barely daylight when they left the bunker with hardly a chance to look around. Now he could see a fine cloud of dust on everything as though sprinkled with a gigantic powder puff. Further down, a building seemed to be leaning toward a small crater. In the other direction, a lamppost stood in a circle of sprinkled glass. "We go this way."

"Oma likes that store," Peter said, navigating a cluster of rocks and pointing. "She takes me with, sometimes."

"And does she buy you a piece of candy when you go with her?" Rainer asked, eyeing the boarded up windows.

"Oh yes," Peter declared. "For a Pfennig when she has one." He covered his eyes shyly. "If I good boy."

"And are you a good boy today?"

Peter didn't answer, not sure what it meant to be a good boy. If he said it wrong, Papa would laugh or worse, be angry.

"We go visit Tante Guste. Can you walk that far?" Rainer asked.

Once more Peter was silent, sensing the wished-for candy slipping from his grasp.

"Or maybe we should stop first for a newspaper at the store where Oma goes. What do you think?"

"Do you have a Pfennig?"

"I think so." Rainer dug into his pockets and pulled out some coins, holding them out for Peter to see. "You can have a Pfennig if you tell me you are a good boy."

"Mutti says I a good boy," he whispered. "She says that all the time."

"And we do have to believe Mutti, don't we?"

Peter nodded. Of that he was sure.

They entered the store, its one light trying to compensate for the covered windows, the sweet scent of candy emanating from inside the case. "Do you have something for a good boy who obeys his Mutti?" Rainer asked.

The woman looked up and scowled, tucking the duster under her apron bib. Then seeing Peter's upturned face, her expression softened. Reaching inside, she withdrew a tray, bending so the little boy could choose. "We were supposed to get more yesterday but the roads are bad. I have just a few."

Standing on tiptoe, Peter took the red one then hid behind Rainer, hugging his leg so tight he couldn't move. "Ja, Peter, and how can I pay the Fraulein if you hold me here?"

Giggling, Peter moved a few steps toward the door, waiting for Rainer to hand him his prize.

Rainer gave a quick glance at the front page then tucked the newspaper under his arm, ignoring the headlines that touted the final solution in Poland and the massive executions in Holland and Czechoslovakia. The news could wait until later. Once more, he took Peter's hand. "You have to be careful how you walk."

By the time they arrived at Guste's the sun was warm on their backs. The house appeared undamaged. It would feel good to sit down before returning home.

He knocked several times before Guste opened the door. She was dressed in a bathrobe, her face creased with sleep. "Oh Rainer, what a surprise. I wondered who would be here so early."

"What early? It's almost eleven." He looked her up and down. "Are you sick? Did something happen? The bombings come close?"

"Oh no." She paused. "Come in. I didn't know it was so late." She grabbed a mound of laundry from the chair, motioning him to sit down. "You walked over? Are you feeling better? Your feet must be hurting."

"I'm better. Hilda has a few hours of work at the café so I took Peter for a walk. Gets us out of the house." He sat down, motioning Peter to the other chair. "Are you all right? You not sick?"

She shook her head. "No one can sleep at night anymore. You too, I guess. Siebold and Wilhelm went to work, Elvira for school." She leaned against the door. "My stomach's a little upset. I thought I would lie down for a while."

"Something you ate? Maybe indigestion?"

She flushed, smoothing her tangled hair. "Well, I should be telling this to Alma first." She gave a short laugh. "You know how that goes. You forget to be careful. Elvira says she always wanted a sister…"

Rainer looked away. "Oh, I see." The warm blood throbbed on his cheeks. "A little business in the hopper. Woman talk."

"I go change. Elvira comes home soon and I have to fix lunch. You should stay and eat with us." She bent down and kissed Peter on the cheek. "And Papa can wash the sticky from your face."

"If it's no trouble…"

"No, no. There's mending that waits and I need to get to it." She scurried upstairs and soon emerged in a wash dress and apron, her hair combed, her face once more composed.

When Elvira arrived, the tone brightened and there was animation between the children. "I won't be going onto Landjahr this summer," Elvira announced. The BDM is going to stay in Bielefeld, high up in the old castle and I've been chosen as a leader for my team. They allowed Mutti to sew my uniform herself because there was such a shortage, but only this once. We will do calisthenics and have inspections every morning. Then there is gymnastics and after that we take showers and go to classes until suppertime. I will be in charge like a foreman or supervisor – like Onkel Wilhelm."

Peter clapped his hands. "Papa in the army too!" he cried. "And Onkel Gunter."

"Peter knows how to count to twenty and can recite the whole alphabet," Rainer said proudly.

"He's a bright boy," Guste was at the icebox taking out a block of cheese and some sausage then slicing bread on the cutting board. "But come and eat. Elvira needs to go back soon."

"There is so much to do, even after school," Elvira sighed. "Then on Saturday…" She looked at the clock. "Today I have to go back and drill the girls before a test."

"But you eat first, and not so fast." Guste admonished.

Elvira nodded obediently, then after a final bite, grabbed her sweater and danced out the door.

"She makes the room bright," Guste smiled, beginning to pick up the lunch dishes. "Today we plan for a new tomorrow. Hitler is making things happen."

It was another motto. *One folk, one Reich, one Fuhrer. Strength through Joy. Honor, loyalty… Hitler promised.* "I think I better start back before Peter gets sleepy," Rainer got up. "I don't think I can carry him."

Outside, they ducked past chunks of plaster and loosened concrete, nodding at housewives who were wielding their brooms to clear the shards of glass. Their progress was slow, and Peter was clearly ready for a nap. "Just a little more and we be home," Rainer murmured. "I know you are a big boy."

At the top of the steps, he reached for the key just as the door swung open. "Papa was home when I got back," Hilda whispered. "He was pale and went to lie down. He said he will tell us everything when Mutti comes home and we are all together."

Just then, Alma appeared. "Why are you standing here? What's wrong?"

"Papa came home and went straight to bed. He didn't tell us…"

"I'm awake." Helmut voice was like gravel as he emerged. "I'm not sick and there was no accident. I was just in shock and couldn't talk…" He reached for a chair and sat down heavily.

"Did someone do something to you? Did you lose your job?"

"They're sending me to Czechoslovakia. Orders from the Central Office. They just said I should go and now I'm going. The permit and train ticket will be waiting at the station tomorrow."

Peter had moved toward the sink and after a brief examination of the pots and pans, curled up on the floor beginning to doze, his head cradled in his arms.

"You mean just like that?" Hilda gasped. "Did they say why? Do you know what you will be doing?"

"I'm an Oiler. I guess that's what it will be, what I will do.

Factories were shipped to Poland and Czechoslovakia. For them the bombing is over so they can work without danger." Helmut shook his head bewildered. "For years there was no work. Now they can't find enough workers."

"But what about us? What is going to happen to us?" Alma demanded.

"It's not right! You sacrificed in the last war…" Hilda chimed in, close to tears.

"I know. Nothing makes sense anymore."

But an order was an order and one had to obey. So the next morning, Helmut left for an unknown destination carrying a dilapidated suitcase and a sack lunch.

Two weeks later Rainer was called back to his unit, leaving the women, like so many others, to deal with the war as best they could.

CHAPTER 21

Chicago, 1943

ELSIE CROSSED THE STREET AND hurried into the store. "Sorry I'm late. Us kids got to talking…" She glanced at the scraps of baloney, paper and string around the slicer and cutting board. "You've been busy?"

"Trudi had to leave early. They're taking graduation pictures." Her mother motioned toward the display case. "Put the lunchmeat away. You can finish cleaning up when you have time. It's going to be a warm night."

Elsie had entered high school with high hopes. But Business Training turned out to be nothing more than filling out forms in triplicate. Algebra required mounds of homework for which there was little time. Girl's choir was pleasant enough, but more like a popularity contest. It mattered terribly, but it didn't, since she had no social life anyway, for they had moved into a three-flat her parents had bought on Whipple Street outside the school district. Oh, the new furniture was nice enough and she had a room of her own for the first time in her life. But there was little chance to meet anyone in the neighborhood and she missed her friends.

The move had taken place shortly after the FBI visited on Addison Street. Dressed in suits and ties, sporting dark glasses and thrust-out jaws, the agents were enough to intimidate anyone. Even their cars looked menacing, black with chrome bumpers, their wide running boards reflecting the blinding sun.

At first August was belligerent. "Who are you? Why you here?"

They flashed their badges. "We have a report that you own a short-wave radio. Mind if we have a look?"

"I don't have to let you…"

"We can get a warrant, sir. Our records show that the Missus is an enemy alien."

Suddenly alert, August stepped aside, and along with Marichen, sat watching while the men confronted the Philco.

"Where are the short wave programs coming from? Are you sending any messages? Have you registered as an alien, Ma'am? May we see your papers?"

Yes, she had registered, having learned too late that citizenship applications had been frozen because of the war. It made Herby's Philco a security threat.

The agents were polite but firm. "Strip out the short-wave band or we will confiscate the entire machine. You have ten days to make it right."

It was done with fear and trembling, but it compromised the beloved Philco, its rich sound never quite the same.

Elsie pulled off her sweater and reached for a uniform. By tonight, it would be dotted with chocolate and pistachio as people crowded into the store for summer's last hurrah. "Where's Dad?"

"He went to the bank. He'll be back soon."

Elsie nodded and waved her mother off as she moved behind

the counter. "Go soak your feet in some ice water. I'll call if it gets busy."

The sky was streaked in an autumn sunset when August returned with his shopping bag, pausing first to check the ice cream dispenser as Elsie moved aside. The shopping bag. Along with the bank deposits, he always carried a hammer – just in case. It was a family joke. Who would bother to rob this little grocer whose weekly profits amounted to less than a steelworker's eight-hour pay?

She leaned against the counter, easing her feet as two boys wandered in smelling of sweat, their conversation proclaiming the start of the football season. They were followed by a girl that Elsie recognized as Betty, one of the snobs from school.

The girl frowned for a moment. "I should know you, shouldn't I?"

"Choir," Elsie murmured. "I sit in front of you."

Betty's voice was vague. "So what are you doing…?"

"I work here. My parents own it."

August moved toward the back. "Don't just stand around and talk," he muttered. "There's plenty work to do."

"We sell a lot of frozen malt," Elsie said hurriedly, addressing Betty and the boys. "It's really pretty good."

One of the boys eyed August as he disappeared into the back room. "*Dere's verk to do.* Imagine that."

Betty gestured. "We've just come from football practice. Tom lives across from me and Ralph is quarterback." She began to giggle. "At least, he hopes…"

Elsie kept an eye at the back, mindful of her father's presence. "So what'll you have? We've got pineapple, black walnut, vanilla, chocolate, fresh strawberry…"

They chose the frozen malt and watched Elsie ring up the amount.

"So where you from?" Tom asked, dropping the change into his pocket.

"From Chicago." Elsie took a deep breath. "Where are you from?"

Tom leaned against the wall. "I mean your folks."

"Tomorrow is the pre-season game," Betty chirped. "Everyone will be there. You going?"

Marichen came out from the back. "Can I get you something or are you done?"

"We were just talking." Tom cleared his throat. "Betty here wondered where you were from. Just kinda interested."

August stood looking over Marichen's shoulder. "Time to go, boys. We're too busy to stand around talking."

"C'mon. We're late and my Mom'll be getting mad," Ralph muttered, tugging at Tom's sleeve.

Tom began to hum, *"There'll be a hot time in the town of Berlin when the Yanks go marching in..."* Then the three scurried out the door.

Elsie stood immobilized, then grabbed a towel and began wiping the counter. "I really don't know her," she mumbled. "I don't know why they came."

"Never mind. It's not your fault."

Soon people began flooding in, savoring the warm night and the moon that hung low in the sky. Boyish-looking sailors with pretty girls clinging to their arm, wizened granddads with little ones trying to decide between strawberry and chocolate, moms and dads standing too close to their soldier boys, their eyes fearful but proud.

Finally it was nine o'clock, and Marichen came from the back to flip the front door sign. CLOSED. It had been a long day.

Now the work shifted, racking napkins and cups, serving the last customers, wiping off the spattered mirror. In the back, August and Marichen loaded shelves, straightening up for the morning.

Suddenly, the door flew open. "Hey, Elsie, we're back!"

Pushing the last customer aside, Tom and Ralph charged in smelling of cigarettes and beer.

"We're closed." Marichen's voice rang from the back, her eyes sending Elsie a warning.

"The door was open," Tom grinned. "You're supposed to serve customers once they're inside. Everybody knows that."

"Not after we're closed." Marichen's voice was soft but firm.

"We just wanted to check things out. I mean, you're not foreigners or somethin' are you?" Ralph ducked into a half-crouch looking back and forth, mockingly sinister. "*Loose lips sink ships...*"

Emitting a drunken giggle, Tom began to sing. "*When der fuhrer says, vie iss de Master Race, we Heil! Heil! right in der Fuhrer's Face...*" each *Heil!* punctuated with a Bronx cheer that sent drunken slobber all over the counter shelf.

August moved behind the milk counter, one hand on the shopping bag. "Okay boys, time to go. Outside."

"We're just being friendly, Mr. Schicklgruber." Tom raised his hand in mock salute. "*Heil Hitler!*"

Suddenly everything went into slow motion. With one powerful leap, August swung himself over the counter, the shopping bag bouncing against his thigh as he charged forward.

The boys stood for a moment in stunned disbelief, then dived toward the door. "Jesus Christ! The guy's crazy!"

"No, August!" Marichen cried. "Let them go. Don't go after them."

But August was in hot pursuit. Within a block he had closed in on the lagging Tom, the shopping bag catching the boy across the shoulders, sending him to the ground, retching and gasping for breath while August stood over him silently watching before he turned to walk back to the store, the street eerily silent.

"What have you done?" Marichen cried, standing at the front door in a halo of light. "*Liebe Gott*, now what?"

"My house is my castle. I have the right. And next time, make sure you lock the door when we close," he growled.

"Yes, yes. Next time. But what happened?" Marichen cried.

"They ran away. That's all."

"And what else?"

"Nothing else. He fell down." August's face was grim. "The other one ran away. Now go inside. It's over."

Retreating into the store, Marichen turned down the lights, and the three worked frantically, stocking, sweeping, stacking empties at the back door for the next day's pickup. Within an hour they were ready to leave.

It was warm outside and people nodded as they passed. Looking neither to the right or left, they boarded the bus with Elsie escaping toward the back staring at an open book, mindlessly turning the pages until they arrived at their stop. Running ahead, she gave a brief "Hi" to Trudi who was in her room listening to the radio, then into her own room where she changed, tossing books and clothes helter-skelter before flinging herself onto the bed. She heard her parents moving about, heard the toilet flush, the lights click out, the murmured voices. Maybe no one had noticed. Maybe this was only a dream.

When she awoke, both parents were gone. It was Saturday, and Elsie wasn't scheduled for work until noon, with Trudi coming in later. Her mind in a fog, she lingered over a bowl of cereal, got dressed and tried to do some homework but nothing registered. Might as well go to work. At the mailbox, a note from a tenant with bold letters, SECOND REQUEST.

Arriving, she brushed past a half-dozen customers waiting to be served, moving behind the counter to help. "Where's Dad?"

"He had to go somewhere. I called Trudi. She's coming as soon as she can."

"Anything happen?"

"I'll tell you later." Marichen handed the customer her purchase and counted out the change, turning to the next in line.

When Trudi arrived, things slowed enough for Marichen to explain. "The police came and took him," she whispered.

"Wow! How long ago? Has he called?" Trudi asked. "He's entitled to one phone call, you know."

Marichen shook her head. "They didn't say nothing to me. They just took him. I don't know what will happen. I had to stay here."

He returned two hours later, stumbling into the back, his face a mask.

"Are you all right?" Marichen cried, dropping the stack of grocery bags she was stuffing into their respective slots. "Let me get you something. You want soup? Maybe a sandwich…" She gestured for Trudi and Elsie to go up front.

"Is okay. I just have to…" Unbuttoning as he went toward the bathroom, he came back with his face washed, his hair combed. "The boy's family called the police. There were papers to sign. They took my fingerprints and asked for my Social Security Card." He took a choking breath. "We need to get a lawyer."

Marichen's eyes widened. "Where do we find a lawyer? We got no money."

"It's getting busy, Mom," Trudi called from the front.

There were already a dozen people waiting as Marichen and Trudi worked the counter with Elsie up front while August remained in the back.

"Aunt Martha called," Trudi murmured. "She said something about coming over tomorrow. But maybe that's not such a good idea."

Marichen brushed it aside. There was plenty more to think

about. Better August should go home and clear his head. They could finish without him.

At five o'clock Elsie gulped down a frozen malt. At six-thirty, she popped a slice of lunchmeat into her mouth, quieting her stomach. At six forty-five, she was back to scooping ice cream. At seven o'clock she signaled Trudi and escaped to the bathroom, running a comb through her hair, adding a light touch of forbidden lipstick. It was Saturday – date night. What did that say about Trudi who was getting ready to graduate? What did that say about her own social life? Her feet hurt and she knew her mother's hurt even more. Two hours to go.

She returned to the ice cream counter. A fresh container of orange-pineapple meant the dig was even harder. Another hour and she could begin the cleanup. Tomorrow would be a day off. She hoped she didn't fall asleep on the bus and miss her stop.

"Are you finished?" Her mother's voice rang through the now silent store, making her jump. "If you are, you can go. We'll close up."

Elsie nodded, placing the freshly washed scoops on a towel the way she'd been taught.

"Just be quiet so you don't wake Daddy when you go in."

The light was on in her parent's room as she tiptoed past. If her father was awake, he didn't call out.

Asleep almost before her head found the pillow, she awakened as the bright sun came through the window. She'd forgotten to lower the shades. It was Sunday and she could have slept in. Suddenly there was the doorbell braying and she was fully awake.

Aunt Martha's voice drifted in from the front room followed by the smell of cigarettes. She threw on some clothes and crept into Trudi's room, both straining to hear.

"Did you tell Aunt Martha about Dad and the cops?" Elsie whispered.

"No. She called way before I knew anything happened. Mom

must've forgotten to call her back." Trudi gestured impatiently. "Just be quiet and listen."

The voices rose and fell, each a monologue before another interruption. "Divorce? What did Wally do this time?"

Elsie clutched at her sister's arm.

"She won't be allowed, because he's in the army," Trudi muttered, pulling away. "That's the law."

Martha's response was followed by a long exchange punctuated by Martha's bitter laugh. "Lawyer? You can borrow mine."

Now the conversation shifted, with words like Court Date, Legal Retainer and Citation, as Martha began coaching August on what he should say when he called in the morning.

Seeing the girls huddled inside Trudi's door, Marichen motioned them into the kitchen. "You can bring these biscuits to the front room. I'll bring the coffee."

"How come..." Elsie asked.

"Never mind. And Trudi, you go get dressed. Just because it's Sunday doesn't mean you should be lazy all day."

Back in the front room, Elsie placed the tray on the end table. "Will you be staying home all the time now, Dad?"

His smile was humorless. "You think I need a vacation? You gonna run the store for me?"

Martha took a deep drag on her cigarette. "My lawyer is gonna take care of it, Elsie. Daddy will go to the store just like every other day, and you go to school like nothing happened, you hear?"

Early the next morning, Marichen called the lawyer's number, her voice barely a whisper. "I need to talk to Mr. Landsman, please. Martha Raschke told us..."

She motioned to August who was sitting across from her. "They're getting him."

The booming response sounded garbled at first. "Oh yes, Martha called me. Tell you what. Have your husband come in and we'll talk it over. Don't worry. No charge for the first consultation." Then the rustling of papers and some muffled conversation. "Let me give you to my girl for an appointment." A pause as his voice softened. "We'll get you in front of the right judge. It'll be a slap on the wrist. Don't you worry."

"Business will go down, and that's for sure," Marichen whispered, handing the phone to August. "All our hard work for nothing."

"These were bad boys," August snapped. "I am an American citizen. I have rights."

The hearing was scheduled for three months later. August went alone, meeting Mr. Landsman in the hall a few minutes ahead of time. August was instructed to remain silent, to let the lawyers do all the talking. It was followed by a reassuring squeeze on the shoulder as they entered the courtroom, an expanse of dark wood and leather with the American flag providing the only color. Their case was number five on the docket. No reading, no sleeping, no talking allowed. It took an hour as other lawyers murmured their Latin phrases, defending tired old men or flashy women at the bar of justice. Then it was their turn.

The judge looked up. "What have we here?"

A man at the next table got to his feet. "Judge, this isn't my case but I would like to start while we wait for my supervisor to arrive. It's a complaint that the defendant beat up a boy outside his store, a minor who was only…"

Landsman jumped up gesturing dramatically. "Your honor, this was strictly an accident. One of the boys was harassing my client and when my client urged him out of the store, the boy tripped and fell as he and my client collided. There was no injury beyond a few scrapes and bruises. Judge, my client is of German descent who has led an exemplary life, never had so much as a traffic ticket. He's an American citizen, the owner of a successful dairy store. He would like the family to know how sorry he is..."

The judge lifted his hand, cutting him off. "I want to hear from the prosecution."

The supervisor had arrived and was conferring with the other man. Now he looked up. "Your honor, we've decided to go to *nolle pross*. The complainant is willing to drop the charges in view of contributing circumstances."

The judge's face was impassive, looking at both, then back at the folder in front of him. "So served. Case dismissed."

No smile, no slap on the back. The wheels of justice...

The bailiff motioned to August. "You're free to go."

"I have another case upstairs in five minutes," Landsman whispered with a studied smile. "Congratulations. Call me again if you need me."

Back in the hall, August paused, trying to grasp what had happened. Fifteen years in America yet certain things remained universal. Very simply, it was all about money. The bill from Landsman would be in the mail, items headed by words like *consulting* or *research*. Martha had warned it would be in the thousands, but he had no choice. Where else could he find a lawyer with contacts at City Hall?

Near the elevator two uniformed officers stood fingering their holsters. Downstairs, the people milled about as though this was an ordinary day. He had been to court and was found innocent. Surely there was nothing to fear.

Back on the bus he stared at the trees, the patches of green outside the window. He pictured Marichen shaking her finger at him. *So much money, and all for nothing*. He tried to remember how much Creamix he had ordered. If the weather got warm, they'd need extra. Maybe it was time to expand, buy the property next door. There was no such thing as wanting too much, being too hungry. His jaw tightened. What was done, was done. Time to move on.

He got off the bus, lightening his step. Marichen had to see that he'd won. The charges were dropped. It was over, and he'd sleep good tonight. As for the lawyer's fee, she'd have to understand. It was only about money.

CHAPTER 22

Germany, 1943

THE ATTACKS HAD BECOME INDISCRIMINATE with bombers blackening the sky both day and night, pulsating terror. German defenses picked up signals from Holland, their sirens screeching in response to the RAF. People in rumpled clothes would spill out of houses, boys of fifteen and sixteen buttoning their Hitler Jugend uniforms, running to man the anti-aircraft guns while the old and infirm pressed babies to their breasts, comforting words drowned out by their screams.

Hilda would snatch Peter in her arms and stumble over broken glass and concrete, racing for the bunker with Alma a few feet behind. The flak-guns aimed at the sky, their searchlights reflecting metallic shards like confetti dancing in the sky. At dawn, going back to a home covered with dust and concrete or finding it so damaged it meant another move to another nameless street with a meaningless address. Sometimes they'd lose their way, orientation muddled in the collapse of buildings and rubble. Other times, the sirens would send them into the nearest basement, praying against a direct hit. One time Hilda fell, with a missile large enough to take down a fighter plane landing inches from her head.

Guste had given birth to a baby girl, both of them evacuated to safety in occupied Poland where she paid for their food and shelter by feeding the pigs and cleaning the chicken coop with baby Ursula slung on her back, grateful that Elvira was safe in Bielefeld. Siebold and Wilhelm remained behind, sharing their ration coupons with Alma and Hilda, combining resources, eating meals together. If rumors of forced labor and the Warsaw Ghetto drifted over the fields, it was beyond comprehension. Personal survival was at the forefront. Nothing else mattered.

Hilda had applied for a permit to evacuate, ready to leave her improvised housing and job at a moment's notice. Meanwhile, Alma was a mainstay, doing a bit of laundry and mending before the rush back to the bunker to grab a bench along the wall, arranging blankets to make a bed, listening as babies cried, the elderly cough and complain.

But this night had been quiet and Alma had packed a few slices of bread and cheese for Hilda, wishing her God's speed as she left for work. Then with Peter at her side, she picked her way down the steps to a market where she hoped to find some bratwurst and green beans to feed five if the owner was willing to negotiate.

Kerchief flapping, she steered around workmen, past little boys not much older than Peter assigned to pick up litter, adding to the mounds along the roadside. With ration books inside her bag, she arrived at Herr Kardorff's, a place that stocked potatoes and powdered milk along with a few pots and pans and secondhand clothes.

A half-dozen women were inside as they entered. Two turned their backs with one moving to the counter, her voice crackling through the silence. "I need a sack of potatoes, Herr Kardorff, and don't give me rotten ones again because I have a good smeller and I know the difference. I brought my ration Karte and want to buy two lamb chops and some cheese."

Herr Kardorff stared for a moment, then shook his head. "Meine liebe Frau, there is no lamb, not even mutton. Remember the bombing over Möhne Dam. Farmlands flooded, cows and sheep drowned, the wheat and corn rotting in the ground. Potatoes I can sell you. Maybe three or four carrots. That is all."

The woman donned a fierce expression. "I saved up on ration coupons and this is all you can give me?"

"Coupons or money, it makes me no difference. There is no fresh meat, and if you find some, don't eat it because it's rotten for sure. Maybe a little sausage. That I got."

Alma peeked inside her shopping bag, cautioning Peter to stay close. She had found a dress under the sink and by ripping out the seams, was creating a child-sized makeover, something she might barter. She counted the hours she'd slept the night before. If it was quiet tonight, she was sure to finish it.

Now she sidled up to the counter. "I have a pair of scissors. Only the tip of one side is broken." She held it up from inside the shopping bag. I'll give it to you for a little sugar."

He scowled. "You have coupons? If you don't have coupons…"

"Yes, I have. Do you have some sugar?"

"Well, I'm not sure. I go in the back and look." He took a few steps, then came back. "But only if you buy a sack of potatoes. I sell you sausage too, but only if you have coupons."

Alma swallowed hard. "How much are the potatoes? I didn't bring much."

She ended up with potatoes that looked like they were ready to sprout, and two skinny sausages instead of the three she'd wanted.

All this for a cup of sugar that might cut through the bitter taste of coffee made mostly from ground acorns and sawdust.

Taking Peter's hand, she hurried back to the flat. There might be water in the tap and a few hours of gas and electricity to wash some clothes with a hoarded bar of soap, hanging them at the window to dry. She might even wash her hair. But first, inventory. What was broken? What could be salvaged? Most of their clothing had been destroyed or stolen. Far more precious were utensils, pots and pans and a working flashlight. It could have been worse. Attic space was less tempting for thieves prowling the streets.

Upstairs and out of breath, she laid her purchases on the edge of the sink. Testing, she was rewarded with a thin stream of water that she promptly collected into containers. There was electricity too. She turned to Peter standing in the doorway. "Take off your hat. I need to do some laundry for Onkel Wilhelm and Siebold."

The little boy climbed onto the kitchen chair. "Papa told me he was going away so he could fix things. Will the soldiers be fixing things pretty soon?"

Alma looked around distractedly, trying to figure what to do first. "I hope so. There's a lot to fix, isn't there?"

Peter nodded. "So Papa needs to hurry home. Did you tell him?"

Plunging a few shirts and underwear into the water, she began to scrub. "He's too far away to hear."

"Onkel Gunter too? Is he far away?"

"Your papa is in France. His unit went there for a rest. I will draw you a map and show you when we have lunch."

"Why didn't he come home to rest?"

"They were fighting far away in Russia. Then they needed him someplace else."

"Does Onkel Gunter get a rest from fighting?"

"Onkel Gunter is in Berlin. That's on the other side. We're in between."

Peter thought for a moment. "Bad boys fight. But our side is good. That's what you always say."

"Our men fight to keep us safe. Your papa fights…" She began rising the clothes. How to explain the logic of war to a four year old? "Peter, go to the other room and find me some hangers. We'll hang the shirts by the window to dry. Go get them for me."

He trotted into the other room, returning with three. "I saw the radio," he announced. "It was inside the dirty clothes basket."

She sighed resignedly. "You have to be sure not to tell anyone. I will let you listen under the blanket tonight if there is still battery power if we don't go to the bunker.

"It's stuffy under the blanket and anyway, I can't hear it very much."

Alma smoothed the shirt onto the hanger. From down below, the sounds were joined by far off rumbling, the air gray with dust and ashes from lingering fires. Would there be enough sun to dry the clothes? "No chance for ironing, but at least the clothes are clean," she murmured to herself.

Sitting down, she began to peel potatoes. There were no green beans but a lone onion would add flavor. "We will eat lunch. Then we both take a nap."

Peter leaned forward, chin in his hands. "Tell me about when Papa was a little boy. About how he played with his sisters and climbed trees and ran races. Tell me again."

"Well, when your papa was a little boy, he liked to play outside. There was grass and trees and flowers," she began.

"And there were children all up and down the road," Peter prompted. "And his Mutti would let them all play together but only after their work was done."

Long thin peels fell off the potatoes, the knife tip gouging the yellow-green sprouts. "Your Papa's chores were to water the peas and beans because they lived in the country and they had a big back yard," Alma continued. "On Sundays, they would pick berries and his Mutti would make a pie. And the pie was so sweet and juicy that they had to eat it with a spoon." It was all a fairy tale. Rainer's family had suffered the same poverty as anyone else.

"When I grow up, I will be like Papa. I will live in the country and have a nice yard." His eyes were dreamy. "All of us together."

She finished arranging the food in a large pot, and moved it to the hotplate next to the sink. "I can show you where is Papa and Onkel Gunter." With a pencil, she drew a rough map on the back of an old letter.

But Peter had lost interest, his eyes turning to the cot at the other end of the room. Ducking his head, he slipped from the chair and taking a few steps, tumbled onto the bed falling fast asleep.

Soon the casserole was done, tucked between two bed pillows to stay warm. Alma had placed sweaters and scarves in a basket to ward off the bunker chill should there be an alarm later on. Now she filled another bucket and three pots with water, anticipating the power being off by suppertime, then curled up beside the little boy and fell asleep.

It was mid-afternoon when they awoke. The wind had picked up and the shirts, now dry, were flapping in the window. Taking them down, she folded them to be ready when the men arrived from work. Sounds from the street had become more pronounced with an ambulance wail announcing an injured worker. Then more clatter as huge machines continued clearing the road.

Still sleepy, Alma went to the breadbox and sliced off chunks of bread. Filling two cups with water, she added a spoonful of Klem, a protein powder that didn't taste like milk, but might slake their hunger, motioning Peter to sit down and eat.

Returning to the makeshift map, she turned it over to re-read the letter. "This was from Onkel Gunter. He is in Berlin where there are some very important people."

"You already told me that." Peter went to the window. "Can I go out to the street? I want to watch."

"You can watch it from here." She roused herself. "Tell you what. Let's sing a song."

They sang. Then they sang some more. Alma began the story of Hansel and Gretel and switched to Jesus at the Temple as a little boy. Peter listened indifferently.

Finally, there were footsteps outside the door as Wilhelm and Siebold swept in, the smell of the mines preceding them. At the sink, they washed up using the precious water Alma had saved. "I have some extra soap at home," Wilhelm offered. "I get it for you after while."

Hilda arrived a few minutes later. "They were talking about more bombing tonight, so we better go to the bunker early," she said hurriedly. "Last time it was so crowded we couldn't get very far inside." She reached for the lamp and the light flickered on.

Placing the casserole on the middle of the table, Alma motioned them to begin. "We better eat before it's too dark to see."

Wilhelm surveyed his meager meal. "Always running to the bunker. I'm getting too old to go back and forth, up and down. Most of the time it's a false alarm anyway."

"Once the bunker fills up, they lock the door and you won't be able to get in. Think about that."

Wilhelm took a small bite. "You go on ahead. I can stop on the way for the soap. There's time enough."

Siebold shot Alma a meaningful glance. "I will stay with him. You just save us a place."

Alma shrugged. "I can't force you. So finish up. No sense leaving it for the rats. Just don't take too long." She gathered the supplies and led the way out as Peter and Hilda followed.

A stream of women and children were already on their way with baskets, boxes and blankets. The workmen were gone, replaced by air-raid wardens and Hitler Jugend, the fading sun reflected on white markings that traced the outlines of doors.

The bunker was claustrophobic with egg-shaped lights wrapped in mesh protruding from the low ceiling. Hollow columns contained cables with water pipes for toilets and drinking fountains at the ends of each floor. In the center was a humming ventilator that could be hand-powered should the electricity fail.

Hilda and Alma found a spot in the middle that offered the greatest protection, laying their blankets and pillows on benches, far enough from others who'd already spread here and there. Pots and pans serving helmets or vomit containers clanged cheerfully as people brushed by.

Now settled, Alma began to fidget. Where were the men? "They didn't have to come very far. How long does it take to eat a few potatoes?"

"You know how Onkel Wilhelm hates this," Hilda murmured. "He will wait until the last minute."

"He never listens, never listens…" Alma's voice throbbed in rhythm with the ventilator's hum.

Another hour as people settled into quiet conversation, the children dozing in their blanketed cocoons. Elderly men played cards and women clustered in a flashlight commune where they mended socks or towels. Hilda talked softly to Peter, playing a game of When You Grow Up, telling him of all the possibilities once the war was over and Alma tried to swallow her concern. Maybe Siebold and Wilhelm had arrived and were on a different floor. One more hour and she'd take a look.

Then suddenly, Siebold was towering over them, his breath coming in short gasps, his face drenched in sweat. "Wilhelm would not come so I left him behind. I had to run. It's really bad out there."

"Is it something new?"

"Bombers over Köln. The whole city is burning. Even the cathedral. We were listening to the radio before the lights went out. Goebbels announced it wasn't so bad, but he lied. Or maybe he just didn't know. The bombers hit the gas mains making big fireballs, one after another. People ran into the river and drowned. Thousands..."

The people began to stir as the news passed from one to another.

"Phosphorus bombs over Wuppertal," Siebold continued, "so bright to make you blind. Some people were in flames and jumped into the river but when they came out, they went back to burning. It sticks to the skin and you can't blow it out."

Hilda covered Peters ears and began rocking back and forth. "...and even God must be weeping."

It was barely light when the all clear sounded, allowing them to emerge. A light breeze stirred curtains that flapped through broken windows catching on shards of glass to form ghostly configurations.

"We'll go and see if Onkel Wilhelm is all right." Alma's voice was frantic. "Hilda, you take Peter home. He shouldn't be there, just in case..."

Taking Siebold's arm they hurried past buildings that leaned like skeletons, their brick and concrete threatening to collapse at any moment.

"The building is still standing! I can see it," Alma cried, and began to run.

Workers were in front, lifting a stretcher onto a waiting truck. One of them waved Alma back. Then seeing Siebold, he paused. "You live here?"

Siebold nodded. "With my brother-in-law. Was there a hit?"

Alma pushed forward gesturing wildly. "He stopped to bring me some soap before going to the bunker. Did anything happen?"

"I'm sorry, meine Frau. There were three of them in the cellar. Concussion waves from the bombs... It makes the lungs explode. It went fast. They didn't know..."

Alma's voice rose to a wail. "I knew this would happen! I told him to come with us. But he wouldn't listen. Now he's dead, all alone, in the dark..." She was clinging to Siebold, almost ready to collapse. "How can we make another funeral?" she whispered, looking up at his face. "Who is there to sew a decent burial shirt? Where to buy a casket or a bunch of flowers? Where to bury him?"

"Tomorrow, Alma, tomorrow. That will be soon enough. There's Ida and the children. Do you know where they are? They will want to say goodbye." Siebold moved aside as the workmen started the engine. Touching her arm, he led her back to the flat where Hilda and Peter were waiting.

"I will go back to see what can be salvaged," Siebold offered. "Maybe there are things you can use..."

No further announcement was needed.

CHAPTER 23

Chicago, 1944

THE BUS BUMPED OVER POTHOLES, past isolated houses and vacant lots along Higgins Road. "An hour on the bus and then we walk even more?"

"We're ready to expand, Marichen. Like Rudy said, only better. A chain of stores all over Chicago. 'Lisbet and Fritz are experienced and don't have to be trained. Herbert comes back from the army. Later it's with Trudi and Elsie. Maybe Eleanor too. Modern Dairy stores all over Chicago."

They had arrived at the end of the line, a few feet from the freshly plowed earth and the cloying smell of spring. "Did you talk to Fritz and 'Lisbet? What did they say?"

"That comes later. For now, we're just looking."

"How come you didn't talk to me?"

"I'm talking to you now. This place rents with no money down, just month to month. We'll sell mostly milk and ice cream just like on Belmont."

A quarter-mile walk brought them to a small building on a

graveled cut-away a few feet from the road. "The landlady lives in that farmhouse next door. She says we can use her toilet whenever we want. She'll keep it unlocked."

Marichen stared at the dead flies and splattered cardboard displays in the window. "It's a chicken coop, August. Not even enough room for six customers. What kind of turnover is that? Where's the profit?" She drew a zero on the dust-covered window. Her voice was firm. "We're too old to start over. Let's go home."

"This isn't starting over," he insisted. "It's having two stores instead of one. Later it's three, and four…" He reached into his pocket and took out a key. "I'm telling you, Rudy had it right. It's time we do it."

"What makes you think 'Lisbet would be interested? Or Fritz either? They don't even like us."

"It's in their blood, just like with us. It's why we came to America."

"You said that was all horse crap."

"If 'Lisbet and Fritz don't want to, we still have three children. Herby has a good head for business and Trudi's boyfriend is a hard worker. When they get married…"

"Herbert is going to college and Trudi likes working downtown. You think she will put in twelve hours a day like us? This girl who gets dressed up in high heels and sits in an office where people call her Miss? And don't even try talking to Elsie. She hates business."

"We'll start small. Just get the store going, then bring 'Lisbet in. After that, the others will come. You'll see."

He'd begun pacing off dimensions, mentally shifting shelves to make room for a bread rack, eyeing the window for placement of signs. One week later he signed the agreement. The keys now belonged to him.

The Higgins store had been a quick-stop for basic needs. It would be simple to add ice cream and gallon milk. In this rural environment, a building boom was certain once the war was over.

They opened in June, the start of summer vacation. Marichen came in once a week to check on inventory with Elsie working full time, bringing home the receipts and cash at the end of the day. The store on Belmont was now open on Sunday afternoon, a bow to the increase in business. With careful planning they could manage.

Three weeks later, Marichen announced that Eleanor was coming to stay for the summer.

"The whole summer? But why?" Elsie paused mid-step, having just come home after a ten-hour day. "Nobody's ever home."

"She'll be working with you at the store."

"You're kidding. All day?"

"Yes. Ask Daddy."

"I can't ask him, Mom. He never talks to me."

"Eleanor will help in the store. You talk about school, about books, things like that. It makes time fly."

"You think we're that busy? Have you looked?"

"Just do what Daddy says. And don't talk back."

And that was that.

Eleanor arrived the following Sunday. She had grown tall and fleshy, her bulk softened by a pretty face and two dimples that danced when she smiled, her dark wavy hair and gray eyes like her mother's.

"You'll sleep with Elsie," Marichen announced, picking up her suitcase. "She has a big bed with plenty of room."

Smiling uncertainly, Elsie led the way, dutifully helping to stash Eleanor's things, the double bed roomy enough, despite Eleanor's size.

They adjusted easily. In the morning, they would nudge one

another awake, darting in and out of the bathroom, catching the bus to open the store at eight. They explored the tiny building from top to bottom, finding an abandoned box of pornography above the artificial ceiling, giggling at the various poses, swearing they would never do *that* even after they got married. Eleanor showed Elsie some steps she'd learned at her ballet class and they practiced balancing on their toes. Eleanor's voice was a clear coloratura, and they improvised harmony to folk songs and current tunes. Voracious readers, they delighted in arguing for preferences, sharing dreams and aspirations, for by a quirk of the calendar, Eleanor was only a year ahead of Elsie in school. Bit by bit, Eleanor's story emerged.

'Lisbet's poverty had been unremitting after Rudy died. Her store had gone bust after the nearby school closed, something August learned as he wandered through the old neighborhood. She'd found a job in a defense plant, seeing less and less of her daughter who was now entering her teens. Still friends with Otto and Sophie, there was little time to socialize. Over the years, she had dated a series of ne'er do wells who came and went like ghosts. Meanwhile, Eleanor remained adrift, indifferent to school despite her bright and curious mind, using food to transport herself into oblivion.

"She's a nice girl," Marichen noted to August. "Doesn't talk back and knows how to handle customers. Elsie has someone to talk to. I think they're getting along."

Introducing gallon milk made the business improve. Later they installed a small freezer and began selling ice cream, planning the big shift to homemade for the following year.

Then it was late summer, a Sunday when the Belmont store opened late, a period of quiet as Marichen moved about in the kitchen preparing breakfast. Eleanor had gone back home to pick up a few things while Elsie went to open the Higgins store alone.

"I talked to 'Lisbet last week," August began, taking a sip of coffee.

Marichen looked up from the stove. "And so?"

"About the store."

"What about the store?"

"She wants to look. So I told her okay. I would meet her at noon." He paused. "Today."

"Without me?"

"Belmont opens at five. We'll be done by then."

"Done with what?"

He looked down at his cup. "You need to listen better. This will be Modern Dairy number two. Then number three and so forth, all under one management."

"Does 'Lisbet know what that means – under one management?"

"I told her. Like Sears or A&P or National Foods. She understands."

Marichen stared at him for a long time, then took a deep breath. "Okay. You wanna get rid of the store? Well, so do I. But just remember to get a fair price. It's my money too." She placed a plate of sausage and eggs in front of him then turned her back.

"If you wanna come with, you can come. Just don't say I never told you."

They arrived just as a black sedan pulled up with Otto maneuvering onto the gravel, his wife at his side, little Dolores, 'Lisbet and Eleanor peering out from the back.

Marichen stared at the entourage, fat Sophie struggling to get out of the car, Otto now bald and thin followed by 'Lisbet who was still pretty, but matronly. It had been five years since they'd seen 'Lisbet, ten since the big fight after the funeral.

"What's going on?" Elsie stood at the open door. "There's hardly any room inside…"

Marichen gestured to be quiet. "You girls go out in front. I'll take care of customers when they come in."

Outside, Elsie sank down on a bench of weathered wood warmed from the afternoon sun, motioning Eleanor to join her. "I've seen old pictures of Uncle Otto and Aunt Sophie but I hardly recognized them," she began. "And I've never seen Dolores. Yet here we were, literally living together, and we never discussed why not."

"No one was supposed to know." Eleanor's voice was apologetic.

"To know what?"

"My mom taking over the store. That was why Uncle August bought it in the first place."

"You're buying the store? And you kept it a secret?"

"You told me that you hated business. So now you're out from under – at least from this one."

Elsie stared at the clouds, at birds swooping over fields of ripening corn. "And you knew all along. And you know Aunt Sophie and Uncle Otto and Dolores…"

The visitors were emerging and Elsie pulled herself together as she stood up, holding out her hand. "It was nice to see you, Aunt Sophie, Uncle Otto. You sure have a nice car."

"Used up all the gas coupons for a month," Otto laughed. "But that's okay. Anything to make my girls happy."

They piled into the car, waving as they pulled away.

Elsie watched until they were out of sight then joined her parents inside. "Eleanor says that Tante 'Lisbet is going to take over the store. Is that true?"

"You should be glad. You're always complaining about work."

August pulled out his watch. "We have to get back. You can close up tonight by yourself."

"Then I can go straight home?"

He nodded. "Just be sure to lock the door." Gathering their things, they walked along the darkening fields to catch the bus.

The sale was completed a few days later. 'Lisbet took over the Higgins store a week before school started.

Meanwhile, August continued looking. In early March he arrived at work, later than usual. "I found it. Another gold mine."

Marichen looked up, stashing her cleaning bucket under the counter. "Where this time?"

He motioned her into the back. "It's in Stickney, not too far from here. The Bluebird bus stops right in front, a nice comfortable ride. The sign says Creamland so we know it's already a dairy store. A Kiddy Land across the street will bring customers in for ice cream and there's a dancehall next door. On the other side is a busy restaurant so there's lots of traffic. It has a one-bedroom apartment in the back of the store with a nice bath and kitchen, all ready to move in. The owner will leave the furniture, so Trudi won't need to buy a thing. It's all part of the price."

Marichen sat down. "Trudi? When did you talk to Trudi?"

August was barely able to contain himself. "Remember when Trudi wanted a fur coat? She begged and begged until we bought it for her, real beaver, not cheap skunk like she got for herself. Cost more than a thousand dollars. She wanted to show off at work and parade in front of the boyfriend so we..."

"What's that got to do with anything?"

"She owes us, Marichen." The front bell signaled a customer and August reached for an apron.

"What makes you think...?"

He was gone, swinging a gallon of milk onto the counter,

dismissing the customer with a nod.

Marichen followed as he moved to the ice cream counter. "You haven't talked to Trudi, have you? I can tell."

"It's always better to work for yourself. Trudi knows she can make more money in business, not sitting in front of a typewriter all day, saying please and thank you. I know my girl."

"Trudi knows what it takes all right, working twelve and fourteen hours a day, seven days a week, with chocolate sauce dripping down the front of her uniform, her feet so sore she can hardly stand up. You'll never convince her," Marichen stormed.

His expression was impassive as he continued checking the stock.

She threw up her hands. "All right, go ahead and talk. But I tell you right now that she won't do it. Not in a million years."

Once more, Marichen was wrong.

By late fall, Trudi had made the move, excited at the prospect of being on her own. Mrs. Turek, the former owner, remained for two weeks, showing Trudi how to order kolacky, pierogi and kielbasa, a mainstay in this Slavic community. Elsie would work there on the weekends, sleeping on the kitchen daybed, her belongings in a nearby cabinet. After that? "Well, we'll see," August said.

At first Trudi delighted in going to bed as late as she wanted, smoking cigarettes at will. The sisters giggled at the names – Dreamland, Creamland and Fairy Land in tight proximity. Then she discovered the loud music from the restaurant made sleep almost impossible and that Dreamland was really a strip-joint, with half-naked ladies pretending to be customers whenever the dancehall was raided. As for the Kiddy Land, it was across a busy street providing little customer traffic.

Elsie was not aware of any of this. Instead, she reveled in her own independence. With business still building, the work was easy. On weekends, she and Trudi would have a cigarette and a late nightcap at the Italian Grotto next door, listening to stories about Al Capone, flirting with the gruff denizens who treated her indulgently like a kid sister. Away from her parents' watchful eyes, her world was expanding, and she embraced it with wide and eager eyes.

CHAPTER 24

Camp Campbell, 1944

ONE PAGE, WRITTEN ON BOTH sides with circles for punctuation. Pseudo-sophisticated, a term Elsie hated. Sophomoric was more accurate. But she did write weekly, more than the rest of the family combined. PFC Herbert Zahn 36744376. A name and a number. He rubbed his forehead, turning the page. *Trudi got engaged to an Air Corps Cadet. His name is Erv and I like him a lot. Aunt Martha got Uncle Fritz drunk so he married Fraulein Kate in City Hall. I don't know who all was there because we weren't. I'm flunking Physics and don't like math any more. I really want to go to the junior prom but it would be impossible to sneak out. But first I have to be asked. I worked at the Higgins store all summer, a lot of it with Eleanor! It was okay, I guess. But I'll probably never see her again because Mom and Dad sold the store to Tante 'Lisbet. That's why Eleanor was there. I'm back working at Belmont with Mom sticking her nose into everything I do. A girl named Vita has become my best friend. She was the most popular girl in eighth grade. We're both in choir and take class voice lessons from a teacher who comes to the school once a week. It cost five dollars for the whole semester and Dad paid for it. We can come in for a lesson any time we have study hall. She even gives us private lessons downtown once a month. I'm paling around with Carol and two Shirleys and we go to the Teen Canteen sometimes because boys are there. Ha ha. Gosh Herb, please, please, please stay safe. We miss you.*

He folded the letter into the envelope. A sister was no pinup, but her letters were a comfort, a return to the familiar. Here, there were a hundred thousand officers and men plus 500 WAACs and female clerks. Barracks and buildings were scattered without landmarks, enough to blanket the mind in a perpetual fog. He was doing his duty, serving his country in time of war. He felt no anger, nor fierce patriotism. Even fear didn't register. But the letters spelled reality, sending his mind back to the store, remembering every case of toilet paper, every loaf of bread, every gallon of milk.

"Hey, you coming?" The voice rang out over the barracks chatter. "Can't be late, my man. It's payday plus a new Danny Kaye movie."

Two years in the army and Herb had finally found a buddy. Other names and faces were part of the haze but Jack Foster's remained. A few years older, his world encompassed most of Herb's aspirations. Educated, erudite, and a bit overweight, he had taken Herb under his wing, teaching him the difference between pinochle and bridge, building a foursome here and there instead of gambling away their pay with poker. They discussed Darwin and Plato and the concept of a super race, agreeing that humanity still had far to go. Together, they sold tickets at the camp theater in return for a few extra dollars and a free seat in the back row once the movie started.

Now outside, their shoes crunched on the pebbled walk.

"Weekend passes have been cancelled. So have overnights." Jack wiped his glasses on a handkerchief. "I wrote and told my wife. Let's hope it gets through the censors." He turned. "Do you get seasick?"

"Don't know. But I almost drowned taking the swimming test. They checked me off anyway."

"Imagine seeing Mozart's Salzburg, or Beethoven's Bonn. But they say it's bombed to hell anyway."

"Well, I sure don't want to go to Japan."

"You speak German so you probably will."

The outside posters reflected the setting sun, blinding them as they entered the dim foyer. They passed a corporal who nodded then returned to his book as Herb and Jack signed their time sheets and entered the ticket booth.

The theater was full by the time the movie started and they took turns sitting in the darkened theater, a quick summary helping to pick up on the plot. Two hours of army spoof cut through the prevailing boredom and their return to the barracks was almost cheerful. If something was going to happen, let it be.

The following morning the call went out. Herb was assigned to Headquarter Company, Jack to Company A, part of the 14th Armored Division given forty-eight hours to make ready. They were to meet again aboard ship two weeks later.

Then back to the old army game: hurry up and wait. First, the scramble to gather personal belongings, then the tally of socks, underwear and t-shirts. Equipment and weapons would come later. In between were calisthenics and marching up and down just to keep busy, finally loading onto a troop train accompanied by the strains of martial music. Bent double under field packs, they flopped onto seats with grunts and curses, watching the miles race by to New Jersey, then New York. Surely their destination would be Europe.

A few passes were issued but most were assigned classes, allowing the command to make last-minute adjustments. They were issued life jackets, not to be removed for the duration aboard ship. It was mid-October. Herded like cattle in the middle of the night, they strained under 100-pound duffel bags, bedrolls, rifles and steel helmets, following one another in the dark through a maze of hatches and companionways. Their assigned area encompassed a forest of hammocks two feet by six stacked in tiers, the man on top staring into a tangle of pipes, those below pressed against the forms sagging from above. Aisles were narrow and packed with gear, so they were always climbing over or around. Just below the waterline with no portholes, the air was suffocating.

Herb's ship was one of twenty-eight, a convoy of converted cruise lines and troop transports. Aboard was the entire 103rd Infantry Division plus the 14th Armored scheduled to set sail the following morning. Officers occupied cabins and ate in salons. Accommodation for the ranks was more basic, their mess a small, crowded area several decks below and near the noisy, smelly engine room. Dining benches were in rows and took up most of the space with 200 men slinging additional hammocks above them at night. Sanitation was simple with rows of wooden lavatories on deck facing the sea. Blackout was rigorously enforced, for German U-boats were prowling the waters. During the day, soldiers in battle gear crowded on deck elbow to elbow, and Herb quickly commandeered his own spot, hugging his knees as one soldier after another stepped over.

In the initial scramble, he had lost sight of Jack and after exploration, assumed that he had been assigned to another ship, a loss he tried not to think about. Instead, he envisioned where they might land. Italy was fighting hard. But please God, not Russia. He tried to tap into memories of Germany, but they no longer existed.

He tried to imagine finding unknown cousins at the wrong end of a rifle but that also failed. No, he was here to follow orders. If he was constipated, sleep deprived, if his muscles got stiff from disuse, so be it. He began to doze then awoke gasping as someone stood over him blowing smoke in his face. The ship was in open waters, rocking gently.

"I thought I'd never find you. You were supposed to let me know…"

Herb leaned forward, blinking to clear his vision. "Cripes Jack, how'd you get here?"

"You were supposed to meet me, remember? Didn't we say we'd stick together?"

"But I thought…"

"Never mind. I'm here with a mission, a summons from the officers' quarters. They needed a fourth for bridge and I told them you were pretty good." Jack thumped his arm. "Pull yourself together. It's in an hour."

"How come…?"

"They're officers, dummy! You do what you're told."

Herb could hear his mother's voice – *Do you hear me?* — or Dad who was more direct. *I'll tell you what you want. Just listen.* He thought hard. Spades, hearts, diamonds, clubs. Aces count as four, kings three, add one for distribution, six in a suit means… "I don't know, Jack. I'm so new at this."

"Just remember Blackwood and the Gerber Convention."

They walked down a very long hallway, their feet silenced by carpeting, the throbbing engine muffled behind heavy doors. Inside the designated room, three bridge tables were set up, some of the chairs already occupied. Motioned in, Herb was partnered with a full colonel. Was he supposed to salute?

"Greetings, Private. We appreciate your filling in. Just a

friendly game for an hour or two." The colonel took out a pack of Camels. "Coffin nail? Or don't you...?"

"No thank you Sir. I'm a pipe man myself. I'll just wait until later."

Then a low buzz of conversation as the colonel began shuffling the cards. "So where you from, Son? Been in the army long?"

"Chicago, Sir. Came over when I was about four." He took a deep breath. "...from Germany. I speak German, Sir."

The cards snapped across manicured fingertips, arranged according to suit. Herb kept his head down as the colonel scanned the room. Would he be told to leave? *Hun, Nazi, Schicklgruber...* The colonel studied his cards then looked up and smiled. "One No Trump."

He didn't remember who won or if he played well. But returning on deck two hours later, Jack was positively giddy. It would be something to tell his wife.

No one noticed they'd been gone. But food in the mess tasted a little better and he was glad to be back with Jack.

They were at sea for two weeks, sighting nothing but white caps and their own ships in the convoy. Rough weather brought round after round of seasickness, and the salty air smelled of vomit. Those who risked a shower discovered that the water had been sucked from the ocean, sending them to the drinking fountains to rinse off the salt as best they could. Meanwhile, sweat remained embedded in their uniforms and their backs ached.

Finally, the sight of land. A warrant officer recognized the port, having served in World War I. They would be landing at Marseilles.

Barnacled hulls poked through the water, the clutter enhanced by civilians parading in and out of torn-up buildings with gaping fronts. Allied bombers had turned the port into rubble as the Germans retreated, transferred to fight in the Normandy landing. The Free

French were about to take control under the watchful eyes of the Allies. It had happened so fast that there weren't enough transports for pursuit, the few that remained, waiting for fuel. "Looks like we'll be here for a while," Jack grumbled.

In disgust, one of the men yanked off his life jacket and threw it overboard, watching it bubble and sink. No one laughed. They were too glad be on dry land.

The dock creaked as men disembarked in scattered order, followed by a long march north. Then to an open field with rows of pup tents reaching toward the horizon interspersed with mess tents and latrines.

Jack commandeered a tent and they dropped their sleeping bags and belongings. "At least we're together," Herb declared. "So now what?"

"Evening mess and then the sleep of the dead. After that we wait. Again."

"How about trying to get a pass to town? The city looked mostly quiet."

"Are you crazy? We just got here."

"Then tomorrow. Hitch a ride, look around. Hey, we're in France. Who woulda thought?"

"Who says we'd get a pass? They can't even gas up the Jeeps."

"Wouldn't hurt to ask," Herb insisted. "Something to bring home. You know, war stories, souvenirs…" The look on Jack's face made him stop. "Okay, so let's go eat. You're probably just hungry."

Dinner was no better than on board ship but after an eight-hour march they would've been happy with bread and water. Then to tepid showers to wash off two weeks of grime.

The night was cold but it didn't matter. Exhausted, they shook out their sleeping bags, crawled inside the tent and huddled together to sleep until dawn.

The next morning, Jack wangled a midnight pass, tradeoff for spending the day filing and typing forms in triplicate. Exchanging dollars for occupation francs, they hitched a ride to the waterfront, sucking in its smell of salt water and fish. Supper would consist of the catch of the day. "And French fries!" Herb cried ecstatically.

Walking past torn-out buildings and an assortment of boats bobbing along the walkway, they came to a place replete with dartboards and ping-pong tables, the paddles clicking away, the enticing smells drifting from the back room. Herb turned to Jack. "I used to play back home. We kept a table and equipment in the church basement."

One of the players gestured, inviting them to come in and play. Surprised, Herb first declined, then took the paddle, each point accompanied with loud laughter and good-natured teasing. They were allies after all.

Seated near the door, Jack ordered from the menu in halting French, the meal excellent and cheap, and after an hour or so, they were ready to leave. It was barely dark as they strolled past shattered windows, broken trees and shrubs standing ghostlike in the fading light.

Aiming for the road, they turned and found themselves in the middle of a plaza with dozens of people hurrying toward a building encased in light. Moving closer, they could hear an orchestra tuning up.

"I think it's an opera house!" Jack's voice was filled with awe. "Out here in the middle of nowhere!"

"Our pass takes us up to midnight," Herb cried. "If it's really bad, we can get up and leave." Approaching the box office, he held up two fingers, and the attendant whipped out a chart. After a careful examination of the options, he and Jack moved inside toward the arched staircase.

The upper level was a cavern of red and gold boxes, two balconies and a gallery. Their seats were second row mezzanine. Crawling over an elderly couple and two women in long dresses, they found their seats and leaned against the worn cushions, blinking into the dim lights.

Genteel applause heralded the conductor's appearance and then the music began, sweeping away war, violence and a yearning for home. It was *La Traviata*, a fully staged performance with singers in full throat, the violins providing enough vibrato to underscore the very soul of love gone awry.

Herb closed his eyes. The city might have been in ruins, the costumes frayed along the seams and thousands of miles from home, but Violetta was dying of consumption, her lover, Alfredo, embracing her at the end, the music soaring as she cried out, *Oh God to die so young...* It was Herb's first real opera.

They remained encamped for a week. Meanwhile, the war stood still and waited. Herb managed a nightly trip into town as the music continued, traveling by Jeep, truck or hitching a ride, sometimes with Jack, other times alone. There were always a few servicemen in the audience, and he felt safe. He saw *Faust*, *Pagliacci*, *Cavalleria Rusticana*, *Sampson and Delilah* and the last part of *Tosca*. Most of the music was familiar, for he'd heard it on the radio or sampled at record stores. But here it reverberated from the lofty walls into his ribs and groin, sending shivers along his spine. Here in the darkened theater, it encompassed despair or joy, and in the face of disaster and death, achingly alive.

On day eight, Herb was summoned by an officious looking corporal, interrupting as he leaned over a bulging file cabinet. "Private Zahn? Colonel Eastman wants to see you in his office."

"Who?"

"You're Private Zahn? That means you."

Colonel Eastman? Trotting in double time, Herb arrived out of breath.

Dressed in battle fatigues, the colonel barely looked up to return Herb's salute. There was no sign of recognition. "We're pulling out, Private. Going across the border into German-speaking territory."

"Yes sir. So we've heard."

"Someone said you speak German." The colonel paused, leaning forward with a puzzled frown. "Do I know you?"

"Yes sir. We played bridge aboard ship on the way to Marseilles."

"Well I'll be damned." The colonel sat back and grinned. "I opened with One No Trump and you raised it to two."

"Yes sir."

"We went down by three tricks."

"I don't remember, sir."

"Good thing we weren't vulnerable."

"Yes sir."

"Well, so much for that." The colonel looked down at his desk. "Now here it is. We need a German translator. Think you're up to it?"

"I can carry on normal conversation, Sir. But I don't have a strong military vocabulary."

"We just don't want to look stupid in front of a bunch of draftees who came to blow our heads off. Can you manage that?"

"Yes sir." Herb was still at attention. "Permission to ask a question, sir?"

"Well?"

"Where would I bivouac?"

"With your unit. But you'd be on call when needed."

"Thank you, sir." Herb took a deep breath. "Is that all?"

"For now. Report to Corporal Jamison, third desk near the door. He'll assign you." He picked up his pen. "Dismissed, soldier."

A German *Dolmetscher* assigned to headquarters. He would be rooming with a driver and a master sergeant. He was still PFC Zahn, doing guard duty and working in the water purification unit during the day. But he would be traveling with the officers whenever needed, and once more separated from Jack. He should have felt proud at such important duty but he hated saying goodbye.

A week later he joined his new unit, marching cross-country to embark on the river Loire, packed elbow to elbow toward Alsace Lorraine, the German-speaking part of France, an area that had been conquered by French, then German, then back to French. For the moment they were allies and should be treated accordingly.

When the ships docked, they encamped in a broad field filled with tents. The wintry sky blended into the trees and underbrush, their frozen twigs and branches crackling as they brushed by. Sunrise told them they were going north, the trucks waiting to convoy them further. Scuttlebutt had their destination as Strasbourg on the German border.

It was Herb's third year in the army and he had yet to fire a gun outside of the practice range.

CHAPTER 25

Germany, 1944

"You're going to make yourself sick with all this crying," Alma declared. "It's wartime. You have the little one to think about."

Hilda dabbed at her eyes. "Why was he sent to Cherbourg? It's a shipping port!"

"Rainer is alive. For him, the war is over."

"I'm not strong like you, Mutti. Papa goes away, Onkel Wilhelm is dead and Gunter is facing all kinds of danger on the front. But you show no feeling."

"You don't know what is inside of me, my girl." Alma turned away, then her voice softened. "We have to survive, Hilda. Rainer is captured, yes. But he is safe in America. They always take good care…"

"He's a prisoner of war! How safe is that?"

"And crying makes it better?" Alma bent over a small container brushing away any further conversation. "We have to move out of here by tonight. It will go fast. Most of our things have been traded away."

Peter stood at the window. "What is that man doing?"

Hilda glanced over his shoulder. "It's a soldier nailing a name or a place on the door. It's what people do to find someone." She tugged at his sleeve. "Come away from the glass. It's dangerous."

"What does it say?"

"It's too far away for me to read."

"Maybe we should nail a notice for Papa so he will find us too."

"He will find us, Peter. There are organizations like the Red Cross…"

Alma gestured impatiently. "You don't have to explain everything, Hilda. He understands enough."

"Papa took a boat to go far away," Peter said knowingly.

"Your papa is in America and gets plenty to eat. More than you." She turned toward Hilda. "Someone said the Red Cross is supposed to deliver letters to the bunker. You think they will?"

"I hope so," Hilda replied, her eyes reddening again.

"We better keep moving. It's already taking too much time." Alma motioned to Hilda and together they lifted a small trunk, placing it in the center of the room. "Peter, take this bag and put in the shoes from the other room."

They would be moving to the back of a bombed out grocery, its roof and walls still intact. With luck, there would be a few useful odds and ends left amid the clutter.

Arms loaded, they stepped over broken glass, brick and concrete. Smoke and dust permeated everything as people milled about. No one reached out to help.

It took three trips to carry all the clothes and utensils. The final load encompassed blankets and pillows that would remain in the two-handled tote, something to counter the bunker's cold as they went back and forth.

Hilda surveyed the chairs, table and a bed waiting to be put in place. A broken-down chest was in the corner and she gave it a push, testing it for stability. "These drawers might be useful. Just a little cleanup…" She turned to Peter. "Take this wash pot and get some water from the faucet we just passed. But be careful how you walk so you don't spill."

The little boy trotted out, armed with the container, proud to be sent on such an important errand. He returned a few minutes later, his pants and shoes splattered with ashes and dirt, the container mostly full. "I stood in line and the Fraulein behind me helped. She said I was a big boy."

Hilda bent over her battered broom scooping bits of hair, plaster and paper, mounding the litter into a pile. There was a flyer picturing grave markers with a foreground of skulls, the caption below plaintively asking, Warum? She frowned. "Why? For the Fatherland. For Lebensraum. For Hitler. And if you believe that…"

"Be quiet," Alma muttered, motioning to Peter. "You don't know who's listening."

The shriek of sirens drowned out her words, its wail sending tremors through the rickety walls. Peter rushed to the doorstep, hopping up and down as the women grabbed for the tote, stumbling over the threshold toward the bunker, preparing to spend the night in boredom or panic in a war that would not end.

Inside, the ventilators would be turned off at the *wrau-wrau-wrau* of incendiaries as everyone sat motionless, children taught to open their mouths to protect their ears from the concussion, all barely breathing until the hum of the fan resumed. Damaged sewers had made personal cleanliness impossible. Especially affected were mothers of young children, without soap or water to wash diapers, no sun to make them dry. Meanwhile, sniffles, skin rash and lice moved from one body to the next.

Outside it was even worse with the sweet fatty smell of corpses or the sour stench of garbage as people rushed out at the all clear, scavenging for anything to barter – a hat, a lampshade or a cooking pot. Then again the siren, sending them to live cheek to cheek with babies being born, old men dying, the bunker reeking of sweat and human waste.

The Red Cross might come occasionally to distribute soup and potatoes, barely enough to slake their hunger. Fresh milk was non-existent and babies were offered little more than soothing words. Army personnel and the Women's Organizations brought bits of clothing and shoes, but there was never enough and the event generated more anger and fear as people scrambled for what they could. Hilda's request to relocate lay fallow, lost in the bureaucracy of war.

Then slowly, the sound would dissipate as people drifted off to sleep waiting for daylight.

A woman on the next ledge lifted her head. "It's getting quiet."

Hilda nodded. "Peter just fell asleep."

The woman lay back down. "My man met someone who works in the Rathaus. His job was to count the dead. There are so many they had to work overtime. All because of the bombing. It's terrible."

"My Onkel Wilhelm…"

"Oh, yes, I knew him, tall, handsome, so much talent." The woman sighed. "So bad what happened. I could tell you about many more. There was a bomb that landed on a gas station. It was terrible. Rows of houses blown up in every direction."

Hilda turned away, trying not to listen.

"When the Americans were outside Aachen," the woman continued, "the Wehrmacht was supposed to fight but instead they broke into the wine cellars and got drunk just to keep the Americans from having it." The woman lowered her voice to a whisper. "They tried to kill der Fuhrer in the Reichstag, you know. A bomb went off inside a suitcase but it missed and our Fuhrer is still alive. He ordered all the men involved to be rounded up. Families too. Wife, children, sisters, mothers... Didn't even knock on the doors. Just dragged them out and hung them from meat hooks. You could hear their screams for miles. Rommel shot himself to save the family's name. Imagine, such a big hero wanting to kill der Fuhrer. I'm telling you, it's terrible, terrible."

"Rommel? His tanks were in Cherbourg. My husband..." Hilda leaned forward, suddenly alert. "Where did you hear all this? How come you know so much?"

"Hitler has a new bomb. A rocket that goes all by itself then whoosh! Kaboom! Now they're testing a plane that goes so fast it has to fire backwards so it doesn't shoot itself. Other weapons are on the table, the buzz bomb, the rocket... We can still win. Sing *Deutchland über alles...*"

Clearly the woman was crazy. Too much time in the bunker, too much family lost.

Hilda closed her eyes, forcing her mind to drift, to picture Rainer in a field of golden grain bathed in sunshine. America had signed the Geneva Convention. America was a civilized country. She began to pray, then began to doze.

At the all clear, they joined the rushing toward the open door. If they hurried, there might be an hour or two of respite before the sirens resumed.

The street was once more covered in rubble and they picked their way back, careful not to drop their cargo of blankets. Peter darted ahead, seeing an official looking envelope beneath the door. "It's a letter from Papa!" he cried. "You said he would find us and he did!"

The letter was addressed to Hilda. Her request had finally been granted for relocation. She would be going to Bad Oeynhausen, some 25 kilometers northeast along the Weser River, a vacation spa with picturesque churches and villas, kilometers from the industrial center. She caught her breath. She once lived there as a foster child. "Mutti…" It was all she could say as she handed the letter to her mother.

There was a long silence. "So you are leaving. Am I to be left alone?"

"Of course not! As soon as we're settled, I will send for you. We just won't tell…" Hilda studied the letter. "We can take furniture and belongings. They'll even send a truck if we need one."

It took close to a month as Hilda waited for a response from Frau Eichmeyer, the foster mother who had been so good to her. Meanwhile, she worked frantically, packing and deciding what to take on the train. This, between trips to the bunker as sirens howled throughout the night.

Finally, it was time. Carrying a box tied with string, she and Peter made their way to the dimly lit station crowded with people. They brushed past women, children and the elderly, all looking bewildered with Hilda's voice lost among the shouts and pleas. "Let us through, please let us through. Be careful, don't step on my child."

Squinting at the signs, she squeezed into the appropriate line, resting her box of belongings on the floor, shoving it inch by inch until she reached the distracted teller, the clerk barely looking up as he handed her the change. The train was to leave in an hour.

Another line in front of the gate was guarded by a uniformed matron. Peter gasped for air and Hilda picked him up with one arm, the box dangling from the other. "If we get a seat, you can go to sleep."

Twenty minutes later, the gates opened and everyone raced forward. Boxes and suitcases bursting open would be retrieved at the owner's peril. Flinging Peter into the car, Hilda scrambled in after him, settling at the back on the very last seat as the doors clanged shut.

Now darkness blanketed throughout, the wheels clicking away from the industrial hub, away from bombers who sought any plant or industry, however small. In Bad Oeynhausen, there would be trees, untrammeled roads and villas, the only sign of war being the luxury hotels converted into military quarters and hospitals. There the grass would be green, the sky blue and only birds would wing their way through the clouds. However small their space, they would be safe.

Two hours later, the train snorted to a stop and people spilled into the night. It was past midnight. Cars and wagons waited at the station, transporting arrivals to their destinations for a small fee. "We will be with Frau Eichmeyer tonight," she whispered to the sleepy Peter. "Tomorrow we will look for our own place."

The Eichmeyers had not moved and Hilda had clear memories as a child of eight. Back then, it was her task to clean the kitchen after meals, doing part of the laundry before school. She would watch baby Oscar while Frau Eichmeyer prepared supper and sometimes help with the little store Herr Eichmeyer ran out of the living room. Then more cleanup before bed. If there was homework or personal care, she didn't remember. Yet, it was a happy time. Frau Eichmeyer was stern, but kind. That she wanted Hilda to call her Mutti was something Hilda couldn't bring herself to do and the only thing that remained awkward.

Frau Eichmeyer was waiting, enveloped in smiles, showing them the bathroom, then into the kitchen for tea and toast before taking them to the upstairs room where there was a large bed, some chairs and enough space for their belongings. It was dark, quiet and safe. They were among friends. For now, it would be enough.

CHAPTER 26

Chicago, 1945

THEY MUST HAVE BEEN THERE a while, puffing cigarettes and sipping wine, their manner clearly congratulatory. Uncle Fritz, natty and suave, still good-looking enough to rival a dozen movie stars. Aunt Martha, newly divorced, attracting men like flies. She'd introduced the family to a few of her admirers, but George kept coming back, a man almost twice her age with a full head of white hair and handsomely distinguished, a musician, singing at selected venues throughout the city, conducting a local choir wearing tails and a red cummerbund. They'd even appeared at Orchestra Hall, which was pretty special. If not exactly famous, he was part of Chicago's music scene with well-known performers among his friends.

Elsie waved, then went into her room to deposit her things, returning to listen to the rambling conversation as they talked about the American Dream achieved through real estate and business, the hope of many families who'd begun with nothing. Buying and selling. Build and Expand. Grow or you die. Watch the pennies and the dollars will take care of themselves. Never mix business with pleasure. Keep your own counsel but listen to advice, the last part observed in the breach.

Then it got specific. Oscar Meyer gives good service. Bread delivery every day. That empty lot next door is just begging... Empty lot? There was one next to the Belmont store. Was this to be another spin-off like Higgins? Elsie squirmed in her chair. "Is this something I should know about?"

Martha turned, then burst out laughing. "August, you better say something before this girl has a heart attack."

Her father's lips curved into a rare smile. "Tante Martha and Fritz are gonna take over the Belmont store. They gonna be partners."

Elsie caught her breath, trying to visualize Martha's damp hair plastered to her forehead, tried to picture Uncle Fritz counting cash and receipts after a twelve-hour day. She knew that her parents made a good living at the Belmont store. How else could they have bought an apartment building and the Higgins enterprise? "Does that mean you're going to retire?"

"You're mom and dad found something else on the north side. It has a softball field and riding stable close by. People come in after a game or after horseback for pop and sandwiches and buy ice cream."

"Sandwiches? But I thought..."

Martha didn't reply. So Elsie excused herself and went to bed. She'd learn soon enough, especially if it meant more work for her.

This was indeed another change, one achieved with dizzying speed. Now there would be four stores under the family name: Modern Dairy on Belmont worked by Fritz, Katie and Martha, 'Lisbet's Higgins Dairy, Trudi's Creamland and a new place on Devon, as yet unnamed. Elsie would be at her parents' new store, an hour's ride on the streetcar requiring two transfers. Weekends would continue at Trudi's as before.

The first afternoon at the new store was almost familiar. There was a milk cooler and side counter with stools for sandwiches and a snack, preparations she'd mastered by third grade, coffee following a simple formula. Selling cigarettes, was a bonus, for she could sneak a pack into her purse when her parents weren't looking.

Now it was a Monday late in March and Elsie was halted by her mother's expression as she entered the store.

"Is something wrong? I'm not late, am I?"

"Erv's coming home on furlough," Marichen whispered. "Trudi wants me to take over for a few days so they can be together a little bit more." She rubbed her hands nervously. "You and Daddy here, with me staying there."

Elsie's eyes widened. "Are you asking me or telling me? Does Dad know?"

"I gonna talk to him tonight."

"Oh man, I sure don't want to be around when that happens."

"Never mind. Just don't say anything."

Marichen waited until bedtime to present her case. It began reasonably enough. Erv was coming home on furlough. He and Trudi were eager to see one another. After all, they were young and newly engaged. Marichen wanted to help.

"What help? He keeps his car at his mother's house. So he drives out to see her."

"She wants to be with him a little bit more. Visit friends, go out to dinner…"

August stared at her. "And so?"

"They need to have time just the two of them. You talked her into buying the store. You're the one who found it. That makes you partners. You have a responsibility."

"Getting engaged was her idea. Nobody forced her. So let them be together in the store. He should learn about the business for later on."

"What kind of furlough is that? What would you have done if it was you and me?"

"With us, the war was over." He tugged at his socks, then ducked down, looking for his slippers under the bed. "Elsie is there on the weekend. That should be enough."

"His furlough is for a week." Her voice was pleading.

He sat back up. "What's that supposed to mean?"

Marichen took a deep breath. "They could stay at his mother's house then go out, just the two of them. You and Elsie should be fine without me. Business is still building up. "

"With extra-long hours and not enough sleep? For this I worked day and night, year after year?"

"Remember what it was like? When we were young…" She reached to unhook her corset.

"So which is it – a few days or a week? Did you promise or just say maybe?" He pulled at the blanket, getting into bed. His back was toward her, his voice muffled. "You're always for the children, always, always." Then a long pause. "Well, maybe a few days, but not a week."

It was more than she'd hoped.

Erv arrived a week later, handsome in his Air Corps uniform. With a flourish, he took Marichen's bag, smiling his thanks to August who stood at the door, scowling. "Elsie's at the store but she's okay with taking the bus back tonight like always."

August nodded. "Just watch out for the snow. It's slippery out there."

The next morning Elsie awoke to an empty house. No cereal. No orange juice squeezed just for her. She gulped down a glass of milk and got dressed. On the bus she looked out the window at it passed the Teen Canteen. She liked one of the boys who was really nice. He seemed to like her too, stopping at her locker, walking her to class. What if he asked her to the Junior Prom? She sighed. Her father would kill her.

After school, it was business as usual. August spent most of the evening in the back going over the accounts while she handled customers in front.

"It's boring up here, working by myself," she muttered as he emerged. "No wonder Trudi wanted some time off."

"Since when is work supposed to be fun?"

"I'll finish college and have a real career, not just a job. That'll be fun."

"Then better you stop listening to the radio and all that crap you like so much. Better you help your Mama a little more."

"I don't listen to crap, Dad. I wouldn't, even if I had the time," she sniffed, "which I don't."

"It's late and you're crabby." He looked at the clock. "Go home and go to bed. I'll close."

The next two days were much the same, with Elsie doing homework between customers, returning to an empty house, hearing her father's key in the door as she drifted off to sleep. Four days, including Sunday. No more. That was the promise and her father was becoming testy.

Now it was Wednesday and as she arrived her father emerged from the back. "Is Mom coming here or will she go straight home from Trudi's?"

"They were supposed to be back by now."

"Has something happened?"

"I don't know. Mama said she's waiting."

Elsie dropped her books in the back. It would be a long afternoon.

At nine o'clock August called Marichen again. Trudi and Erv had still not returned. Maybe there had been an accident.

Elsie stood at the door. "I have a test in the morning and I need to review it before going to bed."

"Do you have Erv's phone? Mama called Information but they don't have it."

"It's probably unlisted. I guess you'll just have to wait. Is Mom okay?"

He nodded distractedly. "You can go. No use us both staying."

At home, she read for an hour then heard her father's key in the lock. It had snowed on and off for several days, leaving a light dusting over the icy roads. Maybe they really were in an accident. *A soldier and his sweetheart dying in one another's arms.* It might make the papers.

A clatter at the front door brought her up short. Finally! She rolled over, ready to greet her mother, only to hear loud voices, then a shout from her father sending her tumbling out of bed. "What are you doing here? Where's Mama?"

It was followed by Trudi's soft murmur. "I needed to pick up some clothes, Dad. Erv had the car and so…" She turned to her sister who stood peering around the bedroom door. "It's okay, Elsie. Mom's still at the store."

August's voice reverberated against the walls. "Mama was supposed to be back this afternoon. So what are you doing here? You have a business to take care of. Go back to where you belong!"

Erv stepped out of the shadows, moving protectively toward Trudi. "It was only for a few days. After all…"

"The few days was finished this afternoon," August stormed. "Twelve, fourteen hours a day isn't enough from us? How much do you need, going dancing, drinking, playing games like children?" He moved toward Erv, his chin thrust out. "You think money grows on trees? I get Trudi the store so she can make a decent living, have a future, not run after you each time you wave hello."

"We were told..." Erv protested.

"Never mind what you were told. My wife belongs here, not waiting for you and Trudi to run around while the rest of us have to work double."

Trudi's face was chalk white as she dropped a box half-filled with clothing, pulling her coat closed. "There's no use talking to him, Erv. I told you what he was like."

"That's right! Get out. And you send Mama home. You should be ashamed. First you go behind my back, then you come in late."

Erv picked up the box as Trudi started to cry. "Let's go before things are out of control," he muttered, nudging Trudi out.

Kicking the door shut behind them, August flipped the lock then turned to Elsie huddled in the hall. "What are you looking at? This is none of your business."

"Where are they supposed to go? It's still winter out there."

There was no reply.

The next day was eerily quiet with August at the store all day and Elsie coming in after school. She asked no questions, remaining cautiously at a distance, returning to an empty house.

Late that night, Marichen finally came home, pausing before opening the outside door. Tiptoeing to the bathroom, she changed into her nightgown, listening for August's heavy breathing before curling up beside him.

"I'm not asleep." His voice was filled with expectation.

Startled, she took a shuddering breath, turning to stare toward the ceiling. "You shouldn't have done it, August. What difference was one or two more days?"

"A promise, that's the difference. People are supposed to keep their promise."

"Well, it's wartime and they didn't have much time together. So last night, after you threw them out, they drove back to his mother's house. This morning they went to City Hall and got married. Just like that."

It was a long silence. "So he's gone?"

"He goes back on Sunday."

"And what else?"

"Mrs. Turek will watch the store until Elsie gets there tomorrow after school. That gives Trudi a chance to say goodbye. After that, everything is the same, except now she's a married woman."

"They should have thought of that before."

"It all went so fast, August. I never thought…"

Down the hall, Elsie heard her mother come in, heard her tiptoe into the bathroom, heard the bedroom door close, the murmured words followed by silence. She lay for a long time then turned over, tucking her arm under the pillow, as the quiet descended. Her mother was home and that was a comfort. Whatever had happened, Trudi would explain – or maybe not. It didn't matter. Her path would be different. Of that she was sure.

CHAPTER 27

Somewhere in Europe, 1945

It was simple duty. Transferred to the command center of Tank Company Easy, Herb was there to serve at the officers' convenience and command. Still in Allied territory, the bursts of light along the horizon were followed by nervous rumblings a few seconds later. The war was getting closer. News from the front was sparse but a sense of geography said that equipment rolling in and out placed them on a north-south route not far from Aachen, the birthplace of Charlemagne and a short distance from Herb's birthplace. A few hundred kilometers beyond, The Battle of the Bulge had begun, a final putsch of massacre and retaliation on both sides. President Roosevelt had been elected to his fourth term and Herb pondered events, yearning for Jack's perspective. In the persistent discomfort and cold, he was sure they were about to see action.

He roomed with a driver and a Master Sergeant in charge of company mess, all billeted in commandeered housing. Charlie was about his age from Alabama with a year of chef's training who would bring them the roast beef or potatoes au gratin left over from the officers' mess. "A good cook always allows for a little extra," he'd grin. Lance Wilson, the driver, was a few years older, a North Dakotan, planning to make the army his career. Both were good guys.

Then the company was ordered to move out, pressing toward Strasbourg bordering the Rhine, Herb and Lance riding in front of the open Jeep, officers in the back, leading a convoy of tanks and trucks loaded with personnel, pulling their chins into their collars, the wind whipping into nostrils and eyes. They stopped some forty kilometers south of their destination, a cadre of draftees pitching tents in an open field while Herb joined non-coms scouting for housing, pounding on doors as wary eyes peered through the windows.

The first door was opened by an elderly man and a wrinkled woman, their faces pinched with cold. "Americans? You have food? We have nothing to give you."

"How many bedrooms are here? *Wie viel?*"

The gentleman stared at Herb's uniform, private first class. "For what? For who? You do not touch my daughters..."

"We need beds for our officers. Office space as well." Herb brushed past the man, surveying the dust-covered living room. "This will do." His eyes skimmed past their crestfallen faces. "Only for a few days. We promise."

He motioned to the soldiers a few feet back. "This can work as a conference room. There are probably bedrooms upstairs. Officers can make this their headquarters."

It continued throughout the evening, houses, barns, buildings commandeered with no alternatives offered. By nightfall the mess tent was up, officers ensconced into their new quarters, mechanized units and tanks neatly lined in a row, supply trucks paced off and parked, the troops stowing their gear as best they could. They were there to offer support as the Allies retook one city after another. The war was winding down, the heads of government eyeing the spoils of war even as combat continued. Meanwhile, they waited for orders to follow the quick-moving front.

Retrieving a cot from another house, they carried it to one of the bedrooms, billeting all three, their gear stashed in cabinets and drawers. Furniture was moved out of the living room and dumped outside despite tears of protest. Toward evening, Charlie returned from the officers' mess with boiled eggs and smoked fish, giving it to the owners who had been moved into an unfinished attic to live as best they could.

Herb now spent mornings translating the nervous chatter of civilians, soothing the frightened, sternly berating those who demanded restitution. Once there was an intercepted memo but it ended as a curiosity, its value long gone. Germans were instinctive record-keepers, even in times of war.

A few nights later, the threesome stole a Jeep and drove into Strasbourg, creeping along deserted streets flanked by empty houses, the city in total darkness. It was too eerie, and after an hour, they went back to base. No doubt the enemy was in retreat. For a moment Herb thought he should report what they'd seen but decided to sleep on it.

A few hours later there was a pounding on the door. "Get dressed! We're moving out. Formation in an hour!" The enemy had not retreated after all.

Barely awake, they stumbled downstairs with Charlie sprinting to pack up the Mess. In the conference room, officers moved about in full uniform, conferring in muted voices. The files would have to be taken or destroyed, nothing left behind. "How much time do we have?"

"Depends on you, soldier. Get busy."

Outside, Lance was checking the Jeep, making sure it had enough gas. Supply trucks stood waiting and tanks were readied. In the field, men gathered their belongings, stamping their feet against the swirling snow. Their orders were to return to Alsace, circling around Strasbourg before continuing toward the industrial Ruhr.

By the time the files were loaded, the rest of the company was gone. "We can follow in their tracks," Lance declared, climbing into the driver's seat. "They can't be too far ahead."

They were three Jeeps driving in tandem, their headlights glowing in the snow and fog. Herb was in the second car, a major and captain in the back, noncoms and lieutenants in the other cars as they picked their way along the rutted trail, the sky slate-gray without the stars to guide them.

Morning broke to reveal the roadway under cover of new-fallen snow, any tracks having disappeared. Were they in enemy territory? Herb clung to the two rifles in front, flexing his fingers numbed from the cold, not sure he'd be able to feel the trigger let alone shoot. The officers had pistols, but their short range made them useless under attack.

Suddenly there was a loud *Pow* and *Tsing-tsing* as bullets flew above their heads. Herb felt himself catapulted out of the Jeep, his rifle flying into a ditch, the Jeep capsized onto its side with white smoke spewing from the front. Grabbing his helmet, he crawled to the edge of the road as bullets whizzed around, feeling a tug at the seat of his pants and a warm ooze of blood. A German patrol emerged from the fog, rifles cocked. "*Hënde hoch! Waffe weg! Waffe lassen. Runter.*"

It was like in the movies, a unit surprised by an equally surprised contingent. "They're calling for Hands up! Drop your weapons," Herb shouted. He didn't need to say it twice.

It was a Wehrmacht patrol, headed by a lieutenant. "*Nicht schießen. Dies sind A-Dur, Kapitän, Offiziere…*" Herb paused. "You lucked out. Our Jeeps are full of officers."

The lieutenant's expression was first quizzical, followed by a broad smile. "Officers?" He nudged his companion. "We take them behind the lines for interrogation." He pointed to Herb. "You come with. Others stay behind."

Herb felt through his back pockets. "I think I've been shot."

The lieutenant motioned to a Wehrmacht soldier standing off to the side. "Take a look." Then to Herb, "*Rum drehen.*"

Herb turned and dropped his pants trying to keep from shivering. It didn't feel like anything was broken, just a nasty sting. But there was blood. He could feel it.

The German soldier's touch was quick, but not harsh. After a moment, he looked up. "Flesh wound. Only a graze."

The lieutenant nodded. "Get the first aid kit and cover it. Doctors can see him later."

Herb looked at the lead Jeep crumpled on its side, the second Jeep having crashed into it. Lance had been thrown for several feet, his head bare and bloody with bits of brain matter spattered on the ground. The others stood shaken and dazed, hands in the air, eyes darting back and forth. The third vehicle was still intact.

"*Er ist schon Todt,*" the soldier declared, glancing at the wreckage.

It was Herb's first experience with death. There'd been no time for fear or panic and even now his mind was clear, trying to evaluate his options while the Wehrmacht leaders conferred.

Finally the German lieutenant gestured with his rifle, motioning the officers to the back of the surviving Jeep, Herb next to a German driver in front, the others to remain with the patrol. Then mounting onto the hood, the lieutenant signaled them to proceed.

They drove slowly as the lieutenant called out directions, passing buildings, fences and narrow bridges into a town lined with rusted vehicles and uniformed soldiers moving about, their manner dreamlike in the fog-swept air. A woman darted from a building crying out that the Americans were coming, and the Jeep slowed down, then brushed past.

It was evening and a road sign said *Schweinfurt* as they stopped in front of a building that looked like some kind of headquarters. Dismounting, the lieutenant returned the guard's salute and motioned them inside. The surge of warm air made Herb feel lightheaded and his eyes began to sting. He hadn't eaten in two days.

Interrogation took place with English-speaking officers. Name, rank and serial number. It didn't take long to determine that Herb knew nothing, so they turned him over to the doctor who dressed his wound and directed him to a cluster of POWs waiting to be processed. His only possessions were the clothes on his back. Even his watch had disappeared.

The following morning some one hundred Allied prisoners of varied nationalities were moved out, flanked by armed guards. The sun said they were going further into Germany. Maybe the Wehrmacht was in retreat after all.

Now each day blended into another, with nights sleeping under the stars in the Black Forest or covered with hay in some farmer's barn, the prisoners standing at attention to count off before setting out again. Food was spasmodic and Herb could feel his belly shrinking. His greatest fear was that his wound would become infected, but that never happened and finally, it began to heal.

They arrived at Stalag 4C, a camp of 2500 prisoners, a virtual Tower of Babel, the prisoners in various stages of neglect. Barracks were filled with beds stacked three or four high, too cramped for anyone to sit up, their wooden slats covered with lumpy straw mattresses that had a musty smell. Food consisted of watery soup and black bread two or three times a day. After being processed, there was nothing for the men to do but sit and shiver with thoughts drifting from food to sleep, studying the bare floors, scratching themselves or one another. They'd been allowed to elect leaders in each section, but no one paid attention or cared. There wasn't even enough energy to fight.

After a week, his section received packages from the Red Cross, each box a foot square and a few inches deep filled with Klem, raisins, coffee, corned beef, chocolate, cigarettes, and soap. Herb ate eagerly, then paced himself when he realized the bonanza would arrive only spasmodically. Later he pocketed a small can of Spam, a good luck charm he carried for the duration of the war.

Eventually the cold modulated, turning the ground to foot-sucking mud. Then, a rustle of activity at morning inspection. Pacing up and down, the officer in charge began pointing toward the men. "You and you, step out." Within a half hour, they were assembled under the eye of fellow officers. "The rest, dismissed."

Those remaining consisted of about fifty men, the strongest, most able prisoners that would be moved to a work camp down the road. Herb was among them.

The new *Arbeitslager* was pristine clean. The outhouses had never been used, the sleeping mats covered with clean canvas. They were there to work, and working felt good, even though it was for the Wehrmacht.

Each morning they marched out to straighten the railroad tracks and ballasts or re-set the heavy logs. They did what they were told, staying within the range of declining energy. It could have been a sweet assignment, especially when the weather improved, until they realized that the Red Cross packages had stopped. Hunger was now real.

It was on such a day that they came upon some *SS* soldiers loitering under a clump of trees. It was early and the sun hadn't yet taken the chill out of the air. Herb had been a prisoner now for three or four months, and having nothing to barter, was filthy, his clothes in tatters. Worse, the morning gruel was half of the usual amount and he knew there would be nothing more to eat until their return.

Looking straight ahead as commanded, he was still able to turn his eyes toward the *SS*. Here among the rubble and stench of war they remained military crisp, their buttons and medals glistening in the sun, their stance at razor sharp attention even while at rest. These were the Hitler elite, claiming murder as their right. What would Mozart have thought? Or Beethoven, whose music cried out for freedom and brotherhood? What about his own father who'd abandoned the country of his birth for something more, something better?

Suddenly, a catcall from across the road. "Hah, you American soldiers. Your crippled President Roosevelt is dead! He makes war on us, and now he is dead. How you like that?"

There had been rumors about the president's fatal stroke, though his death had not been confirmed. Still, this was too much. Cold and hungry, Herb turned toward them. "He might be dead, but you lost your chance to do away with him yourself, Oh Master Race! How you like that?"

The response was swift and totally unexpected as an *SS* soldier leaped across the road, downing Herb with a punch on the chest followed by a kick to the groin.

Rolling on the ground, Herb tried to protect his head, his face, his stomach as the *SS* continued kicking arms, shoulders, knees… The rest of the prisoners had stopped, then moved to get out of the way, their Wehrmacht guards standing silent, watching. Finally, the *SS* wearied of his task, going back to his group to straighten his collar with a satisfied smirk.

Commanded to stand up, Herb staggered to his feet, barely able to breathe, his throat choked with shame. Almost three years in the army yet never in battle or under fire, his wound less than dignified, and now beaten like a dog, too weak and helpless to fight back.

The Wehrmacht guard called for the work party to continue. Then matching stride, turned his head slightly in Herb's direction. "Don't do that again," he muttered. "I can't protect you when you behave that way. He could have killed you."

All that is necessary for evil to exist is that good men do nothing. Herb had read that somewhere. The Wehrmacht solder meant well. Herb had been sleepwalking throughout the war. He also meant well. Yet all he could think of was whether there would be enough food to eat, enough warmth for sleep.

A week later they were moving out again, marching deeper into Germany. Once more they filled the roadways, sleeping a few hours huddled against one another to stave off the cold, then hustled back on the road, stumbling along in boots with worn stitching, the linings frayed or totally ripped. Crossing a stream, they drank from helmets or cupped hands, desperate for anything to put in their stomachs, even when water was mixed with mud. The Wehrmacht trucks bounced along, a clatter of supplies and the smell of gasoline while the prisoners marched behind. To their credit, the guards shared whatever food they had, but that meant that everyone was hungry.

They must have marched a hundred miles or so when they finally arrived at another camp. Then as before, there was nothing to do from morning to night, their chilled sleep intermittent at best. The guards themselves were becoming indifferent, telling them to do their own prisoner count, caring little about any escape.

Misery yearns for company and Herb attached himself to Joe

and Sam, sharing their wretchedness, forming a buddy system of sorts. Total strangers, they would remain so, but for now, survival depended on looking after one another.

It was a sunny morning in April when Herb and Joe rolled out for inspection once again and were greeted with – nothing. The outer gates were wide open, the surrounding field with a few dazed prisoners wandering about. The camp had been abandoned.

With a quick look, they raced toward the gate just as a truck came lumbering across the field, the back end filled with Allied soldiers. Seeing Sam in front, Joe gestured wildly, heaving himself over the tailgate and with surprising strength, pulling Herb aboard as the truck lurched through the gate and onto the deserted road.

"General Patton is in Pilsen," Sam yelled over the roar. "We're gonna try to connect. Damned well gotta get out of here. The Russians are moving in fast!"

The Russians. Communists. Easterners. Slavs. Everyone knew they'd been treated by the Germans as the *Untermensch*, worked harder, given less food and fewer facilities. Hate festered on both sides. They were American allies, yet greatly feared.

The truck bounced over the uneven terrain and soon the road was filled with ragged and emaciated soldiers some hobbling along the side, others hanging onto stray vehicles that coughed and snorted, threatening to stall out at any moment. They were at the outskirts of Prague where the truck shuddered and stopped, unable to go further.

The city had become a Dickens' portrayal, *The Best of Times, the Worst of Times…* crowded with soldiers of every stripe, a cacophony of British, American and Scottish accents and a smattering of French. Smiles were everywhere, grim faces once more made young. Czech civilians were negotiating, trading, exacting whatever they could. The Germans had left, the Americans known to be near. For now, the city was in a blissful state of anarchy.

"Gotta get off the street, find a place to sleep, maybe some food. We need time to figure things out." Joe's voice was close to Herb's ear. "Where's Sam?"

They found him in front of a small hotel, talking earnestly with a gentleman dressed like a doorman or concierge, the man's broad gestures describing a sleeping room on the second floor where they could stay. Payment? "Americans will pay when they come through. We keep count. Just no Russians, okay?"

The room was small but clean, its one bed heaped with assorted pillows and two thin blankets. It allowed them to sleep crosswise on a real bed, an almost forgotten luxury. And sleep they did, despite the activity below, as more and more soldiers arrived, waiting for governments to set up a re-classification center that would bring them home.

Morning brought ersatz coffee and a crust of bread, repeated midday and evening, about a third of what had been the *Sturmlager* diet, with neighboring farms and gardens now stripped bare. They were grateful for what they had and Herb's can of Spam remained unopened.

Lingering in front of the hotel, they listened to stories told in broken English, or read gestures and facial expressions that described the German occupation, the accidental bombing of Prague by Allies on their way to Dresden, and the never-ending fear of fellow-Slavs. Some said General Patton was on his way to Prague. Others said it was the Russians on their way and Patton was pulling back, abandoned by the Allies. All the while they were wary that someone would confiscate their space.

After three days, Herb decided to go on a walkabout looking for food – maybe a dried apple or overlooked potato. He returned after dark empty handed, hoping to slake his hunger with sleep. Instead, he almost fell into Joe's arms as he opened the door.

"Christ, where the hell have you been? We almost gave up waiting," Joe whispered. "The Russians are coming. This time it's for sure. We don't dare hang around. Especially you. They'll think you're a Kraut and then..."

Herb felt a surge of adrenaline. "Where'd you hear this? Maybe it's only a rumor. We've heard lots of things before..."

"Sam and me met this here resistance fighter heading toward the American lines. He said he could sneak us through."

"Just like that? He picked you guys out of all the grunts walking the streets dying to get out? Gimme a break."

"He will meet us tonight at the edge of town. It's a long shot but we gotta go for it."

"He's using you, an American sucker." Herb insisted. "He wants to milk you for all you've got. What did you give him? Your watch? Your shoes, your...?"

Sam was sitting on the edge of the bed. "My wedding ring was good enough. But I'd be willing to give him the shirt off my back."

"Very funny." Herb took a deep breath feeling slightly dizzy. "Okay. If you're going, I'm in."

They arrived at the designated spot where a pickup heaped with scrap metal and assorted cardboard boxes shuddered, its engine snorting uncertainly. The driver was pacing up and down, looking from left to right. As they approached, his expression contorted into a scowl. "Three guys? You didn't say..."

"Sorry, but that's the way it's gonna be," Joe declared. He scanned the back of the truck. "You've got plenty of room."

"We're Americans," Sam added. "That should be good enough."

The driver was outnumbered. More important, there was no time to waste. Under cover of darkness, they might be able to sneak through the Russian lines while the border was under minimal guard.

Climbing up, they huddled under rags and boxes, the rough edges scraping their backs, the truck bumping past checkpoints, past guards sleeping off their drunken celebrations, the threesome barely breathing when the truck slowed, afraid they were being scrutinized.

After two or three hours, they careened into a dip in the road, the truck coughing to a heart-stopping shudder as the driver reached for a cigarette. "You can sit up now," he called out, turning around. "You're here."

Herb squinted through the dark. Off in the distance, there was the hint of light with outlines that might have been tents and vehicles. "Are you sure?"

"Just get out." The driver's gravelly voice had turned menacing.

Tightening his jaw, Herb dropped to the ground, moving toward a line of American Jeeps as Joe and Sam followed. Walking stiffly, he ducked into a huge tent where clusters of soldiers were milling about. A lieutenant glanced up, then stood with his mouth agape.

Smoothing his filthy clothes as best he could, Herb stepped forward and saluted. "PFC Herbert Zahn, 36744376 Tank Company Easy, reporting sir…"

CHAPTER 28

Germany, 1945

THE ALLIES CROSSED THE BRIDGE at Remagen facing a German army that had been ordered to fight to the death. Meanwhile reports of concentration camps and wholesale murders were too awful to believe.

Hilda had found a two-room flat, relying on government allotments and Frau Eichmeyer's occasional help, knowing that jobs were unavailable, even at the small tank factory nearby. Peter's thin arms and legs began to flesh out, his cheeks rosy. They went for long walks, inhaling the spring-scented air, followed by a nap or quiet reading in the afternoon. A year had passed, with Alma arriving under the pretense of a visit, then forgetting to leave.

Today Hilda was preparing for Easter, cleaning and washing their few things, hanging them in the breeze, telling stories to Peter as he sat watching her, his chin resting on his fists. "People color Easter eggs as a sign of re-birth. The springtime lamb stands for the Lamb of God. Easter baskets and lilies are for all the beginnings in the springtime just like Jesus is a new beginning."

"Will there be Easter baskets in church?"

"Oh no. We just go and praise God for his son Jesus. The Easter basket is something else."

Frau Eichmeyer had come to visit and stood at the door smiling at the little boy's excitement. "Ilse might have some eggs for you. Her hens are good layers, enough for her family with some left to sell. You can take the bicycle and be home before dark."

Ilse was Frau Eichmeyer's sister-in-law who lived on a nearby farm, coming to visit with Heinz along with their sons in the mild winter, making the trip in a horse-drawn wagon. A bit younger than Frau Eichmeyer, Ilse radiated good health, her freckled face framed in thick yellow braids, her husband the picture of a round-bellied Bauer. Hilda liked them, and Peter delighted in the visits that brightened an ordinary day.

Hilda paused, clothespin suspended in the air. "You think I could?"

"Why not? The weather is nice and the fresh air will feel good. When you come back, we boil a few cabbage leaves to make red, or onionskins for yellow, coloring eggs in the old-fashioned way. Maybe you even find some blooming violets near to the warm rocks. That would make for blue." Frau Eichmeyer reached down and tousled Peter's hair. "We make it a festival."

Hilda looked at Peter's upturned face. There had been so little joy in her childhood, so little in his.

"If you go tomorrow, is soon enough," Frau Eichmeyer continued.

"Well, maybe. I think about it."

The next morning Hilda awoke to find Peter's face pressed against the pillow next to hers. Clearly, he hadn't forgotten. Even her mother relished the thought.

So after conferring with Frau Eichmeyer, she tucked a roughly sketched map into her string-woven bag, waving to Peter and Alma as she mounted the bicycle, praying that the roads were passable, that she would not get a flat tire, that she not be confronted by thieves. It was Good Friday. There was still time to prepare.

The morning chill was invigorating, the rutted road passable in this once graceful town. Neglect had made the buildings ragged and worn, but the villas and spas wore clean façades, their grounds carefully trimmed. Here and there, tufts of grass and shoots of yellow-green poked through. Meadowlark, sparrow and goldfinch warbled the songs of spring. It was a storybook moment as she bent forward to capture a basket of eggs. Bumping past high fences and distant estates, she was soon on open land where a few enclosed horses and goats rooted the earth. The sun had come out, glistening on morning dew, warming her arms and cheeks.

It was almost noon when she arrived at an uneven lane, walking past a mailbox then toward a cottage where an orange cat looked up before scooting under the porch. A hutch just past was undoubtedly a chicken coop. Baying hounds announced her arrival and Ilse appeared on the porch. "Ah, what a nice surprise! Come in, come in."

Propping the bicycle against the porch, Hilda entered a large room furnished with high-backed chairs and a long table to accommodate the farmhands at harvest time. At the far end were a sink and a stove with pots and pans dangling on hooks overhead. A ladder off to the side hinted at sleeping quarters above. "I hope it is all right. Minna Eichmeyer said…"

"Of course, of course. I am so glad to see you." Ilse moved toward the sink and filled a kettle, lifting it onto the stove. "I was ready to have some tea and now you can keep me company. Heinz is out looking at the fields for spring planting. He took the boys with him."

Hilda pulled out a nearby chair. "So much sunshine. It makes you smile."

"Drafty in the winter but we don't complain." Ilse sprinkled tea leaves into a pot and added hot water, seating herself across from Hilda.

"We were talking about Easter and how we used to color the eggs. I was hoping to find some here."

Ilse got up, coming back with a platter of bread and goat cheese. "Oh yes. We need to celebrate such things for the children. My boys will pass on the practice as well."

Outside, there was the cluck-cluck of chickens and wagon clatter as farmers hawed their horses forward. Inside there was warmth and peace, a life close to nature and God. They talked about parents, church, and cooking, woman-talk outside of politics and war. Hilda related stories about her Opa, of Onkel Wilhelm, of the ever-present music in her life and his. Ilse told of being a four-year old, watching one dog mounting another, wondering at the rules in this strange game. There were murmurs of Papa saying this, the pastor cautioning that, and of women who were relentless and strong.

When Heinz returned with the boys, Hilda realized she had been there for hours. "Oh my, I meant to leave long ago. You should have said something."

"It was a pleasant afternoon for both of us." Ilse reached for Hilda's hand. "And you must do this again, now that you know the way. But first, let's see how many eggs we can find for you."

They captured eight from the squawking hens to be placed carefully inside Hilda's bag. Then a quick goodbye, for Hilda was anxious to be home before dark. She bicycled hard, past a stray dog sniffing at a buzzing fly, past a Fraulein urging two children forward, their thin voices ringing like distant bells. A distant rumble signaled an oncoming storm, making the hurry even more urgent.

It was almost dark when she arrived. Placing the bicycle at the back, she climbed to their tiny flat, holding up the bag of eggs.

Inside, she was greeted with the smell of smoke and gunfire. Across the room sat the ghostly apparition of a man with his head cradled in his hands. For a frightening moment it was as if she were back in the bunker, the ventilators cranking forth the scent of war.

Suddenly weak, she reached for a chair. "Papa? Is that you? Are you really here?"

Her mother, standing behind him, held her finger to her lips. Motioning Hilda aside, she guided Helmut onto the cot in the corner of the room, covering him with a blanket as he turned to the wall. "Peter was crying so hard, I told him to go lie down," she whispered. "Come outside where we can talk."

Placing the eggs near the sink, Hilda followed her mother into the yard and sat on the bottom step, trying not to shiver. "What happened? What did he tell you? Can't he talk? Is his mind…"

"He will be all right. It's just the shock after such a long journey. He told me all about…" She paused. "In the East… They knew that it was over so they let people go. He was given a certificate to travel, and he raced ahead of the Russians, going to Wanne Eichel first. But the Americans were in control and he was afraid to ask at the government office. A woman from the old neighborhood told him we had been moved to Oeynhausen. He had just arrived when the RAF began bombing the tank factory. No sirens, no warning, just one bomb after another, back and forth until there was nothing left. We heard it all the way here. Peter was sitting on the steps waiting for lunch. He ran inside screaming."

"And Papa?"

"He was going by just as it happened. He began to run, then wandered for hours, not knowing what to do, where to go."

So the rumblings had been the bombers, not thunder of an oncoming storm. Once more, the joy was too good to last. *'Nach Lachen kommt Weinen'*, a phrase heard over and over as she was growing up. And tears there were aplenty.

Her mother continued, the words coming slow as though each elicited pain. "Papa talked to Frau Mueller. She was the one who lived five houses down, in Wanne Eichel. Remember her?"

"Oh yes, that old busybody..."

"She said there had been a notice from the war department in our mailbox but then it disappeared." Alma looked down at her tightly wrapped fingers. "It said that Gunter was wounded. He was taken to a field hospital outside of Berlin."

"But there is nothing left of Berlin, Mutti. The city is destroyed. Where would they put a field hospital?"

"It was a death notice," Alma whispered.

"But you said..."

"There was a second one where you have to get it yourself from the post office. Frau Mueller said she could tell. It has a special seal, a special look. But Papa was afraid to get it because the Americans were there."

"Two notices, both of them lost?" Hilda's voice rang with disbelief. "Frau Mueller was always the neighborhood gossip. You yourself said she makes up stories. Anyway, how dare she look into people's mailboxes? Or maybe she was crazy in the head from all the bombing. The war department can make mistakes," she continued, frantic for an explanation. "Papa was reported dead in the war but it was his brother who was killed. That's a fact. It happens."

"I know. Things do get mixed up – names, places..." Alma got to her feet. "So maybe you're right. Anyway, we better go inside. It's getting cold."

Back upstairs, Hilda tiptoed into the bedroom where Peter lay with his eyes wide open.

"Can I get up now, Mutti? Did you bring back some eggs to color?"

Hilda bent down, brushing the hair from his face. "Yes, you can get up. We will do the eggs tomorrow. Opa is sleeping in the other room. Did you see him? Did you say Grüß Gott to him?"

Peter nodded. "Is it suppertime pretty soon?"

"After Opa is awake we will have something to eat." Hilda forced her voice to sound cheerful. "Because Opa is home to stay."

Suddenly Peter's face was bathed in smiles. "That means Papa and Onkel Gunter are coming home too!"

"Pretty soon. The war is almost over."

In that, she was right. Within weeks, the Russians connected with American forces on the Elbe River. A quarter million tons of bombs had been dropped, reducing every German city to rubble. Joseph Gebbels and his wife murdered their six children and then poisoned themselves. Heinrich Himmler, head of the notorious SS, swallowed cyanide, writhing in an agonized death. Hitler and Eva Braun followed suit a few hours after pronouncing their marriage vows, *Until death do us part.* Italian dictator Mussolini and his mistress hid like cowards, but were caught and ripped limb from limb, their remains hung like slabs of meat before a cheering mob.

On May 7, 1945, the Allies accepted an unconditional surrender, marking the end of the war in Europe and the vaunted Third Reich.

Meanwhile, the British took over the pretty town of Bad Oeynhausen, wrapping its lush center in barbed wire with only one guarded entryway. A few Germans were hired as cooks, servants and translators, while the rest were left to starve. The war was over but the agony persisted with retribution taking its place.

CHAPTER 29

Chicago, 1946

"I DON'T BELIEVE IT," MARICHEN declared. "They say Holocaust, like it's from the Bible. We know that Jews believe different from us. So what?" She bent over the table that was filled with canned goods and dried fruit. "War is terrible and both sides do terrible things. But nobody kills for no reason. And don't you tell me any different."

"The papers have pictures, Mom. They pulled gold fillings out of prisoner's teeth, used skin for lampshades. Doctors did experiments on people while they were still awake. Men sitting in freezing water for hours, children baked in the ovens…"

"Never mind. I don't want to hear it." Marichen went into the bedroom, returning with an armload of clean potato sacks. "Here, hold this tight while I sew around the edges. The post office wants them sealed, so we seal them. Tante Guste can use them for towels. They need everything."

"Why don't you just send them some CARE packages? So much easier than dragging all this stuff to the post office. It probably wouldn't cost any more and make for lots less work."

"CARE packages are army leftovers. Who wants to eat that? It's enough that Sophie and Martha send them to Alma. Mine are better."

"But if they're starving…"

"Why do you always argue? We send to Tante Guste and she says she is glad. How come you always know better?" She moved to the next box. "We'll mail these on the way to the store."

Elsie went into her room to wait. She surveyed the dressing table's ruffled skirt, the mirrored chest of drawers, felt the carpet under her feet. Her new room was the nicest she'd ever had. Her parents had sold the building on Whipple, buying this Victorian relic that had been converted into a two-flat, moving into the second floor flat. There was an extra room on the third floor with a separate entrance that would be perfect for Herb when he came home from the army. They had gone shopping to outfit his room, buying curtains and bed sheets, everything fresh and new. It was a mother and daughter thing after what had been a bad year.

It began the year before, when they were still living on Whipple Street. Things were already tense, for Elsie had accepted a date to the Junior Prom despite August saying no.

"Well, I'm going anyway and you can't stop me."

"You think so? Just try it and see." His set jaw and clenched fist had always generated terror. This time, it fueled her resolve.

With the help of Vita and Carol, they conspired to make it happen. No gown? Vita knew someone who knew someone, and so on. The borrowed dress was pink and a perfect fit. Now the prom was less than a week away. It was Sunday, and the store opened late. She stood at the kitchen door where her parents were eating breakfast. "I'm going to Vita's."

August looked up. "You be back at the store by three. You hear?"

Wordlessly, Elsie turned to go.

"I'm warning you. You better be there." His voice followed her down the hall. "And you better forget all that talk about the prom. Or I cut you off from Vita and Carol too. They're a bad influence. The school knows you live outside their district, and if you make trouble…"

It had been a threat since they'd moved from Addison Street. "If you make me switch schools, I'll run away," was her retort.

An impasse – for now.

Today she and Vita would be experimenting with makeup and hairstyles, arranging for the boys to pick them up at Vita's on the night of the prom. Three o'clock came and went. Vita's mother invited her to stay for dinner and she lingered afterward, every minute bringing her closer to disaster.

It was after ten when she got home. Her father was waiting.

This time the fists were more than a threat. "You were supposed to be at the store at three. You think you too smart to obey? Well, I show you. I will break your spirit!"

Hurled back and forth, she was pummeled on the back, face, along her neck with glancing karate chops as she tried to protect herself, huddled beside the bed, screaming at the end of every shout, every thud. "Oh no you won't! Never, never! I belong to myself."

Finally he grabbed her arms, flinging her into the closet, fumbling to turn the key as Marichen cried out, "No, August. She will suffocate. You're gonna kill her!"

Then silence, after which the bedroom door slammed followed by footsteps down the hall.

She waited a few moments then crept out of the closet, too traumatized to cry. She'd been spanked many times, sometimes hard. Herb and Trudi too. But never like this.

The next morning she awoke to an empty house. Stiff and aching, she dressed and went to school, showing Vita and Carol the purple bruises on her back, wondering whether they would fade or might be covered with makeup before the prom, her resolve undaunted.

The girls agreed to help.

After school, they went to the silent apartment, helping her pack her belongings including the pink gown. She could stay with Carol for the time being. School had two more weeks to go before summer vacation. After that, well…

Carol's parents said nothing, looking the other way as Elsie arrived to spend the week. Saturday was the prom, which went as planned. Lou Sojka really knew how to dance and kissed Elsie in the cab coming back.

But once the drama ended, she was overwhelmed with angst. She didn't dare call Aunt Martha or Uncle Fritz, knowing they'd send her right back home. As for Carol's parents, how much longer might they remain silent? With nowhere else to go, it couldn't wait. She had to find a job.

She applied at Goldblatt's, Wieboldt's and Sears. They let her fill out the form. They would let her know.

On Saturday, she expanded her search to downtown and was met with scowls, for it was their busy day. Close to tears, she returned to Carol's house, creeping up the steps and into the living room to be confronted by Herb, military-erect in dress uniform with Carol's parents hovering nearby.

Terrified, her eyes darted to Carol's mother and back again. "How did you get here? Who contacted you? If you think…"

"Get your things. You're coming home." His voice was strong and firm.

"You have no idea what happened," she cried. She tugged at her jacket. "Let me show you."

"Never mind. It's over. Now do as I say."

"You can't make me! I have rights." It was a lame attempt to brazen it out.

"You're fifteen years old. The law is on our side."

Elsie looked at Carol's parents, her eyes pleading, but they were clearly ready to have this finished. "All right, but only because I have to."

Her room was as she'd left it, drawers in disarray, clothes scattered helter-skelter.

"You will stay with Trudi for the summer."

"Any place but here."

"Stop feeling sorry for yourself. This was not your finest hour."

Fifteen minutes later she was on the bus, relieved that there was somewhere to go.

The next day, Herb returned to his army base. At summer's end, President Truman ordered the atom bomb over Hiroshima marking the end of World War II.

In September, Elsie came home to the new place on Kilbourn where her parents had moved during the summer. She hadn't seen or spoken to them since the week before Prom.

August was standing at the kitchen window and looked up as she entered. "Come and look at the squirrels. Mama puts out food for them. She likes to watch."

He'd broken the silence. This might be a good year after all.

Now it was two months before graduation. She threw on her jacket and went back to the table as Marichen finished the second box to Germany. "I'll carry it, Mom. You take the other one. It's not so heavy."

"They should let us send more," Marichen murmured sadly. "These people are hungry and that's the truth. Making prisoners work like slaves or sending them to Russia to die of starvation. Countries not allowed to send food. Instead, they burn their crops in the fields. Even lard and nuts are forbidden and the Red Cross is no more."

"*Straffe*. That's what you always say," Elsie murmured. "No deed goes unpunished."

"War itself is punishment, my girl. Land, mountains, forests, lakes, all bombed until there is nothing left and still they bomb. In twenty years they will be friends again, looking to fight with somebody else. It's like a sickness inside, a vomit of filth. I'm telling you, war is *dreck,* and not just for the losers. It splashes over everybody and everything. And for what? To kill - fathers, brothers, sons, even babies…"

"Herb's coming home, Mom. It's going to be all right."

"I know. But it's still wrong." She motioned Elsie toward the door, and balancing boxes they moved down the steps to the post office.

The Saturday line was short and soon they were on their way. "Daddy is not feeling so good. He doesn't sleep, can't eat," Marichen murmured as they climbed onto the streetcar. "Maybe he should go home early today."

Elsie swayed next to her mother, holding the overhead strap. "He should really see a doctor. Have you talked to him?"

"He just needs to rest."

"But if he's not sleeping…"

"He has too much on his head. First Tante 'Lisbet arguing with him about the store. And now Tante Martha getting married. Who knows where that will lead." Marichen turned away, her eyes blinding from the afternoon sun. "It's always something."

Elsie nodded. Tante 'Lisbet was selling sandwiches and salads, offering small packs of potato chips and soda pop instead of gallon milk, adding a few tables and chairs around the parking space in the summer. Neighborhood kids and farmers came to loll about and enjoy the hot summer nights with some cold drinks and pleasant conversation. Business was good, but it was done without consulting August who still held a substantial contract on the store. Labor intensive versus fast turnover. Margin versus quantity. Then it got personal. Had she no gratitude? And a final thrust – Rudy must be rolling in his grave.

'Lisbet had posed her own question: who would want a dairy store with cows a few feet away from the kitchen door? Instead, people wanted a place to meet. She might even add a swimming pool, charging a small membership fee, a real neighborhood draw.

August was horrified. "You wanna clean the toilets and mop the floors after a bunch of screaming kids?"

"I give them what they want. Pride costs money. Time is cheap."

So they went their separate ways with her father accepting their contract as a mistake, cost neutral after being paid off. No measurable loss except that for him, time was money. That he'd copied her format at the Devon store was not mentioned.

Now it was Aunt Martha posing a threat. George had been in the picture ever since Aunt Martha's divorce from Wally, or maybe even before. But George was looking for a wife, not a career woman.

"Wow! They're getting married? Are we invited?"

"I think it's just talk or maybe Martha don't want to work so hard. Instead, they go out, come home drunk... Daddy tries to tell them but they won't listen."

"They're not drunks, Mom," Elsie protested. "And when has Dad ever talked to anyone beside Mr. Hazard?"

"It's just that Daddy has a lot on his head."

"Does that mean you're selling the store on Devon?"

Her guess was right. Maybe business was better than expected.

Or maybe it was worse, swallowing the loss sooner rather than later. Or maybe her father was really having a nervous breakdown. Whatever the reason, there was a buyer who stepped forward, or perhaps a realtor was involved, offering the right price, or maybe not quite the right price, but adequate. However it happened, the sale was quick, leaving Elsie free from business for the first time since eighth grade.

With weeks before graduation, there was no point in joining any new activities. But she had been able to continue with choir, so when Mr. Groom announced an all-day workshop joining with several Chicago schools, Elsie signed up.

The day began with sight-reading drill by a teacher from the other school. After lunch, it was sectionals, an amalgam of sopranos and altos matching quality and timbre with total strangers, learning how to listen while they sang. Then as a finale, the choirs gathered in the now-vacant auditorium to perform as one, coming together like real professionals.

Back in the classroom, Elsie sat waiting for dismissal, her brain still dipping and swirling through the music. Suddenly she felt two hands grabbing her shoulders from behind. "Hey Elsie! Didn't you see me when I waved?"

It took a minute to register. "You've been here all afternoon? But how come…"

Eleanor had not changed. If anything, she'd gotten heavier. Yet her face was lovely with even features, a creamy complexion surrounded by soft dark hair, her smile real. "You're sitting in my school. I told you I was going back."

"You did tell me…," Elsie stammered, not remembering at all.

"How long has it been? Oh man, we need to catch up." Eleanor leaned forward eagerly. "You should come home with me. Stay for dinner."

Elsie was dubious. "Higgins is pretty far…"

"I moved closer to school. It was the only way I could graduate." Eleanor's expression was matter of fact before the smile returned. "Oh, please come. The kids are always bringing guests. We're down a few so there's plenty of room. No one minds if someone drops in."

No after school job, no schedule to maintain. The freedom was downright heady. "Why not? I'll just call Mom to let her know."

It was a large house that had seen better days, yet sturdy and functional with yawning hallways like that of a hotel. The dining room table was already set and after a quick introduction, they sat down to eat. A motherly-type woman moved in and out filling pitchers and plates, cautioning here and there to keep the noise level down. Eleanor referred to Elsie as her favorite cousin, making it sound loving and warm. Banter was lively, sprinkled with good-natured teasing, postponing study hour as long as they could.

At seven o'clock the table was cleared, time for Elsie to leave. Eleanor walked with her to the streetcar, a brief chance to chat.

"I'm graduating in June. You too?"

Eleanor nodded. "Things are better now."

"These kids are nice. They seem to like you a lot."

Then the streetcar clanged around the curve, leaving them with a hasty promise to keep in touch.

Elsie's father was in bed when she got home, her mother just finishing up in the bathroom. She tiptoed into the darkened hall just as her mother emerged.

"Did you have a nice visit?"

"I did, Mom. There were eight kids living in the house, and everyone seemed to be having a good time, like at a party. Then it got to be study time and I had to leave. The housemother seemed nice. Eleanor called it a Group Home."

"'Lisbet did the right thing. It's good that Eleanor went back to school."

"If she lost some weight, she'd be really pretty. Someone should talk to her."

"It would be a start."

"She seemed happy, Mom. That's what counts." She hugged her books. "The workshop was great. I'm so glad I got to go."

Back in her room, Elsie's head still echoed with song. She'd been surrounded by hymns at church, melodies of Mozart and Brahms at school. Herb's Philco provided orchestration and the music had become familiar. She looked at herself in the mirror and smiled. Maybe she could be happy too.

CHAPTER 30

Germany, 1946

Elvira sat up, her heart pounding. It was an ongoing nightmare. "The Americans are coming!" She'd be running from door to door, stumbling into the basement for sanctuary as the army tanks crept closer. Thundering boots and loud voices came next, the soldiers leering at the women and girls huddled in the corner like maidens in distress.

But the Americans had not raped and pillaged, and except for a few ruffians, there was little commotion for there were no German soldiers left to fight.

Then came partitioning and the British took over, maintaining the harsh wartime rules practiced by the Germans for the sake of convenience. Meanwhile, the specter of starvation loomed large. Ursula, now three, had spent her infancy drinking watery milk, eating bread laced with sawdust, wailing piteously as her mother searched for food. Elvira had been sent home from the BDM retreat, the bombing now so terrible that it was dangerous to stay, the family spending the final months in the bunker.

Then the war was over and Guste found a job on a farm, cleaning and cooking in exchange for a place to sleep and three meals a day. It was something she'd negotiated on a trip to visit Tante Gottliebe in Betel, 150 kilometers away, a mission to barter the last of their possessions for food, leaving Ursula under the care of a friend. It had taken two days, living on a pittance of bread and milk from compassionate farmers, sleeping in barns, women on one side, men on the other, her shoes worn so thin that she returned barefoot.

Finally awake, Elvira swung her legs to the floor, the cot sagging beneath her. Tomorrow she would leave for her own job, working the fields, slopping the pigs, shoveling manure, all for food and a place to sleep, another miracle negotiated by her mother.

Moving toward the window, she flexed her fingers then picked up a coat taken from an abandoned building, ripping seams, sewing it inside out to appear as new. Her father could wear it on chilly nights as he cruised the streets in an open Jeep, working as interpreter for British soldiers who enforced the curfew, another result of her mother's prodding, for after filling forms, they'd been de-nazified by the Allies and permitted to work.

She arched her back as her father entered the room, his night shift over. "Your coat's almost done. It looks like the right size."

He took off his shoes. "Will you finish it before you go?"

"For sure. It will keep you warm. Or you might trade it for a sack of potatoes. Mutti says there's plenty to eat on a farm. She plans to can some garden vegetables and the farmer promised leftovers from the sheep at slaughtering time. Ursula is getting fat."

"Your ration cards will get me what I need. With extras from America, I will be all right."

"Just remember that when you see people in line it means there's bread and potatoes or even coffee. Keep your eyes open after work as you come home."

"...and I can sleep standing up. It's an old army trick."

"Don't make fun, Papa. And watch for coal or wood for cooking. Do you know where to look?"

"Yes, yes. I'm not a baby." He moved toward the sink. "There's water for washing up?"

She nodded. "And think twice before you take from the soldiers. If they report you, you could go to jail or even be shot. We hear stories..."

"They're not bad men," he muttered. "They see how things are with us."

Stripped to the waist, he splashed water on his arms and face, shoulders and chest. "You will pass Bielefeld on your way to the farm," he said, his voice now conversational.

"Bielefeld is bombed out. I don't want to see it."

He settled on the cot, wrapping a thin blanket around his shoulders. "I sleep a little then go back. Americans don't know how to read German script." His voice drifted off.

She left the following morning before her father's return, walking past skeleton buildings and narrowed pathways flanked with plaster, concrete and mud. No longer bannered with patriotic posters, the shattered walls were replete with pictures of the Holocaust, one reading, "YOU ARE GUILTY!" another, "These Atrocities: Your Guilt." She remembered her grandfather's agitated reports, remembered Tante Alma listening to the radio at night, or her pastor railing against the Nazis. Now newspapers, cinemas and radio stations fell under the Information Control Act, an echo of Nazi book burning or the Vatican index of forbidden books. *Deutchland über Alles* was no longer allowed. The Morgenthau Plan mandated cities to be stripped of factories and supplies, the Ruhr dismantled and once more placed under the sovereignty of

France. They had lost the war. They were paying the price.

The open train was a cattle car as people scrambled for space, reaching, shoving, elbowing for makeshift seats or a spot along the wall. Some crouched listlessly, shivering despite the press of bodies, their eyes vacant, unaware of where they were going or why. Many were children or the very old, unable to find food, now barely alive. She took a deep breath. Farmers had it good. Her sister was drinking milk straight from the cow. Through Sturm und Drang, they had managed to survive. She leaned against her box, its slim supplies needing to last the summer. If things went well, she'd remain through the harvest. She closed her eyes and prayed for a jovial farmer and his apple-cheeked Frau who would take her under their wing.

But when she arrived, she realized they were struggling like everyone else, doing whatever necessary to keep the farm. Her Landjahr days had been hard, but loving. Here, it was simply hard. She awoke with the roosters, going out to clean the pigsties, returning to wash up for Früstück, stuffing herself with bread, cheese and milk, knowing there would be nothing more until supper. Then out to the fields with a hoe, bending over rows of potatoes, cabbage and beans, keeping up with farmers twice her size.

Friendly talk was discouraged. Granted, meals were plentiful. Granted Frau Rebensdorf was an adequate cook and didn't begrudge them as much as they wanted, even allowing for seconds. But after a day of backbreaking work, two meals were barely enough, and too often Elvira remained hungry.

The only relief was the few hours allowed to visit her mother and Ursula, crossing the fields between stalks of corn, their tassels waving in the breeze. Sometimes it would rain, with saucers of mud sucking at her shoes. Or if she lingered, the mosquitoes leaving welts on her arms, bedeviling her throughout the night. Yet these visits kept her nourished, for her mother would always provide a treat, a clip for her hair or a welcome bit of news from home. Siebold might write about someone's de-nazification process being lost or denied which meant certain starvation, and she would return to her place, grateful for two meals each day.

The job lasted until autumn. Her reward for the summer's work was five sacks of potatoes which she could sell or exchange back home. Packing her belongings, she fashioning a sledge to maneuver them onto the train. Then with a brief nod, went to say goodbye to her mother and sister who would remain behind.

"You will be all right. Just go every morning to watch for the lines," Guste said, kissing away her tears. "Papa needs someone to cook and do laundry. It's important that he always has a clean shirt for the job. You could help him with his reports. You have such a fine hand."

Elvira turned to her sister, holding her tight. "They expect a cold winter and you don't have any warm clothes, not even a wool sweater. What if there's no heat? Ursula is still so little."

"The farmer's wife is expecting a baby so they will keep it warm. If they need me now, they will need me more later on. You'll see."

"It's just hard, knowing you are both staying here."

"By spring we will be together again, God willing."

So after a final embrace, Elvira set out for home, fighting for space on the crowded train, clinging to the cargo that would provide some small sustenance in the following months.

But this was to be the hunger-winter of 1946-47. With France in charge of the coal mining industry, German exports were sold for one-third the world price with no profit allowed and only a miniscule salary for the miners. Food shortage and strict sanctions reduced food calories to a little more than one thousand per day, one-third of that consumed in America. Food imports, paid by Germany itself, were only allocated to non-ethnic Germans. German patents, copyrights and trademarks were confiscated or stolen, the scientists and technicians jailed if they withheld trade secrets despite the Hague Convention that prohibited the seizure of property. Chocolate and cigarettes, preferably American, were now the medium of exchange, the Reich's mark entirely worthless. In the city, where venereal disease was rampant, young girls, desperate and hungry, would exchange their favors for a pack of Camels or Pall Mall. Yet despite such threats and challenges, Elvira was happy to be going home.

CHAPTER 31

Chicago, 1946-47

AFTER DISCHARGE FROM THE AIR Corps, Erv joined Trudi at the Stickney store. Elsie would continue there over the summer but come fall, she and Herb would join ten thousand returning veterans at Wright Junior College, a school intended for fewer than half.

Now the days were bright with work cheerfully done. On weekends, the foursome that included Erv's brother, would go miniature golfing or bowling, piling into the car to sing old songs and tell jokes or riddles along the way. Never mind the hour. They were young and greeted the morning refreshed.

Between customers, Elsie and Erv might sit at the kitchen table playing a game of Battleship. Other times she'd help sort the bills, deducting outgo from receipts, a simple process of balancing the books. It made her feel competent and useful. But soon the down time became pervasive, the store shelves rarely re-stocked, the bread counter half-empty with little turnover to maintain freshness, making her wonder why she was there.

It was now the end of June, another session of bills versus receipts. "I thought there was supposed to be more income than outgo," she ventured.

"Well, the idea is to make it up on weekends."

"And do you?"

"Supposedly..."

She couldn't ask further. But the question remained. The war was over with jobs aplenty as war plants switched to making washing machines and cars instead of tanks and guns. Television had become the rage, their screens suspended in every restaurant and bar, the customers filling every seat, every stool, every night. For them, business was booming.

By the end of summer, Creamland's decline was crucial, the vendors paid with small bills or rolls of quarters and dimes, making customer change critical for the rest of the day.

Trudi went into Chicago to contact her former employer. Maybe they could use an experienced secretary? She was hired on the spot. It would keep their heads above water for the time being. Three months later the business was sold and Erv returned to his previous job. By then Elsie had returned home, getting ready for college.

The rest of the family was going through its own transition. After eight years in business, August and Marichen were spending their days at home with August puttering in the basement or curled up with the newspaper, Marichen mending or hemming things to send to Germany. August was sleeping better, his disposition much improved. Tenant rent took care of the mortgage, and payments from Fritz and Martha subsidized a quiet life.

Herb had come home at the end of June, tall, slender and handsome with a well-trimmed moustache, an ever-present pipe tucked into his breast pocket, his Purple Heart casually stored on the bottom of a dresser drawer. He found a job working nights at a printing company, the hours coordinated with a return to school.

The week before Labor Day, he shepherded Elsie through college registration. Psychology at eight, Biology at noon, a six-week orientation class at four and American Lit twice a week ending at ten, all in all a terrible schedule.

It didn't matter. She would be sitting at the feet of PhD's from the University of Chicago as new ideas resounded, hearing the rough responses of war-hardened veterans who treated her as an equal. She would study Freud and Plato, learn about Communism and the cosmos and use words like *existentialism, connotation* and *peon.*

Then the cashier's line. "Fees? Isn't junior college free?" She turned to Herb in a panic. "I didn't bring…"

He pulled out his wallet, his face stern. "It is, except for activity fees, lab fees and a service add-on, plus buying your own books. You wanted to grow up? This is part of it. You'll need to get a job."

She'd worried about it all summer, tossing and turning in the middle of the night. What was she trained to do?

She'd stayed in touch with Vita who was working at Martha Washington Hospital as a nurse's aid. It might be a good prospect for a starving student. Hospitals were staffed day and night. Surely their schedules could match.

The phone book provided several addresses, a few within easy transportation, and miracle of miracles she was hired.

Manor Hospital had been a nursing home with sixteen beds, newly converted into a medical facility by an enterprising cardiologist, his staff hired from the nearby Hospital. After a brief training, Elsie was scheduled making beds, emptying bedpans and giving an occasional back rub. She answered lights, changed linen, distributed trays, filled water pitchers and prepared patients for the night. The pay was modest, the work light but interesting.

Now she could finally organize her life. School was wonderful with Social Science and Psychology the favorites, other classes basic enough to keep up. School, hospital and home were all within five miles, the transportation quick and easy. Sororities surveyed the incoming freshmen and Elsie was invited to pledge, but chose instead to join the Women's Club where Herb's new girlfriend was assigned to be her "big sister." Soon, they were a threesome, with Marilou joining them at school performances or debating politics, religion and the purpose of life at the local pizzeria.

Second semester was easier with enough money to pay for registration and books, her schedule a better fit with the job. By the end of her first year she'd accumulated thirty college credits. She'd also re-connected with Jim whom she'd met at her voice teacher's studio and they'd begun dating, taking long walks in the drizzling rain, playing cribbage on the college lawn or in the cafeteria. He and Herb liked one another from the start and soon their threesome became a foursome, exploring museums and galleries or joining the group activities at Marilou's church. The Depression was a fading memory, the war, America's triumph. Newly built highways stretched for miles and Park Forest was born, housing young families who bought cars, TV sets and washing machines, generating a baby boom that would last for more than a decade. Nylon had made the ironing board passé and penicillin could cure almost anything short of the common cold.

Herb had returned from the war an agnostic, reveling in its intellectual gymnastics, his bookish nature well suited for midnight sessions with priests and professors at the pizza hut, joining other students to challenge beliefs, their minds giddy with new ideas. He became a fixture within Marilou's church, a place that offered warmth, ritual and an open forum for new ideas and an indulgent ear. They'd even drawn Elsie into the youth group, persuading her to attend summer camp where there were the usual summer activities along with music and prayer, community and the fun once frowned upon, if not actually forbidden. It made August and Marichen uneasy, yet there was little they could do.

It was during summer camp that Elsie got to know Marilou, learning about how she, a child of a single mother, had spent time reading books or sitting on the stoop, yearning for companionship. Then her mother married the bombastic Glenn, and instead of loneliness, Marilou found herself the brunt of sarcasm, ridicule and name-calling disguised as humor. Her solace was through the church where she was feted for her lovely voice. With God's grace and her own fervent prayers, Herb's path would follow in the Christian way. They became engaged on a cold wintry night standing beneath a lamppost with the snowflakes dancing on her upturned face.

At the end of the two-year curriculum, Herb transferred to the University on the GI Bill, Marilou switching to a four-year college to major in music, a marked change in Elsie's social life, for they had encompassed much of her free time.

So in a burst of nostalgia, she decided to look in on Uncle Fritz and Katie at the Belmont store, hoping to see Aunt Martha as well, depending on who was scheduled. Class had been dismissed early and she didn't have to work that night. Meanwhile, the harvest moon hung like a lantern in the cloudless sky, the air musty with the scent of burning leaves. The store was only a few miles from Wright. It would be fun to drop in and say hello. She hadn't seen them in ages.

The bus passed Carol's house on Rutherford Street, now over-run with weeds, the family having moved to Wisconsin. Approaching Overhill, her eyes sought out the neon sign of Landsman Drugs, remembering how old Mrs. Brodski had taken her there for a banana split as a thank-you for delivering groceries, remembering the hair salon that smelled of pomade and the dry cleaners' steamed-up windows. She alighted and crossed the street.

Inside, the bell rang in the back just like before. Had the store always been this small? A punchboard rested on the back counter with a sign that said *Three Chances for a Dollar,* the prizes pictured like in a circus carnival. Her father would never have permitted gambling in his store. And who had brought in the cigarette rack?

"Look at you! Surprise, surprise!" Fritz emerged from the back, his crisp shirt and tie covered with a clean apron, his face crinkled in smiles. "Well don't just stand there! You're not a customer. Come in the back for coffee and a sweet roll. You been at school? Everything going good, Miss College Girl?"

"I should have come before. You're really so close to school." She looked around, feeling a surge of affection. "There's been a lot of changes."

"You don't know the half of it. We bought the empty lot next door. Next year we build. Better to own than to rent. Didn't your Papa always say that?"

Following him into the back, she sat on a stool, placing her books on the makeshift table. "You're planning to expand?"

"No, no. It will be the same but with an apartment upstairs so we don't have to run back and forth. We get tired of that."

"What about Aunt Martha? Is that okay with her?"

"George wants her at home. That's how it goes when you get married. So I'm buying her out. The landlord gonna put a liquor store in here so there's no competition." He sat back and folded his arms. "But first we gonna take a trip to the Old Country, just Katie and me."

It was after eight o'clock and there had been no customers since she'd arrived. She thought of Trudi and Erv, struggling to make ends meet, of herself slogging over snow and ice, delivering groceries for pennies, of her mother doing without. "Germany's not exactly a vacation spot, you know. It's really a wasteland…"

"I wanna see for myself. I need to see what's what. Katie does too."

"But everything's bombed out. There's nothing left. The papers are telling the truth, Uncle Fritz. Pictures don't lie."

"Truth or lie, it makes no difference. I'm talking about family, about Tante Alma and Guste, Onkel Helmut, Hilda, Elvira. I want to see for myself."

The sound of the front bell heralded a customer. Elsie started to get up then laughed as Fritz moved toward the front. "You can take the girl out of the store, but you can't…"

Fritz's return brought George who ducked past the dividing curtain, his white hair long enough to make him seem scholarly, his face a youthful tan. He was now Uncle George.

"Well hi there, Kiddo. You're looking good. College agrees with you. How're things?" His head moved around distractedly. "I just dropped in to pick up a few things. Martha's out in the car, waiting. Why don't you go say Hello?" He began rummaging through an assortment of boxes, muttering as he felt through the disarray.

"She's here? Wonderful! I'd been hoping…" Excited, Elsie hurried out toward a black car with its engine running, the shadow of Martha in the front passenger seat. As she approached, Martha looked up surprised, then motioned her into the back. "What a nice surprise! Long time no see."

Elsie sat down and shut the door. "I know! Oh gosh, I've been thinking of you so much. Uncle Fritz says you're not going to be in the store any more. But you're so good at schmoozing customers, building up the business. When did all this happen?"

Martha's voice was muffled by the hum of the engine. "I just had a miscarriage, Elsie. Five months along – a baby girl." She took a deep breath. "We had a funeral because George is Catholic. Her grave is next to his mother's."

Elsie sat back, stunned. "A baby! Oh my God. I didn't know."

"It was our last chance…"

George's return came with a rush of cool air. "Fritz couldn't find it, Honey. He said Katie would know. You should call her tomorrow or maybe when we get home." He looked toward Elsie, suddenly aware she was there. "We were in the neighborhood and stopped to pick up a couple of sweaters Martha left behind. But we do have to go. Can we drop you off somewhere?"

"Aunt Martha just told me about the baby," Elsie stammered. "I'm so sorry. I didn't know."

"Well, we can't always get what we want, can we? The baby's in heaven with Jesus, and that's a comfort, I suppose."

Elsie fumbled for the door. "I really should stay and visit with Uncle Fritz a little more. My books are in the store. Oh gosh, I'm so sorry…" Her leg scraped as she got out, leaving a scratch she would find when she got home.

"I know that comes from your heart, Honey. Just remember us in your prayers."

The car pulled away from the curb as Elsie stood watching for a long moment before she went back into the store, her eyes smarting under the lights that suddenly seemed too bright.

CHAPTER 32

Germany, 1947

THERE HAD BEEN LETTERS FROM Rainer, loving, hopeful, reassuring. Yes, he was fine, working on a farm, something allowed under the Geneva Convention. He was allowed to eat half a chicken with fresh vegetables from the field along with potatoes and gravy, all in just one meal. The sun was warm and the guards were friendly and kind. He'd gained so much weight that he couldn't button his pants.

Hilda replied, saying that all was well. Peter had started Volkschule and was a bright, sunny little boy, respectful and devout. They were safe, the war having skirted the borders of Bad Oeynhausen. They slept well and had made many friends. Yes, they were crowded. Yes, the food was monotonous, but all things considered…

Then the war ended and the letters stopped. People said it had something to do with the concentration camps. Death Camps. That's what they were called. Hilda had heard it mentioned from time to time, but paid little attention. After all, every country has prisons with police serving as monitors, didn't they? Then Palavia, a friend from Wanne Eichel visited from Poland, telling her the whole ugly story about Buchenwald.

That was shortly after the British had taken over Bad Oeynhausen, the beautiful Hotel Koenigshof now serving as headquarters. Private homes were confiscated, the residents given 24 hours to leave, their belongings burned or trashed, their rooms smeared with excrement that the owners were forced to clean up. Outside the central area, the population lived under prison-like restrictions. As winter settled in, it got worse, for along with the shortage of food, there was a shortage of fuel.

It was on such a day that Alma returned from the market, having stood in line for more than two hours in the freezing cold, the food from Ilse's farm having vanished long ago.

"Frau Bilder and her daughter were behind me in line. They'd heard about a fortuneteller on Goethe Street and paid her a visit." She set a package of flour and three onions on the table, the most she was able to buy.

Hilda looked up from her mending. "It's all baloney, Mutti. If God wanted us to see into the future, He'd show us where to buy bread and tell us how long this winter would last." She snapped the thread between her teeth and turned the shirt to the other side. "So what did she say?"

"Frau Bilder's Heinz was captured about the same time as Rainer. They got no letters for more than a year. So she asked if he was alive or dead."

"And?"

"The woman said she couldn't see Heinz coming home for a long time."

"Hah! I told you," Hilda snorted. "What is a long time supposed to mean?" She turned toward Peter, sitting on the floor. "And the next time I tell you to change your clothes, you better pay attention. I can't patch your pants when there's nothing left to hold the stitches."

Alma's face was grim. "We need more than shirts and shoes. We need to eat. You have to ask for a job, Hilda. Beg them if you have to…"

"Mutti, I told you many times. I want nothing to do with those monsters. Let them keep their damned jobs."

"We can't be proud, Hilda. Think of Peter."

"We get boxes from America and Frau Eichmeyer shares whenever she can. I trust her."

"The British want us to starve and die. They even said so out loud. I can tell you…"

Hilda covered her ears. "I will not be shamed, Mutti. We have done nothing wrong."

"They are cutting our soldier's allowance," Alma hissed. "And there's no more allotment for families. The Wehrmacht are now called captured enemies, not prisoners of war."

"We can trust the German government, not to…"

"There is no German government!"

It was another few weeks of shivering in the cold, of everyone being hungry, before Hilda faced the sentry at the gate, her shoes covered with snow, her face buried in a collar that provided little warmth. Directed to a side office, she described her skills, listing ingredients and cooking processes. Clearly, she had been well trained. Within a week, she was hired to work in the kitchen, cooking for the non-coms.

It was hard to get through the first few days because she was so hungry. But she was a quick learner. A long coat could hide potatoes taken from the bin and tied around the waist. A chunk of meat retrieved from a scalding pot of soup could be hidden in a corner until quitting time. Never mind if mice or bugs had nibbled at it. Further cooking would kill the germs.

Then Helmut found a job in the boiler room of an ancient building, keeping the machinery running with cobbled-together parts. Surely their fortunes would continue.

Meanwhile, a stream of visitors arrived desperate for anything to eat, the cities suffering under rationing and price controls, stories so heart-rending that Alma would wrap up a few potatoes and drop some coffee into a bag, the Christian thing to do.

Guste came the most often, and on this autumn afternoon, there was more sharing, with Hilda walking back to the train with Guste, carrying a small box of flour, potatoes and dried beans for her to take home. Then a quick Lebewohl, as Guste disappeared into the crowd.

Back outside, Hilda gazed at the road before her. Impulsively, she turned toward Goethe Street and the house with a fortuneteller's sign, making an appointment for the following day after work. Frau Bilder and her daughter might be crazy, but no stone should be left unturned. It was followed by a restless night as she shifted between fear and prayer.

Rising at dawn, she tucked two photographs in her pocket, retrieved while her mother was asleep. The September leaves were turning color, the air crisp and cool. It would be a long day.

When her shift was finished, she hurried to Goethe Street, her heart pounding, her throat throbbing with fear. She looked through the window at the velvet-covered table, the small upholstered chair, then reached for the door. The foyer made her voice seem timid and strange. "Hallo? I am Hilda. I made an appointment..."

A reply emanated from inside a room, the door standing slightly ajar. "Come in. We talk in here."

She entered, the sounds muffled by pictures and soft fabrics.

Seated on a couch was a dark-haired woman dressed gypsy-like with bangles and beads that glistened under the nearby lamp.

Motioned forward, Hilda perched on the chair across from her. "My brother was in Berlin and my husband is a prisoner in America. We did not hear from them for so long…" she began. "The war does terrible things and records get lost, or maybe nobody reads them properly because the files are disorganized or lost. My uncle was killed in the other war and they thought it was my father but it wasn't, so I know that can happen." The words spilled forth, anxious and eager. "Some people say you have a gift, that you know things the government doesn't…"

The woman gestured impatiently. "Did you bring something of theirs like I said so I could make contact?"

Hilda handed the pictures to the woman. "They were taken a while ago. My brother was only seventeen but he was going to war so he had to be called a man because boys don't fight wars, and that's what I said to my mother who signed for him. The other is my husband. I'm the one sitting next to him. I always tried to be brave…"

Feeling along the picture's edge, the woman pressed each to her cheek, to her forehead, to her chin, her eyes closed.

Hilda leaned forward. "They both served in the Wehrmacht."

The woman passed one of the pictures over her lips, then taking a tiny bite from the corner, ran it over her tongue. "This one is on his way. You can expect him in three days."

Hilda stretched to see which picture she was holding. "And the other?" She could barely form the words.

The woman looked away. "He is dead." She handed back the pictures. "I'm sorry."

"He's dead? I come all this way, pay you my hard-earned money and that's all you can say?" Hilda could feel a chill as she ran her hands over her arms. "You need to tell me more. What makes you so sure?"

"I feel, I touch, I just know."

"But what do you do, what do you think? Do you pray? Do you hear voices? Tell me!"

"If you didn't want to believe me, you shouldn't have come. And now you have to go. Someone else will be here in just a few minutes."

Hilda's every muscle tightened. "Believe? That's supposed to be left for God!" She reached toward the woman, too angry to speak further, snatching the pictures and running all the way home. At the bottom of the stairs, she caught her breath and forced a smile before going up, gesturing apologetically as she entered the room.

"Papa is already here and waiting," Alma scowled. "I keep telling you to let me know when you will be late."

"I went to see the fortuneteller that Frau Bilder talked about. I didn't want to tell you because I had said it was a waste of money. Turns out it was."

Helmut had come from the other room, leaning against the doorway. "On Goethe Street? Ah, I heard about that old Schwindler. She only tells people what they want to hear. Yet she is making money…"

"She said that Rainer will be home in three days."

"See? I could have told you that for free. So how much did she charge you?"

"Papa's coming home?" Peter looked up from the table, his face radiant. "So we will have a nice house and a yard and lots to eat?"

"She's a fortuneteller, Peter. They make things up, just the way Opa says. I shouldn't have gone."

Alma face had turned pale. "Then what about Gunter?"

"I'm telling you, these old women…"

"What did she say, Hilda?"

"She said one was coming home. The other one is dead." Hilda pulled out a chair and sat down. "She probably told that story a dozen times to poor people like us, taking our money and proving nothing. I told you I was sorry. So let's not talk about it anymore." She bent over her plate, an end to the conversation.

Although Hilda's job had provided sustenance, the relief was temporary. Within a week, a new directive stationed inspectors at all the exits, the rampant stealing to be punished with dismissal or jail. Now amid the delectable smells and abundant food, hunger cried out from morning until night.

It was on such a day that Hilda came home, tired and weak, her stomach grinding with hunger. Never mind. She would go right to bed, leaving her pittance for Peter. Inside, Alma sat at the table, a bag of mending on her lap, Peter seated across from her, with Helmut a few feet away, having just come from work. Supper would consist of bread and watery coffee, for nothing had come from America in almost a month.

She turned to take off her jacket when the door swung back open. She had forgotten to lock it behind her.

Suddenly it was as though time had stopped, a camera's eye frozen with Alma's arms wrapped protectively around Peter, her mouth opened to form a scream. Helmut's face had gone chalky white. In the doorway a gangly presence hunched forward in a rumpled coat two sizes too big, his face pinched and creased with grime, his stringy hair down to the collar.

Spreading his arms, he broke into a broad smile. "I'm home!"

Hilda stared at the skeletal figure of Rainer, so altered she hardly recognized him. Night after night she had dreamed of his return. But never like this. Where was the proud posture, the firm chin, the glowing voice that sang Schubert Lieder? Was she supposed to kiss him, embrace him, this ragamuffin, this refuse from a once proud military corps?

The agony on Alma's face bespoke a different response. If the fortuneteller was right, then Gunter was dead.

"We have nothing to eat." Her sob summarized the moment.

His sunken cheeks swallowed the smile before she could retract the hurt. "That's all right. I brought something…" Reaching inside his coat, he withdrew a chunk of bread and some butter. "I saved it on the way back. …for you and the little one."

It was a scene that Hilda would remember for the rest of her life.

CHAPTER 33

Chicago, 1947-48

THEY WERE MOVING AGAIN, LEAVING the house on Kilbourn where she had the nicest room ever, where Herb had his own space on the third floor, where school and work were less than an hour away. Elsie didn't know why, but once more, she didn't ask. If they'd fallen on hard times, if they'd made some poor choices, it remained a mystery, something for her parents to solve or savor. Instead, she watched the movers load the truck then mounted her bike for the ride to Iowa Street, skimming past brick houses embellished with verandas, then rows of two- and three-flats standing slender and proud. She cut across the main roads, past department stores with their flashy displays, toward streets with small shops and saloons emanating the smell of beer, the sound of jukeboxes braying jazz, jarring memories of her former neighborhood nearly forgotten. Then to Leavitt Street, past the Baptist Church where the minister's daughter had been her best friend in second grade, past Columbus School and St. Mary Hospital with its blinking sign declaring Slow Danger.

Arriving, she circled the tiny fenced yard in the back to park the bike. Then to the entrance, scanning the buildings along the street neatly painted in various pastels, the addresses printed over the doors. A young woman emerged, her eyes questioning. "You the new owner? They said you'd be coming. I'm Dora. We live on the second floor."

Elsie looked her up and down, a young woman near her sister's age with hair pulled back into a matronly bun, her face and arms blotched from the sun. "My dad's coming with the movers," she replied. "Mom will be here a little later."

She entered through the front into the living room as Dora followed, eyeing the closet door and a space heater under the windows its cord coiled around the controls, at a hall leading to a bedroom on either side. A few feet beyond was the kitchen containing a sink, refrigerator and pot-bellied stove. A toilet rested in a room so small that the door had to open out. Beyond, an enclosed porch would serve as a third bedroom.

"I got two boys. They like the back yard, but we are moving soon. Your parents know that," Dora said.

Just then the moving truck lumbered up, and Dora sprinted upstairs. August was the first to get out, followed by a man that released the loading ramp.

Marichen arrived a half-hour later. By then the couch and two upholstered chairs had been brought in, the Philco placed in the middle of the front room, with assorted boxes and miscellany cluttered about. "You think it's gonna be all right?"

"Don't worry, Mom. Herb and I are never home anyway. We just need a place to sleep."

"It's like living in the old country."

Elsie calculated the added distance to work and school. Maybe she should look for another job.

By the time Herb arrived, they had finished unloading, leaving him to sort his records onto a set of makeshift shelves.

"Had you seen this place before?" Elsie whispered as her mother left the room.

Herb shook his head. "They never tell us anything. You know that."

"At least you'll be close to work."

"It's rent free, Kiddo. Don't knock it."

"I passed by the old place on Division Street. This is even worse."

He gestured impatiently. "Can't talk right now. Marilou said she might have an apartment lined up. We've got to find a place to live and the wedding is getting close."

His voice was hopeful, the housing shortage being real, with returning veterans snapping up whatever they could find, the landlords snatching the moment, filling apartments with every conceivable piece of junk, declaring it furnished in order to raise the rent, or tying the lease to the purchase of a worn sofa or sagging bed, clearly illegal but hard to prove.

"There'll be one available here. The woman upstairs is moving out."

"Very funny."

Marichen had come in from the kitchen. "You going out again? What're we supposed to do with all these boxes?"

"We've talked about buying. But only if we can't find something to rent. Wedding's only a few months off and we need to find a place pretty quick."

Elsie stared at her brother. His army allotment had been put aside as savings just for him. But he'd used some to buy Marilou's engagement ring. So how much could be left? "I'm going to unpack. Let me know if you need me."

In the end, there was no choice but for Herb and Marilou to cobble together a down payment for a large house that had been converted into four small apartments. They would live on the first floor rear, with the rental income paying most of the mortgage. With that out of the way, the wedding plans moved forward.

Immanuel Baptist was a small church with a long sanctuary separable by sliding doors at the back and a kitchen off to one side. It would be ideal for a wedding reception with food, coffee, and punch served by the Lady's Aid Society.

Herb contacted Joe, the pal with whom he'd shared the momentous announcement of the Pearl Harbor attack, the friend who'd taught him to drive on his Willys-Knight and even lent it to him once or twice. Joe would be delighted to serve as best man. Marion, a mentor from church would be Marilou's maid of honor with Elsie as one of the bridesmaids. Marilou's Uncle Randall would come to Chicago and give the bride away.

None of the details impacted Elsie who only worried about whether her gown would need to be altered and whether her hair would look right. She would also need a manicure. Red nail polish was no longer a sin.

Finally it was Friday, the day of the great event. Presents had been put on display. A hum of activity and good smells emanated from the church kitchen. By evening, the sunbeams would be dancing on the white tablecloths, offering a blessing from on high. Martha and George would be there as well as Katie and Fritz, along with the many friends from church. Elsie's boyfriend would not attend, it being his Army Reserve weekend in Wisconsin.

The sanctuary began to fill with relatives softly whispering, nodding and smiling at one another. Marichen was ushered up front as mother of the groom with August following. Then the mother of the bride, followed by Glenn. As the music swelled, the procession stood ready. One slide, two slide, three… Elsie, on the arm of a stranger in a black tux, someone whom she would never see again, followed by Edna, the second bridesmaid, on the other tux's arm. Long pause, followed by Marion all by herself. Then the familiar, Here comes the bride with Marilou and Uncle Randall moving forward to meet Joe, the reverend Ed McKearnan and Herb before the altar of God.

It was over in a half hour, the recessional joyous and proud with people spilling out toward the receiving line and buffet.

Suddenly there was a small commotion toward the back with Jim in his army uniform, having snuck out of bivouac to attend.

It was the first time he'd met Elsie's family. It took only a minute before Fritz and Martha claimed him as their own.

Fritz scanned the table. "What? No schnapps?" He nudged George and together they drew Jim into the bathroom for a nip from his hidden flask while Elsie shepherded Aunt Martha and Katie around, introducing them here and there as her parents stood off by themselves, looking vaguely uncomfortable.

Finally the newlyweds were ready to leave. By then, Marichen and August had gone home, and Jim was on his way back to camp. The bride and groom would spend the night at their new place on California Street, going to Wisconsin the following day for a short honeymoon. Ed McKearnan had lent them his car, a thoughtful gesture far beyond the duties of a minister and more than generous as a friend.

Elsie moved toward the back of the empty sanctuary as the Lady's Aid Society worked at cleaning up. It had been a busy month and she was scheduled to work the following day. A wedding was supposed to mark a beginning, but that wasn't true. Herb was barely back home and now he was gone. Oh, she liked Marilou and sympathized with all that she'd gone through, much of it too familiar to be remarkable. But she'd wanted to talk to Herb a lot more, asking about the army, about why he wanted to be a lawyer and whether he believed in God after all. She wanted to thank him for taking her to the museums and the library, for taking her inside the streetcar barn to warm up before continuing on to school, for being there when her cat was struck by a car, sending her back to school so she wouldn't see the cat die. He'd given her money for movies when movies were still a sin and played Beethoven and Brahms on the Philco until their melodies became familiar. There was college and the back and forth at Tony's Pizzeria, with lessons in learning how to think. Surely he'd had his own yearnings as well.

In a few weeks, her parents would celebrate their twenty-fifth anniversary. She tried to imagine them as young lovers. Did they have a wedding? Did her father look all melty-eyed and sentimental like Herb did when he was with Marilou, or was he always angry and sour? Had Mom always deferred? Had Dad always said little but received much?

She sighed as she boxed up her gown. She had decided long ago that she would never marry. Education would save her. She would be her own person like Aunt Martha or Katharine Hepburn, a woman who belonged to herself. And if Jim didn't like it, too bad for him. Or maybe not...

Getting on the bus, she pressed her face against the window, watching the lights inside the department stores. One more transfer and she'd be home.

CHAPTER 34

Germany, 1948

THEY HAD MOVED TO BAD Oeynhausen under a government mandate. But Alma and Helmut were not part of the package, hence, never reported. Now that Rainer had returned they were five, crowding into two small rooms with little hope of finding something else, for the British had commandeered anything larger than an outhouse.

"The boiler room is warm and quiet," Helmut offered. "I can bring in a straw mattress and sleep there, stashing it behind the pipes during the day. Nobody will see." His eyes shifted to Alma. "It makes no difference anyway."

"I should be the one taking care of you," Reiner protested. "I am the man…"

"You are still not well," Hilda declared. "If you get a chill…"

Alma surveyed the table pushed against the wall, the narrow cot, the boxes serving as cabinets with dishes, pots and pans crammed to the very edge. The tiny bedroom was even more crowded. Clearly, something had to be done. "We have to make do when we have no other choice. I could still cook, iron, clean like always," she offered. "It would be just for now."

And so the new routine was established, with supper together then dispersing for the night. Rainer told them about Cherbourg, about how his machine gun battery was overrun by coastal bombardment, of hovering next to shattered walls for protection. He told of the crossing to America with prisoners allowed on deck for an hour, of rampant seasickness and U-boat attacks despite being clearly marked as a POW transport. Then the ride on a plush passenger train and his introduction to life in the United States.

Opened in the summer of 1942, the prison camp at Aliceville was already established with a movie theater, prisoners' orchestra and choir as well as a weekly newspaper called Der Zaungast. Classes in philosophy, chemistry and English were taught by conscripted scholars, their schooling having been interrupted by the war. There were soccer fields and a greenhouse to beautify the camp. By the time Rainer arrived, the hardened Nazis had been separated out making it safe.

Six thousand prisoners of war were filling a labor shortage in America's Deep South, harvesting peanuts or working at a sawmill for eighty cents per day, paid with chits exchanged at the PX. Food was equal to that of American soldiers, something mandated by the Geneva Convention, and Rainer gained so much weight that his clothes barely fit. Leisure time enabled him to carve a chess set out of yellow pine with a fitted box to house them. It was something he guarded throughout his ordeal, displayed with gentle pride when he returned.

All this changed when Germany surrendered. For the Allies, Germany no longer existed, the Swiss legation no longer required. Food rations were cut in half and then cut again. Recreation and cultural activities were limited, then curtailed, with all mail suspended. *Der Zaungast* ceased publication. Prisoners were treated as conscripts rather than volunteers. Retribution was the order of the day with little medical care for the growing malnutrition. Thousands would be reclaimed by England and France, worked at repairing the damage of a lingering war.

But after his return, the British rules softened, fearful of an uprising and embrace of the Communist strength. Rainer was hired as a janitor, then as a landscaper on the estates commandeered by the British. By spring, the little family was able to move into two rooms of their very own. Lying in the arms of her husband, it wasn't long before Hilda was pregnant.

Spring always heralds hope and a new beginning. This year's Easter would be festive, with Guste's family coming in for the day, the family gathered at Hilda's new flat.

Dressed in their finest, the women donned aprons and chatted as they bustled about the kitchen before the blessing and sharing of food. Guste talked about the pastor's sermon at the Gemeinschaft. Ursula announced that she had a seat of her very own on the train, while Peter declared that he'd taken the train lots of times even though he hadn't.

"I wasn't sure everything would taste right," Hilda began, moving away from the stove. "I don't have much appetite these days."

"You can't be too careful," Siebold declared. "With all the shortage, people will put anything in their stomachs, then pretty soon, they're sick." He turned toward Alma, whose lips were working into a sly smile. Suddenly aware, he looked away, his face flushing crimson red. "Oh I see. This is woman's business."

"Well, I think that's just fine," Guste declared. "And what better day to celebrate?" She winked at Hilda. "We talk later."

"It will be in October," Hilda offered. "We are happy. Really."

Everyone nodded politely. "It will be all right."

"You still have your job."

"Oma is here to help."

"But we have our own good news," Elvira interrupted, barely able to contain herself. "I'm getting married. His name is Renaldo and…"

"Married? But where…?" Alma gasped.

Guste laughed. "That is how it is today with young people. American soldiers buzz around Elvira like flies to honey, and the Germans wanting a girl who can cook."

"…and be friendly," Siebold added dryly.

"He is a good man," Guste insisted. "He looks like a wrestler, thick and strong but quick. The family is from Italy or the Balkans so he has a lot of dark hair and a ruddy complexion."

"And eighty thousand marks in the bank," Elvira added.

Hilda stared at her cousin, so round and ripe though barely eighteen, clearly ready for marriage. If it included love, so much the better. But this was still news.

"All of you have to come," Elvira continued. "Afterward we celebrate at home – I mean at Mutti and Papa's place.

The wedding would be at the end of May, allowing six weeks to deal with the bureaucratic maze. First, the official notice and proof of citizenship plus a series of forms to send to the registrar's office including the bride and groom's names, ages, birth dates, birthplaces, residences, occupations, and whether single or widowed. Another form would list the parents' names, residence, occupations and marital status. Witnesses' names, ages, and relationships to the bride or groom were required along with identity of the person giving permission for the marriage.

Once the papers were in order, there would be a simple ceremony at the registrar's office followed by festivities at the home of the bride. "Tante Martha is sending a dress, something nice and fancy," Elvira declared. "Americans know how to do things right."

"May your husband be good as my own Rainer," Hilda murmured. "And may there never be another war."

Now everything focused on the big event. Hilda borrowed a loose-fitting sheath from a neighbor to wear during the ceremony. She and Alma would take an early train to help prepare.

Elvira greeted them with her hair rolled in curlers, her face shiny with lotion and sweat. The room was lined with borrowed chairs, the kitchen stacked with assorted plates and cups. American chocolate and cigarettes from CARE packages had bought extra cheese, potato salad, herring and bread. There was coffee and cake from the black market. "You can help with the wedding soup. I already added the peas to the broth. Dumplings are almost ready to mix in."

"But first, the dress!" Guste cried, clapping her hands.

It was hanging on the bedroom curtain rod, yards of blue chiffon, the tight bodice ruffled along the edge, the shoulder-length veil adorned with tiny embroidered flowers. "It came last week and it fits perfectly."

"Renaldo rented a suit with white tie, gloves and a top hat," Elvira giggled. "Papa rented a top hat too. He says it makes him look like an undertaker. Ursula's yellow dress will make her looks like a flower. Oh, this is going to be so fine!"

Hilda scanned the room. "Is this where we sleep overnight?"

"No. You will use Frau Wiedermeyer's flat downstairs. She leaves right after the wedding to visit family in Dortmund. I told her about the trains not running so late and she said you could stay there. Renaldo and Elvira will stay here and go to their new flat in the morning. Ursula comes in the bedroom with us."

"And maybe I could take a nap? You know how it is…"

"Oh yes, the sleepy months. I remember," Guste laughed. "Just go downstairs and knock on Frau Wiedermeyer's door. I told her you are coming."

By early afternoon, the preparations were complete. Ursula was dressed. The women had finished primping the bride, combing her hair and applying a touch of color to her cheeks, smoothing the bodice of the dress.

Renaldo arrived at half-past two, the rest of the family at three. It would be a short walk to the Community House followed by snapshots taken out of doors. Then back to the flat for a festive celebration.

All brides are beautiful and clothes make the man. Arms linked, Elvira and Renaldo climbed the marble steps into the hushed interior of officialdom. They paused at the desk and after a brief wait, were motioned into the wedding chapel, a room of paintings, nymphs, and an arbor of artificial flowers where the registrar would formalize the event.

Soft music came from some hidden spot as the family crossed the carpeted floor, seating themselves on tiny velour chairs, Alma and Hilda with Peter beside her, Siebold, Guste and Renaldo's mother on the front row, Helmut and Rainer behind.

Soft voices instructed the bride and groom where to stand. Then more words. *Are you both free and willing to marry?* to which they replied, *We are.* Then the bride and groom transferring their rings from left hand to right. Bending down, Renaldo turned to Elvira and kissed her on the cheek. They were now man and wife.

Outside, the photographer stood ready to pose the family as the sun began to fade.

"The neighbors will be waiting at the flat," Alma whispered, motioning to her sister. "I can go back while you finish up here."

Guste nodded, handing her the key.

By the time they returned, the room was warmed with activity. Renaldo doffed his jacket and tie, and someone began humming a song as he danced with Elvira in the middle of the room. Platters of food were filled, then re-filled, the noise level rising with each new cry of *Prost*. Then as evening fell, the cake, followed by a toast to the newlyweds. The wedding celebration was over. Visitors began drifting off with hearty handshakes and cries of best wishes. Finally it was only the family, the men capping off the last of the wine as Hilda struggled to stay awake.

"I think it went well," Guste declared, leaning back in her chair.

"And better with all the tomorrows to come," Renaldo murmured, stroking Elvira's hand.

"We can put the food away and finish in the morning." Guste turned to Hilda. "Where did you put the key?"

"You gave it to Mutti," Hilda replied, rousing herself.

"I mean Frau Wiedermeyer's key. She said she would give it to you when you came to take a nap."

"She only showed me the bedroom then walked away," Hilda stammered. "She was gone when I awoke, so I just closed the door and came back upstairs."

"Liebe Gott!" Guste turned frantically to Siebold. "Go downstairs and see if they're still there."

"You should have said something," Hilda cried, her chin quivering. "How was I supposed to know?"

"No, no, it's just a mistake. Siebold will find out." Guste opened the door, staring into the dark, waiting for Siebold's returning footsteps.

He returned, out of breath. "The door is locked and no one answered when I knocked."

Guste turned to Alma. "Are you sure the trains have stopped? Maybe you can still…"

"We studied the schedule together," Alma replied. "Don't you remember?"

"What is done, is done." Helmut said firmly. He peered into the next room. "We have two rooms and two beds. Maybe we can sleep crossways."

"For ten people? Are you crazy?"

"Women and children on the beds. Men on the floor." Guste commanded, now fully in charge. "There are some extra pillows in the closet. We'll just have to make do."

It was a sleepless night. Early morning saw Elvira and Renaldo gathering their things to leave. The others grabbed leftovers, munching on whatever could be found as they went back to work.

Alma stayed behind to help with the cleanup. By noon, it was done, the sisters too exhausted to be angry. The wedding had been festive and well attended. Elvira and Renaldo were about to begin a new life. Hilda would soon be bringing a new life into the world. In the final analysis, they had survived. That's all that mattered.

CHAPTER 35

Chicago, 1948-49

THE SILVER ANNIVERSARY WAS A simple gathering. Marichen had prepared a traditional meal and bought a cake for dessert, a sheet of plywood enlarging the small table to seat all seven. Herb and Marilou were there, adjusting to their role as husband and wife, Trudi and Erv resplendent in a new car, Elsie primped in a suit and high heels bought with an employee's discount at her new job at Wieboldt's.

Chicago could be beautiful in September and dinner was tasty. They talked about the weather, politics, the Truman Doctrine, the Marshall Plan, and Herb's entering Law School. After clearing the dishes, they went outside to admire Marichen's tomato plants and the last of the marigolds. Erv took pictures – first the women, then sisters plus sister-in-law, husband and wife, married pairs, men alone… Then as the sun began to fade, it was back inside for coffee, cake and more conversation.

The evening ended early with Monday being a work day, leaving August and Marichen alone as they reflected on the past.

"Twenty-five years, August. I never thought it would go so fast. Trudi and Herbert married, the house almost empty..."

"We could have been millionaires, Marichen. But Fritz was never a hard worker and Otto was no good once Sophie came over. Then Rudy died and everything went *kaput*."

"'Lisbet got the best and so did Fritz..."

"Nickel-dime business with punchboard and a gumball machine," August grumbled. He brushed past the pot-bellied stove, going into the bedroom to change his clothes. "We should get rid of this place before winter," he muttered. "With upstairs and downstairs empty, it should sell in a hurry. Herbert said his basement flat will be empty next month. The rent is cheap. We could move there and start saving again."

Marichen sat quietly for a long moment, mulling it over. "We could open a little business, just you and me," she said finally. "I'm tired of sitting around doing nothing. You too?"

"Something small, not so many hours..."

And so once more, there was a move, turning the house over to a realtor who ultimately sold it at a loss.

Their new flat was one room with a Pullman kitchen and small bathroom with a shower that drained into an opening in the middle of the floor, the entryway large enough to serve as Elsie's room. Given where they had been, it was a step up.

August and Marichen opened a diner serving breakfast and lunch to factory workers along Elston Avenue. Up at five, they'd walk the half-mile to work, finished by late afternoon with weekends off. By keeping prices low, they developed a regular clientele and earned a small profit.

Elsie shifted jobs to the telephone company, working nights, going to school days, seeing her boyfriend whenever there was time.

Then came the event that sent August into another paroxysm of rage. Marichen couldn't even remember what the quarrel was about. Maybe it had to do with Elsie coming home at all hours, or being too much with her Jimmy boy. Maybe it was the continued fight over Elsie's smoking, or maybe because Elsie was planning to join Marilou's church, without so much as a *By the way...*

It was another Sunday and they were at the kitchen table finishing lunch. "Elsie is being baptized next Sunday," Marichen began. "She wants us to come."

"What do you mean, baptized?" August demanded, looking up from his plate. "Elsie is already baptized."

"That's the way you join in Marilou's church. It's like Jesus in the River Jordan. They have something under the altar like a little swimming pool. The pastor takes you down the steps and holds your nose while you go under."

"So God is supposed to take her twice, like the first time wasn't good enough?"

"I know, I know. She always thinks she knows more than anyone."

August looked down at his plate, his mouth grim.

"Smoking, always running after her friends, out late at night," Marichen continued. "Now this."

"Well I don't go, and you don't go either. You hear?"

"She always has to argue. Elsie's the worst but it's Herbert and Marilou too. A little college and they think…"

"I'm just telling you. We stay home."

Marichen's voice was more sad than angry. "I don't wanna see it either."

And so on this ordinary Sunday, Elsie came home with her hair frizzed, her clothes still damp after changing too quickly from the baptismal gown. She and Jimmy had lingered over lunch at a favorite restaurant, then gone their separate ways. Ducking her head into her parents' room, she announced, "I'm home," then closed the door, knowing there would be no response.

Meanwhile, Elsie and Jim continued their courtship in coffee shops or over an after-movie nightcap. She met Jim's family, enchanted by his sister and aunts who worked in corporate or government offices and were savvy about restaurants, makeup and the latest movies. Sometimes they'd visit Martha and Fritz or have dinner with Jim's mother in a cheerful setting. And when the pall of silence lay too heavily upon her, Elsie would go upstairs to be with Herb and Marilou for a breath of fresh air.

It was on such a visit that Herb mentioned that the attic flat was going to be available. "Lolly was looking to move in but she needs a roommate. What do you think?"

It took a few minutes to register. "You mean me? It never occurred…"

"You remember Lolly from church, don't you? If you could manage it…"

Lolly and Marilou had grown up next door to one another. Daughter of a physician and herself an RN, Lolly was blessed with a jolly personality and an earthy sense of humor. Deeply religious, she had given herself to God to become a missionary at some future date. Handsome rather than pretty, she wore little makeup and dressed for comfort. "You mean living on my own with a date actually coming in for a cup of coffee or a drink? Or coming over to sit around and talk, or even laughing out loud? You mean living normal, like everyone else?" She took a deep breath, dizzy with the prospect. "Do you think the folks would go along with it?"

His expression said it had already been arranged.

They signed the lease a month later, splitting expenses down the middle. It was a simple task to carry her belongings up two flights of stairs to their tiny attic space. She had purchased a set of bunk beds a few years before, immersed in a fantasy that she could invite a friend to sleep over, all the while knowing it would be impossible. It had been bought with the wages from Creamland, probably the final blow that forced Trudy to sell the business. Lolly's mother provided the kitchen set and together they bought a 9x12 shag rug from Sears. With tables and lamps from here and there, it was enough to furnish their small apartment.

Now there were evenings with Jimmy and friends, eating popcorn and drinking beer or Coke, philosophizing or just having fun. Elsie might be ironing, Lolly baking cookies in the kitchen, both chatting over their shoulders as they finished their chores. With opposing schedules, they could easily move around one another. All this, while Elsie was carrying a full load at school.

Then came a Saturday morning when Elsie and Lolly were still asleep, a pounding on the door followed by a loud voice. "Open up! We need to talk."

Startled, Elsie threw on her robe and stumbled to the door, flinging it open just as Herb was reaching with his master key. "What's wrong? What happened?"

He was dressed in rumpled shorts and tee shirt, his hair uncombed, his voice grating. "What time did you get in last night?"

"About nine. Why? Was there an accident? Is somebody sick?"

"And when did Jim leave?"

"Right after Lolly got home. She was working three to eleven. We talked a little and then he left – about midnight."

"That's what I thought. Just you two up here alone. I won't allow it. You are my sister and I am responsible."

"What are you talking about? How dare you imply…"

"There is a certain decorum expected of young unmarried women. As your landlord, I have the responsibility to set the standards. You do not entertain young men up here alone especially with the door shut. And if you don't like it, I will take the door off the hinges. See if you like that better."

"Good grief, what's gotten into you? Have you lost your mind?"

"This is my place. I set the standards."

She felt her throat tighten. "Lolly and I have signed a lease. We're two adults. You said so yourself." Her voice was getting louder. "Who made you God?"

"Shouting won't change a thing. You have always been headstrong and I for one will have none of it. Just remember what I said." Turning, he stormed back down the steps leaving the door ajar.

Lolly stood at the kitchen door, her face creased with sleep. "What happened? Is everything all right? What did Herb want?"

Elsie sank into a chair, burying her face in her hands, too shaken to cry. "You met my dad. Now Herb is behaving just like him. He used to be so sweet, so different..." She looked up, her face woebegone. "It must be in the blood."

"He's a good big brother," Lolly soothed, stroking Elsie's back, "and you should be grateful. It's hard to see your little sister grow up. Just wait until tomorrow. It'll be all right."

"I'm so embarrassed..."

"He'll get over it. Wait and see."

"Not because of him – in front of you."

"Well, you have to admit that appearances..."

"That's just what I mean."

Herb's anger was eventually mollified but the shame lingered on.

Soon she and Jim started talking seriously. She was eighteen, he past twenty-one. They wanted to spend the rest of their lives together. Why wait?

They chose December 26th when families would be in for the holidays, a candlelight wedding with Christmas decorations on display, living with Jim's mother until they found a place of their own. Elsie would finish the semester then work full-time until Jim's graduation. After that, it would be her turn.

Vita's mother, a professional seamstress, made her a cocktail-length dress in heavy white nylon. Edith Lang, one of Mrs. Gross' students who was now singing in grand opera, would provide the music.

The next step would be more complicated, that of talking to her parents. She decided to approach her mother first. The opportunity came when she caught sight of her mother on the way to the Laundromat. Throwing on a coat, she followed, arriving just as Marichen finished loading the machines. The place was not very busy, but noisy enough to cover a private conversation.

"I was out for a walk and happened to see you," Elsie lied. "It's been a while." She reached for the chair next to her mother. "Herb tells me that your new place is going well. I'd like to stop in if that's okay."

Her mother's expression turned from surprise to serious. "I'm always glad to see you, Elsie. Just don't come when we're busy. You know how that is."

"Maybe for a cup of coffee in the afternoon." Elsie paused, waiting for her heart to stop pounding before taking a deep breath. "Has Herb said anything to you? I mean, about Jimmy and me?"

"You mean about getting married?"

Elsie nodded.

"Because he didn't come talk to Daddy first? You think your Jimmy is so smart but he doesn't know what's the right way?"

Elsie's laugh was more nervous that amused. "Mom, people don't do that anymore. Jimmy and I are adults. We don't need your permission. And anyway, Dad never came out from behind his newspaper. He probably wouldn't recognize Jimmy if he bumped into him on the street."

Marichen's eyes were fixed on the washer spinning a rinse cycle. "Don't do it, Elsie. You're too young. Wait a year or two. Finish school. Follow your plan and be by yourself for a while. Once you finish school, there will be plenty of others. Jimmy's a jerk. He's gonna beat you when he don't get his way. I know his kind. Like Uncle Wally. They're all the same."

"You just don't know him, Mom. I've never been with anyone so gentle, so sweet…"

"You think you know everything. Well, just remember what I said. You're going to marry a bum, supporting him for the rest of your life."

"That's it? You think it's all about money? You don't wish us well? You're not glad that I'm happy, that I found someone? That I'm in love?"

"You are too young to know what you want. Next month you'll change your mind like you always do. Like always changing jobs." Her voice turned to pleading. "Give it some time, Elsie. Just wait a little – a year or even a few months. Something can happen, something around the corner…"

Elsie sat for a long moment, her face screwed up like a child holding back tears. "It'll be the day after Christmas at the church, Mom. I hope you and Dad will come. But whether you do or not, it's going to happen."

On her own, Elsie began to put plans into place. The library provided books and magazines that helped, while friends offered a few tips here and there. By mid-October, she was on her way.

Herb offered grudging congratulations. Marilou, newly pregnant, declined to serve in the wedding party. "With a brand new baby…"

Trudi also declined. "You know what it's like to cross the Old Man..."

Elsie understood. She really did. So Vita would be her Matron of Honor and only attendant. She would walk down the aisle alone.

The day after Christmas was a Sunday, the wedding scheduled for four-thirty. Invitations had gone out and thank you letters sent, one for a pair of lamps from Otto and Sophie included with a note conveying their regrets. Eleanor and 'Lisbet did not respond. Fritz and Katie sent a floor-standing ashtray with a pearl handle similar to the one Elsie and Jim had foolishly admired. Martha and George sent sterling salt and pepper shakers and Vita and her mother hosted a bridal shower with gifts of linen and household items, all packed away for future use. Their wedding reception would be at the Oak Park Arms at six.

Morning dawned clear and cold with a thin layer of ice covering everything. Elsie walked to church alone, sitting next to Jim despite the tradition that banned seeing one another on the day of the wedding.

Back in her apartment, she tried to take a nap but failing that, soaked in the tub. At three forty-five, Vita arrived, her husband waiting in the car while they did the final check of gown and makeup.

The sun was going down when they arrived, the Christmas tree providing a silvery glow and scent of pine. Edith was there with an armload of music, conferring with the organist at the front of the sanctuary. Bob and Jules Spiegel, Jim's high school pals, served as ushers at the outer door. Jim would be driving in with Ray Melone, the best man, and his family.

At four fifteen Elsie began to pace. Jim was supposed to have arrived at four o'clock.

At four thirty-five the sanctuary was full and people began

looking around. Edith handed the organist some music, and they filled in the time. Another fifteen minutes and Edith was halfway through her repertoire. Still no Jim. In between, Lolly scurried back with whispered reports, first that Elsie's parents had arrived and had been ushered to the front, then that Ray's car had been in an accident, with Ray's sister taken to the hospital, the message received at the parsonage and brought over by one of the children. Jim would be taking a cab to the church, the rest remaining at the hospital.

He arrived at five thirty. Bob Spiegel would fill in as best man.

The rest of the ceremony was seen through a haze, walking to the altar, hearing words, prayers and more music. Finally the kiss that said they were man and wife.

Surrounded by well-wishers, Elsie caught sight of her mother and father hurrying toward the exit. Then just before reaching the door, her mother turned, cutting into the receiving line to thrust a small package into her hand. "Daddy wants you to have this," she whispered, after which they disappeared into the cold.

It was past midnight before Elsie thought about the package again. By then they were in Madison, Wisconsin to spend their honeymoon in Jim's Aunt's apartment while she visited her sisters in Chicago.

Retrieving it from her suitcase, she carried it to the bed and began to open it. "I can't imagine..."

"If it's a sermon, just put it aside," he said reassuringly.

With trembling fingers, she tore at the wrapping, pulling out a small white box. Inside was a Hallmark card with no notation or signature. Puzzled, she turning the box upside down and in the dim light watched ten one hundred dollar bills flutter like butterflies onto the sheets.

CHAPTER 36

Germany, 1949-50

IT WASN'T FAIR. NO SOONER had they gotten a few pennies ahead when they were faced with another disaster. This time it was the devalued Reich mark, now worthless. In its place, everyone would be allocated forty Deutsche marks. Start over, they said. Throw the old money away. Burn it. Feed it to the goats.

Looking around the room, Hilda pictured what might have been. If only they'd been warned.

Her musings were interrupted by Peter. "Baby Karl is awake. Do I pick him up?"

She moved toward the bedroom. "I do it. Papa will be home pretty soon. Then we go to Oma's for supper."

"I wanted to go with, but Papa said no."

"He goes to his *Singverein* on Sundays. That's no place for you." She went toward the bed and lifting Karl, carried him into the bathroom and onto the toilet. "Do it for Mutti," she murmured as she rubbed his back, her words rewarded by a reassuring tinkle.

"Baby did good boy," she declared as Karl trotted forth, eager to see what his big brother was doing. Weekends were for family but Sundays were never long enough. She was grateful to have Rainer back, though getting re-acquainted was hard after so many years of separation.

The noise from the other room interrupted her reverie. Although seven years apart, the boys still managed to roll around on the floor like a pair of puppies. At first Peter had held back, watching the fuss made over the bright-eyed towhead. But pretty soon he was charmed by the baby's smiles, as was everyone else. They were clearly brothers.

"We need to take sweaters because Oma likes it cool inside," she called over her shoulder.

Just then Rainer arrived, snatching Karl up and swinging him toward the ceiling, as the baby squealed with delight.

"You're playing with danger," Hilda admonished. "Better I get him dressed first."

"This has been such a fine day," Rainer murmured, handing the little boy to Hilda. "I tell you, no one can be sad or weary after singing."

"We sing in school," Peter declared, "and I sing the best. Fraulein Weiss says if I study hard, I could go on to Hauptschule or even the Gymnasium."

"You will have chances we never had," Hilda agreed. "Things are changing. At least some good has come from all the suffering."

Rainer glanced at the bed. "Maybe I have time for a nap…"

"Oh no! We're already late and I still have to get dressed," Hilda cried.

"I know. I was just making fun. Don't be falsch."

"Better you take your fun outside with the boys so I can get dressed." She reached for the clothes laid out on the bed for the squirming Karl. "And be sure to keep them out of the dirt."

Rainer winked at Peter. "Mutti is böse. She needs to do more singing."

"Just give me twenty minutes."

"Twenty minutes? Someone so beautiful should take only five."

"Papa makes jokes," Hilda muttered, looking at Peter. "When I need an extra pair of hands, your papa makes a joke."

They left for Alma and Helmut's flat by late afternoon. Swinging Karl onto his shoulders, Rainer led the way with Hilda and Peter walking behind.

Her parents had moved to a one room unit behind a construction supply house, the main building separated from a storage shed by a wide stretch of gravel. There was no green space or play area for the children, but the landlord was a decent sort, making sure the area was clean, knowing that Alma kept things quiet despite Karl being there during the day. And the rent was reasonable, all things considered.

They arrived to see Alma moving from stove to the table, back to the stove to turn over the fried potatoes, then back to the table again. She was clearly agitated.

"Karl slept a little longer and I couldn't bring myself to wake him," Hilda apologized. "Sorry we're late."

"No, it's not you. It's what Papa brought in from yesterday's post. I don't know if I should laugh or cry." She handed an envelope to Hilda. "They're coming to visit. What are we going to do with them? Where can they stay?"

Hilda glanced at the post. "Onkel Fritz is coming to Oeynhausen?"

Alma nodded. "Where will we put them? There's no room."

Helmut's eyes were on the food simmering on the stove. "Can we talk about that later? Supper is already done."

"We know what counts around here," Rainer laughed, moving to settle the boys at the table.

"They'll be here in April. That is less than six months from now," Alma cried. "Where will we put them? There are no rooms even if we had the money. And we don't."

"Never mind. Something will turn up. It always does."

But there was no letup in the Occupation and contact with neighbors and friends produced nothing.

Now it was the first of March and Helmut was on his way to the front office to pay the rent, something he had done every month for almost a year. He passed the storage building, about the size of a fire-house, its barn-like interior jammed with wooden doors, windows, and sheets of lumber. It had a second level with a pitched roof and two windows with narrow door, its stairway making it look like a whiskered chin on a cartoon face. A sudden thought crossed his mind. Might there be living space upstairs? Might Herr Meyer be interested in renting it? Was it livable?

He entered the front office to find out.

"Living space? For what? Pigeons?" Meyer laughed. Then he paused. "Actually, someone did keep pigeons there. We don't use it because of the steps."

"We have family coming from America with no place to stay. Could we maybe take a look?"

"You're serious?" Meyer shook his head, then shrugged. "Why not? If I can find the key..."

The stairs were filthy but sturdy. Inside, the room reeked of pigeon droppings, the windows layered with dust. But the roof and walls were intact, the floor solid. "It needs to be cleaned up," Helmut ventured. "But a little elbow grease could make it nice. It could be rented out afterward. Housing is dear."

"When are they coming? Are they clean and quiet?" Meyer's

questions amounted to assent. After brief negotiations, he agreed to consider the cleanup as payment for Fritz's stay.

The women went to work, washing the walls and dusting the rafters, scrubbing the floorboards three times before making the smooth sanded lumber visible, polishing the windows to get rid of the grime. Then outside to scrub the stairs in the budding spring air. A friend lent them a bed. Herr Meyer found a chest, table and some chairs in the storeroom, supplies garnered from buildings being rehabilitated. It was a transformation and when finished, everyone stood back, amazed. "We did good," Alma murmured. "No one would have guessed."

Fritz and Kate arrived a week later, their first stop before going on to Wanne Eichel. They arrived like potentates, Kate's pudgy ankles wrapped in nylon stockings, Fritz's moustache carefully trimmed.

Rainer and Helmut were there to welcome them, their assortment of luggage carried to the loft. "You know about the British occupation," Helmut panted, pausing to catch his breath. "…about the housing, the barbed wire, the restrictions. This was the best we could do."

"We saw already from the train," Kate nodded. "Houses, and shops, the roads so full of rubble…"

"Like in the first war, only worse. Back then, we didn't have all that machinery. Not until the end." Fritz paused. "But you are here in Oeynhausen. Is not so bad."

"Most of our troubles are hidden. We show you later. Right now, the women make us lunch. After that, we can go for a walk."

They moved to the tiny flat in the back of the main building. Hilda has splurged, buying bread and lunchmeat with cucumbers and potato salad to make the meal special while the children sat transfixed at the abundance.

"I see you still eat good," Fritz observed, shifting his chair closer to the table.

"Your coming has made it special," Alma smiled. "But a good cook can turn a simple dish into a banquet. Hilda is well trained."

"So is Kate. She worked in rich households so she knows about fine quality – Persian carpets, silver tea sets… Our house is full of fine things."

The room was silent. "We do our best…" Helmut murmured at last. "It has not been easy." He forced a smile. "But tell us more. How are you doing?"

Fritz lifted his chest. "Business is good. Soon we move to a new place. Better yet." His story continued, a fable within a fable, embellished over time. They had taken over the store after it had become too much for August and the business had flourished under their command. "Martha got married and has plenty of money so we bought her out. You should see her kitchen with a Mixmaster and a steam iron where you can press woolen pants without having to use a damp towel. She goes to the beauty shop and gets her hair and nails done every week. And George gets tickets to all the concerts because he knows everybody."

He continued, his voice deepening at the lengthening list. Their new building would include a five-room apartment on the second floor, with Kate's figurines on display and a sterling silver tea set plus service for twelve. "Downstairs, we keep it simple. I cut out the ice cream machine right away. Too much trouble. Self-service has people take off the shelf by themselves and bring them to the counter to pay. We ring up and they're out the door."

They listened quietly. Only in America…

"And everyone else?"

"August and Marichen have a little café where you can buy breakfast, lunch or a cup of coffee. Five days a week and they go home by supper time. It's an easy living. Kids all grown so it's just them two."

"So who lives inside the barbed wire?" Kate asked. "Is it like a prison?"

"Oh no. Inside is the good part. We only work there," Helmut said. "Then we come home to this."

"Don't forget that you are German. Always be proud." Fritz swallowed the last of his lunch and stood up. "Now we take a walk before we all fall asleep."

There were few people moving about and they walked easily toward the city's center, seeing the hotel Königshof in the distance and the building that held the British offices. They arrived at Hilda and Rainer's flat just as it began to get dark. "Come in and rest. I make some coffee and a little bread and jam. The children are tired and need to get ready for bed," Hilda declared. "It will only take a minute."

Fritz was still spinning his magical tales when Hilda emerged from the bedroom, telling how American soldiers were going to college for free, a reward for service during the war. Factories were spilling out appliances and furniture answering the pent-up demand. New cars were rolling off the factory floors and workers were able to buy a variety of products with union wages and benefits. Suburbs ringed the cities, with tract houses, rolling lawns and a community swimming pool for the children. When Martha had come to visit, they'd been regaled with stories about America. Now it was Onkel Fritz and Kate singing the same song. Her parents had remained behind. That said it all.

Hilda applauding their achievements. But after a week she was glad to see them go. Yet the impact persisted. While mending socks, she would picture Martha throwing them in the garbage and buying new. When she walked to work, she pictured George getting in his car to pick up a pack of cigarettes – American cigarettes.

A month later, she picked up the mail as she came for Karl after work, glancing idly at the envelopes as she entered. "Tante Guste sent you a post. Onkel Fritz must be back in America."

Alma took the letter and began to read, skimming over the more general parts. "Fritz said he was glad we were doing so well. Kate brought Elvira presents for the baby and gave Siebold some American dollars."

Hilda laughed dryly. "He gave Rainer a carton of cigarettes and the boys' new sweaters. We should be glad that the barter system is behind us."

Then the last line – "'...*and Fritz is sponsoring Elvira, Renaldo and the baby to come to America. He will be sending the papers. The time should go fast*'..."

They stared at one another. "She does have a way with her, doesn't she?"

"She was like that from the very beginning," Alma sighed, "even as a child."

"It's a gift. That's just the way it is."

"Did he offer you? Did Kate?"

"No, but it's no matter, Muttie," Hilda said softly. "We are settled here and we'll make the best of it."

"But he might have said something even if you said no. I mean, fair is fair…"

It took Elvira and Renaldo almost a year to get ready, selling their possessions, staying briefly with Guste and Siebold, signing the papers that moved slowly through Britain's enormous bureaucracy. Then waiting for Fritz to notarize an agreement that made him financial responsible for five years, procuring plane tickets to carry them from Düsseldorf to Bremen, to New York and Chicago's Midway airport.

Fritz, Martha and George were there to meet them, the six crowding into George's car, gazing at the Christmas decorations along the way. Streetlights blinked with ribbons and wreaths, bright red Santas jangled bells over Salvation Army buckets, people dressed in furs hurrying along with bulging shopping bags, the vision enhanced with a sprinkling of snow. Surely their mentors were millionaires. Surely they would be living like kings.

Instead, they arrived at a little grocery story with a flat upstairs, their quarters an enclosed porch barely heated. After a week, Renaldo received a bill from Fritz covering the cost to bring them over. Elvira was handed a bag full of socks to mend.

Little of this was known by the family in Oeynhausen. Yet the topic refused to rest despite Hilda being past thirty, Rainer approaching his fortieth birthday. How much better it would be for the children. How much safer they would be with an ocean separating them from the prospect of future wars. And think of the freedom…

Swallowing her pride, Hilda approached Fritz and after careful negotiations, they followed, a second migration to the American shores. Like those that preceded them, they took any available job, working to master the language, embracing friends wherever they could be found, finding comfort in church, and when there was nothing else, in one another.

It was the echo of so many with stars in their eyes and hopes blazing eternal, repeating the struggle of generations preceding them.

In the final analysis, it was for the children. Always, always for the children.

PROGENY OF FREDERICK AND PAULINE

Wilhelm = Ida
(four daughters)

Fritz = Katie

August = Marichen
Siegfried (died in infancy)
Herbert = Marilou
Trudi = Erv
Werner (died in infancy)
Elsie = Jim

Alma = Herman
Hilda = Rainer
    Peter
    Karl
Gunter

Rudy = 'Lisbet
Eleanor

Guste = Siebold
Manfred (died in infancy)
Elvira = Renaldo
Ursula

Otto = Sophie
Dolores

Martha = Walter
      = George

Rudy, Fritz and Otto emigrated 1926
August emigrated 1927; rest of his family emigrated 1928

ABOUT THE AUTHOR

BETH STAAS IS A FREELANCE writer who has been published in numerous national periodicals including *Southwest Airlines, Chicago Tribune, Entrepreneur* and *North American Review*. She holds a bachelor's degree in psychology and a master's in English. She taught writing at the high school and college level for some twenty years and was listed in *Who's Who among American Teachers*. This book originated as a memoir for her five children, a reflection on historical events as they buffeted ordinary lives. It is her third novel.

www.ingramcontent.com/pod-product-compliance
Lightning Source LLC
Chambersburg PA
CBHW051747040426
42446CB00007B/260